PIMLICO

808

BODY PARTS

Hermione Lee's previous books include the internationally acclaimed biographies *Virginia Woolf* and *Edith Wharton* and a study of Elizabeth Bowen. She has written on many American authors, from Willa Cather to Philip Roth. She is a well-known reviewer and broadcaster, and, in 2006, Chair of the judges for the Man Booker Prize. She is the first woman Goldsmiths' Professor of English at Oxford University, a Fellow of New College, Oxford, of the British Academy and of the Royal Society of Literature. She was awarded a CBE in 2003 for services to literature.

Ex Libris
BARRY CASEY

Amazon,
January 2022

By the same author

The Novels of Virginia Woolf
Elizabeth Bowen
Philip Roth
Willa Cather: A Life Saved Up
Virginia Woolf
Edith Wharton

As editor

Stevie Smith: A selection
The Hogarth Letters
The Mulberry Tree: Writings of Elizabeth Bowen
The Secret Self: Short Stories by Women (Vols I and II)
The Short Stories of Willa Cather
Virginia Woolf: *A Room of One's Own and Three Guineas*
To the Lighthouse, The Years
On Being Ill

BODY PARTS

Essays on Life-Writing

HERMIONE LEE

PIMLICO

Published by Pimlico 2008

12

First published in Great Britain in 2005 by
Chatto & Windus

Pimlico
Random House, 20 Vauxhall Bridge Road,
London SW1V 2SA

www.rbooks.co.uk

Addresses for companies within The Random House Group Limited
can be found at www.randomhouse.co.uk/offices.htm

The Random House Group Limited Reg. No. 954009

A CIP catalogue record for this book
is available from the British Library

ISBN 9781844137466

Penguin Random House is committed to a sustainable future for
our business, our readers and our planet. This book is made from
Forest Stewardship Council® certified paper.

Typeset by Deltatype Ltd, Birkenhead

Printed and bound in Great Britain by Clays Ltd, Elcograf S.p.A.

In Memory of
Josephine Lee
1921–2003

Contents

Note

Some of these essays, revised for this collection, first appeared in the *Guardian*, the *Observer*, the *Journal of Victorian Studies*, *The New York Review of Books*, the *Yale Review*, the *New Yorker*, the *London Review of Books*, and the *Times Literary Supplement*. I am grateful to the Paris Press for permission to reprint a revised version of the introduction to 'On Being Ill', to Oxford University Press for permission to reprint a revised version of my Oxford University Inaugural Lecture, 'Reading in Bed', and to Princeton University Press for permission to reprint in this collection three essays given as lectures at Princeton University in September 2004 ('Shelley's Heart and Pepys's Lobsters', 'Jane Austen Faints', and 'Virginia Woolf's Nose') and the essay 'How to End It All'. The author and publisher are grateful to Julian Barnes, Michael Cunningham, and Mark Doty for permission to quote their words, and to Faber & Faber Ltd for permission to quote some lines from Philip Larkin's 'Aubade'.

I should like to thank the following for help and encouragement: Ian Donaldson and Richard Holmes for inviting me to the Cambridge seminar on 'Biographical Knowledge' where I tried out some of these ideas; Jan Freeman at the Paris Press, Karen Kukil at Smith College, and Michèle Perry for helping me with 'On Being Ill'; Barbara Epstein at *The New York Review of Books*; Lyn Pykett for editorial help with the Gosses; Lindsay Duguid at the *TLS*; Terence Dooley for asking me to write about Penelope Fitzgerald; the late Brian Moore for his friendship; my agent Pat Kavanagh; my husband John Barnard; my students in the biography seminars at Oxford over the last five years; Dinah Birch, Lucy Newlyn, Hugh Haughton and Roy Foster for conversations about life-writing; to Julian Barnes, for a vital inspiration; and my dear friend, the peerless biographer and editor Jenny Uglow, who helped me to make this up.

Introduction: Writing About Lives

When Boswell's *Life of Samuel Johnson* was republished in 1831 in a new edition by John Wilson Croker, it caused a great stir. Those who had always hated Johnson and the English Toryism he stood for took the opportunity to attack him and his biographer – some, like Macaulay, with savage ferocity. Those who had always cherished Boswell's intimate, candid *Life* of his brilliant and eccentric friend welcomed the book. (Its reception, in fact, is a good example of how biography is so often mixed up with politics, personal allegiances and conflicting versions of history.) Thomas Carlyle, who was passionately interested in biography – and whose own *Life*, by his friend the historian J.A. Froude, would be the biggest biographical scandal of the century – used Croker's edition of Boswell's *Life* to air his own biographical convictions. The writing of a life, Carlyle said, should above all be an act of sympathy. 'To have an open loving heart' was the primary qualification for a biographer. With that comes the feeling for detail, the evocation of personality, and the commitment to truth-telling, which Carlyle (like Johnson and Boswell before him) thought were the marks of the best kind of life-writing.

Carlyle singled out one incident in Boswell's *Life of Johnson* to show how a chain of human sympathy can link the reader, not only to the central figure of the biography, but, through 'many a little *Reality*', to the lesser-known people who are brought back to life by the biographer. Boswell and Johnson were walking and talking, as their habit was, by night, in London. As they walked along the Strand, Johnson was accosted by 'a woman of the town'. Johnson, according to Boswell, said to her, but not harshly: 'No, no, my girl, it won't do.' She went away, and they continued their walk, talking of 'the wretched life of such women'. Carlyle comments:

> Strange power of *Reality*! Not even this poorest of occurrences, but now, after seventy years are come and gone, has a meaning for us. Do but consider that it is *true*; that it did in very deed occur! That unhappy Outcast, with her sins and woes, her lawless desires, too complex

mischances, her wailings and her riotings, has departed utterly; alas! her siren finery has got all besmutched, ground, generations since, into dust and smoke; of her degraded body, and whole miserable earthly existence, all is away: *she* is no longer here, but far from us, in the bosom of Eternity, – whence we too came, whither we too are bound! Johnson said, 'No, no, my girl; it won't do'; and then 'we talked'; – and herewith the wretched one, seen but for the twinkling of an eye, passes on into the utter Darkness.[1]

Carlyle, writing in the 1830s, talks about the sanctity of human lives and the sacred duty of the biographer in terms which most biographers wouldn't use now. But his idea of life-writing as the creation of intimate links between the dead and living, his insistence on sympathy as the motivating force, his interest in the rescuing of lives, however obscure, from oblivion, and his belief in the power of small anecdotes and little details – what he calls 'light-gleams' – to bring a whole life home to us: all this still has value.

We all want stories and details and particulars in our life-stories. We are still the readers Elizabeth Gaskell was thinking of when she noted to herself, as she started her life of Charlotte Brontë, 'Get as many anecdotes as possible. If you love your reader and want to be read, get anecdotes!'[2] Richard Holmes, whose now classic formulation of biography is as a tracking of footsteps, a 'pursuit', and who imagines the biographer as a 'ferryman', like Charon, between the dead and the living, always insists on the idea of 'bringing to life': 'If you were lucky, you might write about the pursuit of that fleeting figure in such a way as to bring it alive in the present'.[3] The trouble with death, Henry James thought, is that it 'smooths the folds' of the person one loved. 'The figure retained by the memory is compressed and intensified; accidents have dropped away from it and shades have ceased to count; it stands, sharply, for a few estimated and cherished things, rather than nebulously, for a swarm of possibilities.'[4] The critic David Ellis cites this profound passage as a way into talking about the problems of biography: that it can tend to sound too knowing and firm about the shape of its subject's life, to make it read too smoothly, to be too selective. Alternatives, missed chances, roads not taken, accidents and hesitations, the whole 'swarm of possibilities' that hums around our every experience, too often disappears in the smoothing biographical process.

Whether we think of biography as more like history or more like fiction, what we want from it is a vivid sense of the person. The reader's first question of the biographer is always going to be, what was she, or he, like? Other questions (like why, or how do you know, or do we approve, or does it matter?) may follow. But 'likeness' must be there. And when we are reading other forms of life-writing – autobiography, memoir, journal, letter, autobiographical fiction or poem – or when we are trying ourselves to tell the story of a life, whether in an obituary, or in a conversation, or in a confession, or in a book – we are always drawn to moments of intimacy, revelation, or particular inwardness.

Readers of biography are greedy readers, with an insatiable appetite for detail and story. There are all kinds of ways of satisfying these appetites. Coming at a likeness will always involve a messy, often contradictory, mixture of approaches. It's that all-encompassing quality which gives biography some of its appeal – and makes it so resistant to theorising. History, politics, sociology, gossip, fiction, literary criticism, psychoanalysis, documentary, journalism, ethics and philosophy are all scrambled up inside the genre. But the target of all these approaches is a living person in a body, not a smoothed-over figure – even if seen or caught as fleetingly as the woman on the street who once accosted Dr Johnson. What makes biography so curious and endlessly absorbing is that through all the documents and the letters, the context and the witnesses, the conflicting opinions and the evidence of the work, we keep catching sight of a real body, a physical life: the young Dickens coming quickly into a room, sprightly, long-haired, bright-eyed, dandyish, in a crimson velvet waistcoat or tartan trousers; the sound of Coleridge's voice as he talked magically on and on; Rimbaud, dust-covered and scrawny and dressed in baggy grey khaki trousers, leading a caravan of camels across the desert sands of Abyssinia; Joyce with a black felt hat, thick glasses and a cigar, sitting in Sylvia Beach's bookshop in Paris.

Biography has changed enormously in the last hundred years in what it allows itself to talk about. Johnson and Carlyle called above all for 'veracity' rather than 'panegyric', for a warts-and-all picture which should include the representation of 'the minute details of daily life'.[5] A more protective practice of idealising or censoring biography developed (though not exclusively) in the Victorian period. But with the increasing dominance, popularity, professionalisation and – it must be added – scandal-mongering – of biography in the twentieth century, real warts are now allowed to be included. The life of the body plays much more of a part in contemporary biographical narratives. Masturbation, dental work, body odour, menstruation, gonorrhoea, addictions and sexual preferences are all permissible subjects; the shock and horror which greeted Froude's revelations about Carlyle's marital behaviour and impotence, at the end of the nineteenth century, would now be replaced by sympathy and clinical interest. As Virginia Woolf observes, 'opinions change as the times change', and one of the biographer's jobs is to detect 'the presence of obsolete conventions'.[6] The comparison of deathbed scenes in biography which ends this book suggests how much conventions have changed. But from the time that Dryden, writing in the 1680s, praised Plutarch's *Lives* for showing us the domestic lives of great heroes like Alexander in their 'private lodgings' and their 'undress' ('the pageantry of life is taken away; you see the poor reasonable animal, as naked as nature ever made him; are made acquainted with his passions and his follies, and find the Demi-God a Man'),[7] biography has always directed us to the figure of a real person in all his or her peculiarity, accidentalness and actuality.

Body Parts, which is a collection of writings on literary lives, looks at the variety of ways in which a life can be brought home to us. How do biographers deal with moments of physical shock, or with the bodily life of the subject, or with the left-over parts of a life? How do autobiographers write their bodily sensations and memories – of illness, or reading, or aesthetic pleasure? What strategies do some writers have for masking themselves, making themselves disappear, so as to elude the reader and the potential biographer? How do biographers come at the personality and the life of the writer through the body of their work? How may a life-story be shaped and reshaped by the tools of psychoanalysis, or by a close listening to tones of voice, or an analysis of story-telling? What part do blame, resentment, personal affection, judgement and defensiveness have to play in the courtroom drama of life-writing? *Body Parts* looks at the writing of a good many writers' lives, writers whose work and life-stories have always interested me, and who include Jane Austen, Virginia Woolf, Edith Wharton, Eudora Welty, Rosamond Lehmann, Penelope Fitzgerald, J.M. Coetzee, and

Brian Moore. But *Body Parts* begins and ends, not with whole life-stories, but with relics, legends and fragments, with the parts and bits and gaps which are left over after the life has ended. That's what biographers use to piece their stories together, trying to make a solid figure, embodied on the page, out of what has gone.

Shelley's Heart and Pepys's Lobsters

Biographies are full of verifiable facts, but they are also full of things that aren't there: absences, gaps, missing evidence, knowledge or information that has been passed from person to person, losing credibility or shifting shape on the way. Biographies, like lives, are made up of contested objects – relics, testimonies, versions, correspondences, the unverifiable. What does biography do with the facts that can't be fixed, the things that go missing, the body parts that have been turned into legends and myths?

A few years ago, a popular biographer who had allowed doubts and gaps into the narrative of a historical subject was criticised for sounding dubious. 'For "I think", read "I don't know",' said one of her critics crossly. But more recently, 'biographical uncertainty' has become a respectable topic of discussion.[1] Writers on this subject tend to quote Julian Barnes's *Flaubert's Parrot*:

> You can define a net in one of two ways, depending on your point of view. Normally, you would say that it is a meshed instrument designed to catch fish. But you could, with no great injury to logic, reverse the image and define a net as a jocular lexicographer once did: he called it a collection of holes tied together with string.
>
> You can do the same with a biography. The trawling net fills, then the biographer hauls it in, sorts, throws back, stores, fillets and sells. Yet consider what he doesn't catch: there is always far more of that. The biography stands, fat and worthy-burgherish on the shelf, boastful and sedate: a shilling life will give you all the facts, a ten pound one all the hypotheses as well. But think of everything that got away, that fled with the last deathbed exhalation of the biographee.[2]

We all know stories of what falls through the net of biography. Many of these are bonfire stories. The poet, biographer and editor Ian Hamilton, who had been severely singed in his attempt to write a biography of Salinger, enjoyed himself in *Keepers of the Flame* (1992) with stories of widows and executors fighting off predatory biographers, of conflagrations of letters, of evidence being withheld. These stories all read like variants of Henry James's novella, *The Aspern Papers*, in which the predatory would-be biographer, the 'publishing scoundrel', is thwarted in his greedy desire to get hold of the papers of the great American romantic poet Jeffrey Aspern by the two protective, solitary women who have inherited and who guard his legacy. These are stories like Byron's executor, publisher and friends gathering round the fireplace of John Murray's office in Albemarle Street in 1824 and feeding the pages of Byron's memoir into the flames; or Hardy spending six months of 1919 destroying most of his life's papers while setting up a conspiracy with his second wife that she pretend to author the biography he was actually writing himself; or Cassandra Austen destroying those letters of her sister which may have contained revealing personal material; or Elizabeth Gaskell reading, but feeling unable to use, Charlotte Brontë's passionate love-letters to M. Heger, in a biography which set out to protect her against accusations of impurity; or Ted Hughes destroying Sylvia Plath's last two journals, and then publishing his own edition of the rest.

Many literary biographers are affected by such bonfires. Writing on Willa Cather, I came up against her directive, in her will of 1943, that none of her letters should ever be quoted (with the result that they are paraphrased, usually to her disadvantage), alongside her command that no adaptations or dramatisations should be made of her work 'whether by electronic means now in existence or which may hereafter be discovered'.[3] One of the significant gaps in the Woolf archive is the apparent lack of any correspondence between her and her brother Adrian, so that this relationship has never come into focus. The friendship between Edith Wharton and Henry James is a challenge to her biographers, because James made a bonfire of nearly all the letters he had from her, which as a result have to be decoded from *his* letters to *her*.

James's destruction of Wharton's letters about her private life, or Elizabeth Gaskell's censoring of Charlotte's love-letters, are acts of protection, and are often talked about as illustrations – as in *The Aspern Papers* – of the battle for possession that is always fought over a famous literary life. But such disappearances also raise the question of what biographers do with the things that go missing, or with contested objects. Biographers try to make a coherent narrative out of missing documents as well as existing ones; a whole figure out of body parts. Some body parts, literally, get into the telling of the stories, in the form of legends, rumours or contested possessions. Body parts are conducive to myth-making; biographers, in turn, have to sort out the myths from the facts. There is a tremendous fascination with the bodily relics of famous people, and the stories of such relics have their roots in legends and miracles of saints which are the distant ancestors of biography. But they persist in a secular age, rather in the way that urban myths do, and are some of the 'things' biographers have to decide how to deal with. These 'body-part' stories play into the subject's posthumous reputation, sometimes with suspicious appositeness. We might expect Joan of Arc's heart (and, it is sometimes added, her entrails) to have survived the flames and be thrown into the Seine. It seems fitting, too, that Sir Thomas More's head, boiled, and impaled on a pole over London Bridge, is supposed to have been secretly taken by night by his daughter Margaret Roper to St Dunstan's Church in Canterbury, which, after the beatification of More in the nineteenth century, became a pilgrimage shrine. Charlotte Yonge, in *A Book of Golden Deeds*, retells – without much conviction – the old story that, in the boat, 'Margaret looked up and said: "That head has often lain in my lap; I would that it would now fall into it." And at that moment it actually fell, and she received it.' It's the kind of story probably best ignored by biographers.[4]

There are stranger stories of the fate of relics. Napoleon's penis is said to have been chopped off by the Abbé who administered the last rites, and since then has been sold, inherited, displayed and auctioned many times, last heard of in the possession of an American urologist, but possibly buried all this time in the crypt at the Hôtel des Invalides. Hardy's body was interred in Poets' Corner, but, after an argument between his friends and his family, his heart was buried in his wife Emma's grave at Stinsford Church, near Dorchester, carried in an urn to its resting place with great solemnity by a procession of gentlemen in suits and hats (the church has a photograph of the ceremony). On the tomb, it says: 'Here Lies The Heart of Thomas Hardy'. Rumour has it that Hardy's housekeeper, after the death and the extraction of the heart, placed it in a biscuit tin on the kitchen table, and that when the undertaker came the next day he found an empty biscuit tin and Hardy's cat, Cobby, looking fat and pleased. The story then divides: in one branch a pig's heart replaces Hardy's in the urn. In the other, Cobby is executed by the undertaker and replaces his master's heart. Either way, this rural myth is probably more useful for a Life of Cobby than a Life of Hardy.[5]

The story of Einstein's brain is intriguingly grotesque, too. After a pathologist from Kansas, Thomas Harvey, performed Einstein's autopsy in 1955, he made off with the brain, claiming he would investigate and publish his findings on it. He cut the brain into 240 pieces, and, at various times, doled out bits to scientific researchers. In 1978 a reporter tracked down Dr Harvey in Kansas and was shown the brain kept in two Mason jars in a cardboard box. In *Driving Mr Albert: A Trip across America with Einstein's Brain*, Michael Paterniti described a journey with Dr Harvey and his 'sacred specimen', in which he meditates on the motives for such 'relic freaks'.[6]

Uncertainty also surrounds the bones of Yeats. Yeats was buried on 30 January 1939 in an Anglican cemetery in France, at Roquebrune. His wife George took out a temporary ten-year-lease (she thought) on the grave site. Plans to bring his body home to Sligo in September 1939 were thwarted by world events. In 1947, it was discovered that the concession had run out after five years, not ten, and that Yeats's bones had been removed to the ossuary. Very confused negotiations followed between George, some of Yeats's friends, the municipal and church authorities and the French Government. In March 1948 the remains were identified (though leaving some room for uncertainty) and placed in a new coffin; in September 1948 the coffin was taken in state, from Roquebrune to Galway. The re-interment ceremony at Drumcliff on 17 September 1948 took place with enormous crowds in attendance, and the poet's verse was, some time later, duly inscribed on the tombstone: 'Cast a cold eye, on life, on death; Horseman, pass by!' But rumours persisted that the bones had got mixed up in the ossuary; Louis MacNeice, at the funeral, said they were actually burying 'a Frenchman with a club foot'. Roy Foster's life of Yeats takes a laconic and brisk line on all this, since in his view posthumous legends about body parts have no meaning for the life. 'The legend of a mystery burial, or even an empty coffin', he notes dispassionately, 'sustains a kind of mythic life, as with King Arthur, or – more appositely – Charles Stewart Parnell.' What interests Foster about Yeats's death is that, in the last days, he showed no interest at all in the systems of occultism and supernaturalism that had so preoccupied him, he made no mention of the afterlife, but concentrated exclusively on finishing his last poems. His last conscious act was to 'revise a contents list for an imagined last volume of poems'.[7]

So, what, if anything, are biographers supposed to do with such mythical body-part stories? They can easily be set aside and ignored. But these compelling relics fit with our deep fascination with deathbed scenes and last words – which I'll come back to in the last essay in this book. We are all fascinated by the manner of the subject's death. And if there are legends about the last moments of the subjects, or stories about what happened to their bodies after death – most of which fall into the category of unverifiable things or contested objects – it is a rare biographer who risks taking no notice of such stories. They play a part in the meaning of the life. How such matters should be dealt with in the biographical narrative involves tricky questions of tone and judgement, often involving a stand-off between scepticism and superstition, rationalism and sentimentalism. But most biographies concern them-selves with afterlives as well as with lives.

One of the most complicated and emotionally charged examples in British biography of the contested use of sources, of rival versions and myth-making, in which a body part comes to symbolise the subject's afterlife, is the story of the death of Shelley. Shelley's great biographer Richard Holmes has written several times about this, once in his biography of 1974, once in the chapter called 'Exiles', in *Footsteps* (1985), which movingly retraced his own steps as Shelley's biographer, and once in a more recent essay on the legends about Shelley that followed his death, in which he notes that 'many lives change their shape as we look back on them'.[8] In *Footsteps*, he began that 'looking back' process on the writing of Shelley's life by remembering what he had wanted to do as Shelley's biographer in the 1970s. When he started work, he said, he was faced with a 'received biographical image of Shelley's adult character'. This 'received image' had 'three powerful components', he said, all of which he wanted to 'explode'. One was 'the "angelic" personality of popular myth, the "Ariel" syndrome, with its strong implication that Shelley was insubstantial, ineffectual, physically incompetent'. The second 'concerned his radical politics', which had always been treated 'as essentially juvenile, and incompatible with his mature lyric gift as a writer'. Holmes wanted 'to show that Shelley's poetic and political inspirations were closely identified'. The third was the 'prevailing attitude' to 'Shelley's emotional and sexual make-up'. Holmes cited Matthew Arnold reviewing Edward Dowden's biography of Shelley in 1886, with horror at what it revealed of the poet's 'irregular relations'. Holmes, who described his own experiences and friendships in the 1960s as being rather like those of the Shelley circle, was not shocked or horrified, and wanted to understand how Shelley's principles of free love and equal partnerships could have led to such chaos and suffering.

Matthew Arnold's distaste at Shelley's morals formed part of a nineteenth- and early twentieth-century story of posthumous protection and accusation which Holmes outlined at the start and the end of his Shelley biography. This is how he tells it:

Shelley's exile, his defection from his class and the disreputability of his beliefs and behaviour, had a tremendous effect on the carefully partisan handling of his biography by the survivors of his own circle and generation, and even more so by that of his son's. In the first, the generation of his family and friends, fear of the moral and social stigma attached to many incidents in Shelley's career prevented the publication or even the writing of biographical material until those who were in possession of it, like Hogg, Peacock and Trelawny, were respectable Victorians in their sixties, who were fully prepared to forget, to smudge and to conceal ... Mary Shelley was actually prevented from writing anything fuller than [a] brief introduction ... [and] editorial 'Notes' ... partly by the same considerations of propriety as Shelley's friends, but even more by the fact that Shelley's father, Sir Timothy Shelley of Field Place, specifically forbade any such publications until after his own death ... and made the ban singularly effective by outliving his detested son by twenty-two years ... In the second generation, control of the Shelley papers passed to Boscombe Manor and Sir Percy Florence's wife, Lady Jane Shelley, who made it her life work to establish an unimpeachable feminine and Victorian idealization of the poet ... The vetting and control which Lady Jane exercised over the chosen scholars who were allowed into the sanctuary, notably Richard Garnett and Edward Dowden, was strict ... This crucial period of Shelley studies was crowned by Edward Dowden's two-volume standard *Life* (1886), whose damaging influence is still powerfully at work in popular estimates of Shelley's writing and character.[9]

Towards the end of the biography, Lady Shelley's shrine at Boscombe Manor is described in more detail as 'complete with life-size monument of the poet, lockets of fading hair, glass cases of letters and blue opaque pots containing fragments of bone'. Ian Hamilton, in *Keepers of the Flame*, adds Shelley's baby-rattle to the list of sacred items and blames the women for the sanctification of Shelley: Mary was 'a pious keeper of her husband's flame'. The Shelley scholar Timothy Webb, describing in 1977 the posthumous forces 'which operated to thin the poet's blood and to idealise his memory', said that Lady Shelley 'kept the poet's hair, his manuscripts (limited access for true believers only), his books and his heart (or was it liver?) which had been rescued from the flames at Viareggio. Before you could enter the shrine you had to remove your hat.'[10]

All three of these writers attributed the romanticising of Shelley to Mary Shelley's remorseful, grieving idealisation of her husband, and to the testimonies of Shelley's friends: the egotistical Thomas Jefferson Hogg, the adventurous, self-invented Edward Trelawny, who dined out for years on his Shelley and Byron stories, and the unreliable Leigh Hunt. All of them had their own versions to tell of the end of Shelley's life.

The Shelley story evolved through tremendous battles over materials and versions. Friends and family did battle over 'their' accounts of Shelley, censoring each other (Lady Shelley putting a stop to Hogg's biography after two volumes, Trelawny taking issue with Mary's editing of Shelley's work), and changing their own stories. For over a hundred years, accusations and counter-accusations flew of lies, censorship, and even forgery. A splendidly obstreperous book of 1945 by Roger Smith and others, *The Shelley Legend*, much disliked by the Shelley scholars of the time, puts Lady Shelley at the centre of the battle for custody: 'Lady Shelley, terrified lest the facts of Shelley's sex-life should become public, made herself the centre of a conspiracy to keep these facts hidden.'[11] As Richard Holmes says in his biography, at every point of conflict over the Shelley sources, 'where events reveal Shelley in an unpleasant light' (as with his abandonment of Harriet, his first wife, and her subsequent suicide when heavily pregnant) 'the original texts and commentaries have attracted suppressions, distortions, and questions of doubtful authenticity, originating from Victorian apologists'. William St Clair sums up the matter in his essay of 2002, 'The Biographer as Archaeologist': 'The general intention of the family was to enhance the reputation of Shelley and of Mary Shelley, and to suppress knowledge of matters which contradicted the image, or rather the myth, which they wanted to see projected ... for example by removing evidence of irreligion, and slurring ... the reputation of Shelley's first wife, Harriet.' Long after these attempts at censorship, and now that all the facts of Shelley's life have been scrupulously explored, there are still competing versions of the life-story; blame and accusation are still in play.[12]

In a case like Shelley's, the posthumous life of the subject has as much to do with the writing of biography as the life itself. An interesting essay by the critic Andrew Bennett, called 'Shelley's Ghosts', touches on this. Bennett argues that Shelley had an acute and intense relation to the idea of posterity, and presents himself in his own work as 'a ghostly spirit set to haunt or inhabit the minds of readers'. Bennett begins his piece on Shelley as the ghost-writer of his own life by talking about how we treat the dead: 'What we do with dead bodies is different from what we do with live ones'.[13] This is particularly apt for Shelley, since one of the most important ingredients in the making of the Shelley legend was the story of what happened to Shelley's dead body.

The famous, tragic story, once more. In April 1822, the Shelleys and their friends moved after a winter in Pisa to the Casa Magni, at Lerici on the Gulf of Spezia. The household consisted of Percy and Mary Shelley and little Percy, Claire Clairmont, Jane and Edward Williams. Claire's daughter by Byron, Allegra, died in April. Mary, two of whose children had died, had a miscarriage in July; both women were ill and distressed. Byron and his flamboyant entourage were at the Palazzo Lanfranchi in Pisa. Leigh Hunt and his family were arriving in July; there was a plan that Hunt, Byron and Shelley should start a magazine. Shelley was writing *The Triumph of Life*, Byron was writing *Don Juan*. Byron and Shelley, with the advice and help of their new friend Edward Trelawny and a Captain Roberts, had become addicted to sailing. Byron was having a large schooner built, the *Bolivar*; Shelley's smaller boat was called the *Don Juan*, though he had wanted to call it *Ariel*. In June, it was refurbished, by some accounts unwisely, with new topmast rigging.

Shelley and Edward Williams and Captain Roberts sailed on the *Don Juan* down the coast to meet Leigh Hunt, newly arrived at Leghorn (Livorno), on 1 July 1822, to help them get settled in Pisa. On 8 July, Shelley, Williams, and the ship-boy Charles Vivian set sail from Leghorn/Livorno to return to Lerici, on a stormy day. A squall broke out in the Gulf of Spezia, the *Don Juan* went down under full sail, and they were all drowned. The women were waiting for them at the Casa Magni. It took another ten days of agonised and confused waiting and searching, in which Trelawny played a leading part, before the bodies were washed up and the news of the deaths was confirmed. The bodies were buried in quicklime on the shore to avoid infection. On 13 August, after getting permission from the authorities, Trelawny, Byron and Hunt, with soldiers, attendants and onlookers, dug up Williams's body and burnt it on a pyre; on 14 August they repeated the ceremony for Shelley, on the beach at Viareggio.

The telling of this story formed a central part in the making of the Shelley legend, and it was seized upon with gusto by the main players. Here is part of Trelawny's 1858 version, written thirty-six years after the event. It has been variously described as 'a semi-fictionalised account', 'one of the great purple passages of romantic literature, and deservedly so', and 'a scene which in all its gruesome detail has etched itself onto the Romantic imagination':[14]

The first indication of their having found the body, was the appearance of the end of a black silk handkerchief ... then some shreds of linen were met with, and a boot with the bone of the leg and the foot in it. On the removal of a layer of brushwood all that now remained of my lost friend was exposed – a shapeless mass of bones and flesh. The limbs separated from the trunk on being touched.

'Is that a human body?' exclaimed Byron; 'why it's more like the carcase of a sheep, or any other animal, than a man: this is a satire on our pride and folly.'

I pointed to the letters E.E.W. on the black silk handkerchief.

Byron, looking on, muttered: 'The entrails of a worm hold together longer than the potter's clay, of which man is made. Hold! Let me see the jaw,' he added, as they were removing the skull, 'I can recognize anyone by the teeth, with whom I have talked. I always watch the lips and mouth: they tell what the tongue and eye try to conceal.'

. . . [Williams's] remains were removed piecemeal into the furnace.

'Don't repeat this with me,' said Byron, 'let my carcase rot where it falls.'

The funereal pyre was now ready; I applied the fire, and the materials being dry and resinous the pine-wood burnt furiously, and drove us back . . . As soon as the flames became clear, and allowed us to approach, we threw frankincense and salt into the furnace, and poured a flask of wine and oil over the body. The Greek oration was omitted, for we had lost our Hellenic bard. It was now so insufferably hot that the officers and soldiers were all seeking shade.

'Let us try the strength of these waters that drowned our friends,' said Byron, with his usual audacity. 'How far out do you think they were when their boat sank?'

'If you don't wish to be put into the furnace, you had better not try; you are not in condition.'

He stripped, and went into the water, and so did I and my companion. Before we got a mile out Byron was sick, and persuaded to return to the shore.

The lonely and grand scenery that surrounded us so exactly harmonized with Shelley's genius, that I could imagine his spirit soaring over us . . . As I thought of the delight Shelley felt in such scenes of loneliness and grandeur whilst living, I felt we were no better than a herd of wolves or a pack of wild dogs, in tearing out his battered and naked body from the pure yellow sand that lay so lightly over it, to drag him back to the light of day . . . Even Byron was silent and thoughtful. We were startled and drawn together by a dull hollow sound that followed the blow of a mattock; the iron had struck a skull, and the body was soon removed. Lime had been strewn on it; this, or decomposition, had the effect of staining it of a dark and ghastly indigo colour. Byron asked me to preserve the skull for him; but remembering that he had formerly used one as a drinking-cup, I was determined Shelley's should not be so profaned. The limbs did not separate from the trunk, as in the case of Williams's body, so that the corpse was removed entire into the furnace . . . More wine was poured over Shelley's dead body than he had consumed during his life. This with the oil and salt made the yellow flames glisten and quiver . . . The corpse fell open and the heart was laid bare. The frontal bone of the skull, where it had been struck with the mattock, fell off; and, as the back of the head rested on the red-hot bottom bars of the furnace, the brains literally seethed, bubbled, and boiled as in a cauldron, for a very long time.

Byron could not face this scene, he withdrew to the beach and swam off to the *Bolivar*. Leigh Hunt remained in the carriage . . . The only portions that were not consumed were some fragments of bones, the jaw, and the skull, but what surprised us all, was that the heart remained entire. In snatching this relic from the fiery furnace my hand was severely burnt; and had any one seen me do the act I should have been put into quarantine.

After cooling the iron machine in the sea, I collected the human ashes and placed them in a box, which I took on board the *Bolivar*. Byron and Hunt retraced their steps to their home, and the officers and soldiers returned to their quarters.[15]

No reader can fail to be struck by Trelawny's highly coloured Hamlet-ising of Byron; the deliberate contrast between Byron's worldliness, appetites and cynicism, and Shelley's ethereality (which goes all through Trelawny's memoir); the pathetic fallacy which invests the scenery with the spirit of Shelley's genius; the pagan quality of the event (no prayers, Greek libations), and – not least – the emphasis on Trelawny as the main, heroic protagonist and the only true witness (the others either wandering off or averting their faces). It comes as no surprise to hear that Trelawny was given to showing off the scars he got from plunging his hand and arm into the fire.

This was not Trelawny's first, nor his last, version of the scene. His latest biographer David Crane notes: 'In account after account over the next sixty years he would return to this summer of 1822 with ever new details, peddling scraps of history or bones with equal relish.'[16] Holmes says that he 'obsessively re-wrote his account nearly a dozen times over the next fifty years, accumulating more and more baroque details, like some sinister biographical coral-reef'. Each version became less realistic than its predecessor. As the retellings developed, 'the physical details became gradually less gruesome . . . and . . . the romantic setting which had originally been the backdrop to the cremation of Williams, was later transferred to the cremation of the Poet'.[17] In versions written in 1822, he tells us that Williams's body had 'the eyes out' and was 'fish-eaten', and that Shelley's body 'was in a stage of putridity and very offensive. Both the legs were separated at the knee-joint ... the hands were off and the arm bones protruding – the skull black and no flesh or features of the face remaining ... The flesh was of a dingy blue.' The later version that I've quoted, the one published in 1858, altered and prettified the story for 'his more squeamish Victorian contemporaries'. When Trelawny returned to the story yet again in 1878, he embellished further, with details such as these: 'Shelley ... had a black single-breasted jacket on, with an outside pocket as usual on each side of his jacket. When his body was washed on shore, Aeschylus was in his left pocket, and Keats's last poems was in his right, doubled back, as thrust away in the exigency of the moment.'[18]

Confusion developed over whether he had seen the bodies when they were first washed up, over what happened to the body of Charles Vivian, over whether Byron actually witnessed the burning of Shelley's body or not, over whether it was a volume of Aeschylus or Sophocles in the left pocket, over which page of Keats's last poems the book was doubled back at – was it 'Lamia', or 'Isabella', or 'The Eve of St Agnes'? – or whether anything survived of the volume except its covers – and, of course, over the size of Shelley's heart.

But, notoriously unreliable though they were, such first-hand versions made their way irresistibly into the biographies of Shelley. Trelawny's witness was compounded by that of Leigh Hunt, an even more emotional narrative, with a convincingly ironic coda:

> The ceremony of the burning was alike beautiful and distressing. Trelawny ... [took] the most active part on this last mournful occasion. He and his friend Captain Shenley were first upon the ground, attended by proper assistants. Lord Byron and myself arrived shortly afterwards. His lordship got out of his carriage, but wandered away from the spectacle, and did not see it. I remained inside the carriage, now looking on, now drawing back with feelings that were not to be witnessed.
>
> None of the mourners, however, refused themselves the little comfort of supposing, that lovers of books and antiquity, like Shelley and his companion, Shelley in particular with his Greek enthusiasm, would not have been sorry to foresee this part of their fate. The mortal part of him, too, was saved from corruption; not the least extraordinary part of his history. Among the materials for burning, as many of the gracefuller and

more classical articles as could be procured – frankincense, wine, etc – were not forgotten; and to these Keats's volume was added. The beauty of the flame arising from the funeral pile was extraordinary. The weather was beautifully fine. The Mediterranean, now soft and lucid, kissed the shore as if to make peace with it ... the flame of the fire bore away towards heaven in vigorous amplitude, waving and quivering with a brightness of inconceivable beauty. It seemed as though it contained the glassy essence of vitality. You might have expected a seraphic countenance to look out of it, turning once more before it departed, to thank the friends that had done their duty.

Yet, see how extremes can appear to meet even on occasions the most overwhelming ... On returning from one of our visits to the seashore, we dined and drank; I mean, Lord Byron and myself; dined little, and drank too much ... I had bordered upon emotions which I have never suffered myself to indulge ... The barouche drove rapidly through the forest of Pisa. We sang, we laughed, we shouted. I even felt a gaiety the more shocking, because it was real and a relief.[19]

Such 'eyewitness' accounts, along with other testimonies from Thomas Love Peacock (written forty years after the event), Byron and Hogg, powerfully influenced the earliest full biography (written under the sanitising control of Lady Shelley). Edward Dowden relied heavily on Trelawny and Hunt, though he censors the inappropriate scene of Hunt and Byron returning to Pisa roaring drunk. He takes from Trelawny's later version the added detail that Shelley's heart was 'unusually large', and a conveniently symbolic sea-bird, which in some versions was a curlew, in others a seagull, with (as one of Trelawny's editors put it) 'a ghastly unappeased appetite for roast poet'.[20]

The furnace being placed and surrounded by wood, the remains were removed from their shallow resting place. It was Byron's wish that the skull, which was of unusual beauty, should be preserved; but it almost instantly fell to pieces. Of the volume of Keats's poems which had been buried with Shelley's body, only the binding remained, and this was cast upon the pyre ... Three hours elapsed before [the body] separated; it then fell open across the breast; the heart, which was unusually large, seemed impregnable to the fire. Trelawny plunged his hand into the flames and snatched this relic from the burning. The day was one of

wide autumnal calm and beauty . . . During the whole funeral ceremony
a solitary sea-bird crossing and recrossing the pile was the only intruder
that baffled the vigilance of the guard.

Byron, who could not face the scene, had swum off to his yacht. Leigh
Hunt looked on from the carriage. Having cooled the furnace in the sea,
Trelawny collected the fragments of bones and the ashes, and deposited
them in the oaken box. All was over. Byron and Hunt returned to Pisa in
their carriage. Shenley and Trelawny, bearing the oaken coffer, went on
board the *Bolivar*. The relics of Shelley's heart, given soon after by
Trelawny to Hunt, were, at Mary Shelley's urgent request, supported by
the entreaty of Mrs Williams, confided to Mary's hands. After her death,
in a copy of the Pisa edition of 'Adonais', at the page which tells how
death is swallowed up by immortality, was found under a silken covering
the embrowned ashes, now shrunk and withered, which she had secretly
treasured.[21]

Dowden takes us on to the next stage of the narrative, the quarrel over
the possession of Shelley's heart. And what happened to Shelley's heart
became, like everything else to do with his death, a source of
controversy. There appears to have been an unseemly and passionate
tussle over the heart between Trelawny, Hunt and Mary Shelley. John
Gisborne, Maria Gisborne's husband, gave one version of the quarrel in
one of the hundreds of documents which form the huge compilation of
Shelley materials made by Lady Shelley.

After the funeral rites of Shelley had been performed . . . Trelawny gave
the heart, which had remained unconsumed, to Hunt. Mary wrote to
Hunt requesting that it might be sent to her. Hunt refused to part with it
. . . Mary was in despair. At length the amiable Mrs Williams . . . wrote
to Hunt, and represented to him how grievous and melancholy it was
that Shelley's remains should become a source of dissension between his
dearest friends.[22]

Articles were written with titles like 'The Real Truth about Shelley's
Heart'. Frederick Jones, the first editor of Mary Shelley's letters and
journals, summed up the controversy in his edition of the letters in the
1930s:

Much controversy has raged about Shelley's heart . . . That Trelawny did remove the heart and that it was kept by Mary, there can be no doubt . . . Mary's, Hunt's, and Byron's letters, and other evidence are quite conclusive. After Mary's death Sir Percy and Lady Shelley kept it, and at the death of Sir Percy in 1890 it was placed in his coffin and buried with him in St Peter's Churchyard at Bournemouth.[23]

The battle over the possession of Shelley's heart seems macabrely to embody the contest over who should 'own' Shelley's story. That it was given reluctantly into Mary Shelley's hands by Shelley's male friends points to Mary's position in the posthumous life of her husband. Mary's biographer Miranda Seymour, who set out to defend Mary against what she saw as a concerted effort to sideline and denigrate her by Shelley's friends and biographers (including Holmes, whose picture of Mary Shelley, according to Seymour, is of a 'sulky, nagging wife'), gives a partisan account of Mary's role in the events:

As his bones shrivelled to ashes on the shore, Mary's relationship with Shelley was already being judged. No precious relic was brought back for her from the funeral pyre. This was the age in which, without photographs . . . fragments of the dead were invested with the value of talismans. Byron's choice, the skull, fell to pieces in the flames. Trelawny burned his hands in seizing a fragment of jawbone; Hunt took another. The heart, or the part of the remains which seemed most like a heart, had failed to burn, while exuding a viscous liquid. [Seymour's footnote to this sentence reads: *The heart's survival in intense heat is hard to explain, even if it had been in an advanced state of calcification. It is possible that the object snatched from the flame was the poet's liver.*] Trelawny snatched it out; Hunt requested and received [it]. When Mary asked if she might have the heart herself, Hunt refused to surrender it . . . It took a reproachful letter from Jane Williams to Hunt to compel a surrender. The heart was rediscovered after Mary Shelley's death. Wrapped in silk between the pages of *Adonais*, it had lain inside her travelling-desk for almost thirty years.

. . . The task of defending and enhancing her husband's reputation would be her great work for the future, her consolation for the remorse she now felt.[24]

Clearly, the battle for possession over Shelley's heart – if it was his heart
– has not come to an end.

Mary Shelley's letters at the time of Shelley's death to their mutual
friend Maria Gisborne immediately began the process of Shelley's
idealisation, on which Holmes has commented: 'The legend of his death
transformed his life almost beyond recovery.'[25] In this process, Shelley's
elegy for Keats came to be read as his own elegy, and his soul was felt to
have an ethereal life beyond his death. For Mary, Shelley's heart at once
took on the mythical resonance it has continued to have since then, as
the 'unconsumable' immortal part of the poet.

> Today – this day – the sun shining in the sky – they are gone to the
> desolate sea coast to perform the last offices to their earthly remains.
> Hunt, L[ord] B[yron] & Trelawny. The quarantine laws would not
> permit us to remove them sooner – & now only on condition that we
> burn them to ashes . . . Adonais is not Keats's it is his own elegy . . . I
> have seen the spot where he now lies – the sticks that mark the spot
> where the sands cover him . . . – They are now about this fearful office –
> & I live!

> I will say nothing of the ceremony since Trelawny has written an
> account of it . . . I will only say that all except his heart (which was
> unconsumable) was burnt, & that two days ago I went to Leghorn &
> beheld the small box that contained his earthly dross – that form, those
> smiles – Great God! No he is not there – he is with me, about me – life
> of my life & soul of my soul – if his divine spirit did not penetrate mine I
> could not survive to weep thus.[26]

That spiritualised Shelley would inspire such romantic versions as
André Maurois's *Ariel: A Shelley Romance*, of 1924, translated by Ella
d'Arcy, and highly popular in its time, where Shelley's soul is 'clipt in a
net woven of dew-dreams', his blood is always freezing and his heart is
for ever standing still or pounding in his breast. And the sacred heart of
Mary's, kept in the pages of *Adonais*, is a perfect example of a contested
body part whose possession and appropriation can stand in for the
whole biographical history of the subject. Writing desolately in her
journal for 11 November 1822, after she has been accused (by Leigh
Hunt) of cold-heartedness, Mary cries out: 'A cold heart! have I [a] cold

heart? . . . Yes! it would be cold enough if all were as I wished it – cold, or burning in that flame for whose sake I forgive this, & would forgive every other imputation – that flame in which your heart, Beloved one, lay unconsumed! Where are you, Shelley? . . . My heart is very full tonight . . . I shall write his life.'[27]

That heartfelt quotation seems uncannily to sum up the biographer's question. '*Where are you, Shelley?*' Who do you belong to? Who 'owns' your 'unconsumed' heart? Mary's possessive lament can be set against another act of posthumous appropriation, carried out by Trelawny in the Protestant Cemetery at Rome. Trelawny's 'management' of Shelley's tomb is another gripping story in itself. Joseph Severn, sadly taking care of the plans for his own friend Keats's tombstone, was suddenly confronted with the extraordinary figure of Trelawny, whom he described in a fine letter of April 1823 as this 'cockney-corsair', this 'pair of Mustachios', 'this Lord Byron's Jackal'.[28] Trelawny completely took over, insisted on moving Shelley's ashes to a site nearer to Keats's grave, with a space for Trelawny right next to Shelley, and chose the wording for the tombstone. At the top, he had the words 'Cor Cordium' engraved. (Frederick Jones, Mary Shelley's editor, visiting the grave in the 1930s, noted that 'Roman tourist guides, pointing to "Cor Cordium" on the tombstone, tell travellers that the heart lies under the stone.') Beneath them were the lines from *The Tempest*:

Nothing of him that doth fade
But doth suffer a sea change
Into something rich and strange.

Rich and strange indeed is the posthumous life of Shelley. But Richard Holmes, in his biography, would have none of all this. He calls Mary's identification of 'Adonais' with Shelley, rather than with Keats, a 'sentimental half-truth' and he will have no truck with any of the versions of Shelley's death I have been describing. This is how he tells the story:

The bodies of Shelley, Edward Williams, and Charles Vivian were eventually washed up along the beach between Massa and Viareggio ten days after the storm. The exposed flesh of Shelley's arms and face had been entirely eaten away, but he was identifiable by the nankeen trousers, the white silk socks beneath the boots and Hunt's copy of Keats's poems doubled back in the jacket pocket. To comply with the complicated quarantine laws, Trelawny had the body temporarily buried in the sand with quick lime, and dug up again on 15 August to be placed in a portable iron furnace that had been constructed to his specification at Livorno, and burnt on the beach in the presence of Leigh Hunt, Lord Byron, some Tuscan militia and a few local fishermen. Much later Shelley's ashes were buried in a tomb, also designed by Trelawny, in the Protestant Cemetery at Rome, after having remained for several months in a mahogany chest in the British Consul's wine-cellar.

In England, the news of Shelley's death was first published by the *Examiner* on 4 August, and on the following evening by the *Courier* whose article began: 'Shelley, the writer of some infidel poetry has been drowned; *now* he knows whether there is a God or no.'[29]

Shelley's heart is a deliberate gap here, a body part that goes missing in the interests of dealing with a particular problem in literary biography, and as a way of getting out of a biographical trap, in which, as Holmes put it many years later, 'biography is caught and frozen, so to speak, in the glamorous headlights of Shelley's death'.[30]

To turn from the story of Shelley to the story of Pepys is to make a grotesquely violent jump from tragedy to comedy, from the ethereal to the robust, and from posthumous myth-making to material realities. Pepys's story is simply steaming with body parts and objects of consumption, from the bosoms and bottoms he so loved to fondle, to the Parmesan cheese he made sure to bury in his garden during the Great Fire of London. Pepys's most dramatic 'body part' story is not one of a heart magically unconsumed by the flames, but of a gallstone painfully extracted without anaesthetic. The life of Pepys would seem to raise none of the problems of missing parts and contested legends raised by the death of Shelley. Instead, it provokes a feeling we may have about life-writing which was most brilliantly articulated by the *fin-de-siècle* French man of letters, Marcel Schwob. In his *Vies imaginaires* of 1896 (well ahead of Lytton Strachey) he argued that short lives (preferably of obscure characters) are more revealing than long lives of great men, and that what is most revealing are the quirks, the eccentricities, and the body parts. History books only ever deal with such body parts if they are thought to have had a determining effect on 'general events':

> [History tells us] that Napoleon was in pain on the day of Waterloo . . . that Alexander was drunk when he killed Klitos, and that certain of Louis XIV's shifts of policy may have been caused by his fistula. Pascal speculates about how things might have turned out had Cleopatra's nose been shorter, and about the grain of sand in Cromwell's urethra. All these individual facts are important only because they have influenced events.

But biographies can do more, Schwob argues, with oddities and idiosyncrasies, than 'historical science' can:

> That such-a-one had a crooked nose, that he had one eye higher than the other, that he had rheumatic nodules in the joints of his arm, that at such-an-hour he customarily ate a *blanc-de-poulet*, that he preferred Malvoisie to Château Margaux – there is something unparalleled in all the world. Thales might just as well have said [Know thyself] as Socrates; but he would not have rubbed his leg in the same way, in prison, before drinking the hemlock.[31]

Claire Tomalin, Pepys's most recent and most praised biographer, rather than trying to deal with unverifiable legends, has the pleasure of plunging into all those kinds of oddities and idiosyncrasies, in a life full to the brim with authentic, factual, bodily, everyday materials. She makes the most of the body parts: the most brilliant, and appalling, set piece in her book is the detailed account of the excruciating operation for the removal of that bladder-stone. Pepys kept his stone, had a special case made for it, and showed it to his friends. (Perhaps it survived him, like Napoleon's penis.) His mother, who had the same condition and 'voided' her stone, threw hers on the fire. Tomalin points to this as the crucial difference between the 'classifying' and 'purposeful' son and his 'sluttish' 'tough' old mother. She enjoys Pepys's ambition and orderliness, his endless enthusiasm for and curiosity about himself, and his pleasure in ordinary human activity, from hearing fine music to eating a good dinner to designing a new bookcase. And she relishes the openness, curiosity, plain-speaking and dramatic immediacy of the diary: a diary which might be enough to make any biographer feel redundant.[32]

Sex, drink, plague, fire, city life, music, plays, marital conflict, the fall of kings, loyalty and betrayal, ambition, corruption and courage in public life, wars, navies, public executions, incarceration in the Tower: Samuel Pepys's life is full of irresistible material. His famously candid, minute and inexhaustibly vigorous account of every detail of his daily life filled six leather-bound books written in shorthand. The unpublished nineteenth-century transcription ran to fifty-four volumes; the definitive edition by Robert Latham and William Matthews is in eleven volumes. (The story of the Diary's survival and publication is in itself a remarkable one.) But the Diary, which begins on 1 January 1660 and ends (because of Pepys's eye problems) on 31 May 1669, covers only nine years out of a seventy-year life. The twenty-seven-year story that precedes it – of Pepys's family, childhood, education, professional advancement and marriage, in the context of the Civil War – and the thirty-four years that follow it, when the death of his wife and public disgrace were followed by rehabilitation, distinguished years of naval administration, an active retirement after 1688, and a second long relationship, all have to be tracked without the Diary. This silence is filled by a vast mass of materials: thousands of letters, Pepys's work-papers and trial documents, naval histories (including Pepys's own), Admiralty papers, contemporary diaries and memoirs, and many histories and biographies. Yet it also involves, as Tomalin puts it, much 'obscurity and guesswork'.[33]

Claire Tomalin had two challenges to overcome with Pepys. One is that the Diary provides so much material it is sometimes overpowering. The other is that outside the Diary years, and outside Pepys's own point of view, she has to hypothesise. As in her Lives of Jane Austen and Dickens's mistress Ellen Ternan (*The Invisible Woman*), she often has to proceed by ingenious analogies. Since we don't know how Pepys was brought up, she provides a contemporary manual of manners for children from 1577. Since we don't have first-hand accounts of the sexual activities of young men-about-town in the 1650s, she points us to a book of advice on *The Arts of Wooing and Complementing*, written by Milton's nephew in 1658. In filling the gaps, Tomalin characteristically brings some sympathetic guesswork to the voiceless heroines of Pepys's story – maids, mistresses, patronesses – and especially to his wife,

Elizabeth Pepys, the beautiful, penniless, quick-tempered French girl whom Pepys married when she was nearly fifteen. Tomalin makes her the 'muse' of the Diary: Pepys is 'inspired' to write it 'by the condition of marriage itself'.[34]

But for all his alluring openness and the mass of evidence he provides, Pepys raises some strategic problems for his biographer. If she paraphrases him, as she must, what goes missing? A few tiny examples of the transition from Diary to biography show how the source material has to be tidied up, little bits of it lopped off here and there, in order to give the life-story a clear narrative shape.

Tomalin describes Pepys inviting Elizabeth to join him on a trip to the residence of his patrons at Huntingdon on 13 September 1663, 'with the gallant words': 'Well, shall you and I never travel together again?' 'As soon as they arrived at Brampton', Tomalin continues, 'he took her to spend the day with Lady Sandwich. Later they rode into the woods to gather nuts, and he showed her the river.' She calls this an 'idyllic' 'afternoon together in the autumn sunshine'. In the Diary, this trip is more of a mess. After his invitation to her, they don't in fact set out together, but ride out separately, as he has to wait for someone else. They meet up on the way, and Elizabeth is taken ill drinking beer, and is alarmingly sick. When they arrive at Brampton they are extremely tired. Pepys visits Lady Sandwich on his own, not with his wife, and then leaves Elizabeth behind when he returns to town. It isn't until 19 September, a week later, that they go riding in Brampton woods, eating nuts in the sunshine, and it's she who shows him the river 'behind my father's house', not the other way round. Elsewhere in the biography, Tomalin does refer to Pepys's anxiety at Elizabeth's sickness while riding to Brampton, but she doesn't link the two occasions together.[35]

Wanting to show his mixed feelings about death, Tomalin reports the dream Pepys has after his mother's death. 'He dreamt of her again, coming to him and asking for a pair of gloves, and in the dream "thinking it to be a mistake in our thinking her all this while dead".' She quotes him again: 'This dream troubled me and I waked'. But in the Diary, this is followed by further nightmares: of seeing his urine turning into a turd, or of pulling at something, possibly from the end of his penis, that looked like 'snot or slime', and this substance turning into 'a gray kind of bird . . . [that] run from me to the corner of the door'. This is horrifying to him. But Tomalin – though far from squeamish –

doesn't quote this, perhaps because she is more concerned at this point to draw an analogy between Pepys's dream of his dead mother and Proust's dream of his dead grandmother. (Tomalin frequently compares Pepys to Proust, and she starts her book with Proust's epigram: 'Un livre est le produit d'un autre moi que celui que nous manifestons dans nos habitudes, dans la société, dans nos vices.' But Pepys's Diary is surely the product of exactly the 'moi', the self, which *does* manifest itself in its habits, social life and vices.)[36]

Here is one last little example of an oddity that has been tidied up in paraphrase. On 13 June 1666, Pepys was saying grace at dinner. In the middle, he says, 'my mind fell upon my lobsters', and he jumps up, exclaiming, 'Cud Zookes! What is become of my lobsters!' He had bought two fine ones that day, but had left them in a hackney coach. Tomalin mentions this twice, once to show how Pepys likes to repeat his own sayings, once to display his extraordinary energy. On the same day he loses the lobsters, he also attends the funeral of Admiral Myngs, goes to a board meeting in Whitehall, visits the Exchequer and the studio of a painter who is doing a portrait of his father, and goes to his mistress in Deptford where he 'did what he would with her'. He gets a boat home, drinks a pint of sack, and buys three eels from a fisherman. No wonder he forgot his lobsters! But what Claire Tomalin omits is that he remembers that he forgot them, and bursts out with his exclamation, in the middle of saying grace.[37] (And perhaps that's why he writes it down: he may have been rather ashamed of himself, and wanted to expiate the offence in the Diary.) The story has been slightly flattened, and has lost a little of its idiosyncrasy. But the biographer can't do everything. Biography has to omit and to choose. In the process, some things go missing – in this case, just the whiskers of a pair of crustaceans that fell through the gaps in the net.

Virginia Woolf's Nose

Biography is a process of making up, or making over. The *New Oxford Dictionary of English* (2001) includes in its definitions of 'making up', to compose or constitute a whole (of parts); to put together or prepare something (like mortar) from parts or ingredients; to arrange type and illustrations on a page; and to concoct or invent a story. 'Making over' has two meanings: 'to transfer the possession of something to someone', and 'to completely transform or remodel something' (such as a person's hairstyle – or nose). Since biographers try to compose a whole out of parts (evidence, testimony, stories, chronologies) and arrange it on the page, since they appropriate their subjects and usually attempt to create a new or special version of them (so that we speak of Edel's James or Ellmann's Joyce), and since they must give a quasi-fictional, story-like shape to their material (or no one will read them), these terms seem to fit. But pulling against 'making up' or 'making over', both of which imply some forms of alteration or untruth, is the responsibility to likeness and the need for accuracy.

At a conference on biography in London, in the 1990s, when various practitioners (myself included) were holding forth on the ambiguities and relativity of biography, the biographer of a philosopher rose to his feet and said: 'But there is such a thing as a fact'.[1] Once we get to anything less well attested than a time and a date for tea written in a person's diary, or the outbreak of the First World War, most biographical facts are open to interpretation. But they do exist, and lie around biographers in huge files and boxes, waiting to be turned into story. These facts have owners: they belong to the lives of the biographer's subject and the people whom the subject knew, loved, hated, worked with or brought up, or perhaps met once in the street in passing. All these people will feel a claim over the fact that concerns them. My first experience of being on the receiving end of this was to read, in a biography of my friend the novelist Brian Moore, that I and my husband got lost on our way to visit Brian and Jean Moore at their remote house in Nova Scotia in the mid-1990s, and had to spend the night in a hotel. No such thing happened, and – although this 'fact' didn't have the slightest bearing on Brian Moore's story, except as a useful way of describing how out-of-the-way his house was – I felt a twinge of outrage and bafflement on reading it, as though a tiny part of my life had been for ever traduced. I imagined, then, what it might be like (as for Ted Hughes, for instance) to feel that one's whole life had been falsely 'made over' by biographers: hence his despairing, angry and futile cry: 'I hope each one of us owns the facts of his or her own life.'[2] No: for the biographised and for their friends and family, there is a fight from the death over facts, between the participants in a life and the writers of it.[3] And even if, unusually, no such tug-of-war takes place, the biographer still has to have the internal tussle between 'making up' and 'fact', or 'making over' and 'likeness'.

No wonder that such strong emotions of blame and anger can circulate around biography, or that it is likely to be seen, in the worst cases, as a form of betrayal. For those with an investment in a life-story (whether as relatives, descendants, friends, lovers, colleagues, admirers, scholars or devoted readers) a kind of despair can be felt if what's judged to be an inauthentic version of the life gains currency and prevails. Virginia Woolf provides a particularly interesting example here, because – like Sylvia Plath, or Shelley, or Jane Austen – her life and work have been, since her death, variously and passionately idealised, vilified, fictionalised and mythologised. (An eventful life is not a prerequisite for such passionate make-overs.) Now that this much contested literary life-story has been turned into novel and film, a powerful popularised version of her, for the time being, prevails. In this version, biography and fiction have become blurred together to produce an image of Virginia Woolf which has aroused some anger in those who feel she has been thereby betrayed. I want to look in some detail at this recent making up, or making over, of Woolf, and to ask what these reinterpretations (the technical term is 'versionings') suggest to us about her influence and her afterlife, and about the processes of telling a life-story.

At the beginning of the film *The Hours* (2003) (written by David Hare, directed by Stephen Daldry, and based on the novel by Michael Cunningham), we hear in voice-over the words of Virginia Woolf's suicide note to her husband Leonard, and we see Nicole Kidman as Woolf, looking young and fierce, writing the note, leaving her country house (on a beautiful summer day), walking determinedly, in a tweed coat, down the garden path and towards the river bank, and slowly entering, until she is fully immersed, the green sun-and-shade-dappled waters of a gently flowing river, to the accompaniment of birds calling and a pulsating, emotional score by Philip Glass. Since the film begins with this romanticised version of the suicide of Virginia Woolf, it sets up a life-story which is moving inexorably towards that death. In the next moment that we see her, she is starting to write *Mrs Dalloway*, so that to a casual audience the two things – her writing of the novel and her suicide – might seem to be going on at the same time. As the story of *Mrs Dalloway* unfolds in her mind, it is entirely about the choice between life and death. The other two narratives in the film, which has three inter-cut story-lines, are also concerned with that choice.

I noticed a tiny pause in the voice-over at the start of *The Hours*, which took me back to the work I did on my biography of Woolf, one of the sources used by Cunningham and for the film. When I read the manuscript of her suicide notes to Leonard (she wrote two versions for him, and one for her sister Vanessa, unable to stop revising her work until the very end), with those heart-breaking phrases ('I feel certain that I am going mad again: I feel we can't go through another of those terrible times ... You have given me the greatest possible happiness ...'),[4] I was struck by the organisation of the words on the page. Woolf had written them in short, jagged half-lines, as if she could hardly get to the end of the sentences. I reproduced the letter in my book as it looked on her page, almost like a poem. Michael Cunningham reprinted it in the same way in his novel. As we hear Kidman speaking the words at the start of the film, and see her writing them, she hesitates, almost imperceptibly, on one of those line-breaks, as if she can't quite go on.

The process of creative translation that stretches from Virginia Woolf writing that letter over sixty years ago, to Nicole Kidman playing her character with award-winning, long-nosed intensity, is a long and complex one. It layers Woolf's 1925 novel *Mrs Dalloway* with Cunningham's novel (the surprise American literary hit and Pulitzer Prize winner of 1999), with David Hare's screenplay for and Stephen Daldry's direction of the film of *The Hours*. I think Woolf would have been intrigued by this process. *Mrs Dalloway* (as Elaine Showalter has noted),[5] is an extremely cinematic novel. Woolf was showing an interest at this time in the cinema as a new medium which could express emotions – like fear – without words. She wrote an essay on this in 1926, after going to see *The Cabinet of Dr Caligari*: 'It seems plain that the cinema has within its grasp innumerable symbols for emotions that have so far failed to find expression . . . The most fantastic contrasts could be flashed before us with a speed which the writer can only toil after in vain . . .' However, in her enthusiasm for the new form, she notes that the results of adapting famous novels for the screen are 'disastrous to both'. Take *Anna Karenina* (of which she must have seen a pre–Garbo silent film version). In the film, we just see her 'teeth, her pearls, and her velvet', and scenes of her kissing Vronsky 'with enormous succulence, great deliberation, and infinite gesticulation on a sofa in an extremely well-appointed library, while a gardener incidentally mows the lawn'. In the book, 'we know Anna almost entirely by the inside of her mind'. 'So we lurch and lumber through one of the most famous novels of the world'.[6] A salutary warning, you might think, for the adapters of a novel that itself 'adapted' and 'rewrote' *Mrs Dalloway*.

Mrs Dalloway was the ideal novel through which to fictionalise the life of Virginia Woolf, because it is itself so much about life-writing. Early on in the novel, the aeroplane above the Mall, which the citizens of post-war, peacetime London gaze up at wonderingly and happily, loops its advertisement in the sky, writing a different message for each of them. ('But what letters? A C was it? an E, then an L? Only for a moment did they lie still . . . "Glaxo . . ." "Kreemo . . ." . . . "It's toffee", murmured Mr Bowley'.) To the hallucinating shell-shock victim Septimus Smith, the words in the sky seem to be a signal directed at him, though 'he could not read the language yet'.[7] Everyone in the novel has an unreadable life secreted inside, in layer upon layer of memory, emotion, habit, thought and response, which the language of the novel burrows down into and excavates, but which can only be glimpsed on the surface in the simplified single letters by which we recognise each other externally. Mrs Dalloway's maxim is that 'she would not say of any one in the world now that they were this or were that'. The novel describes people living extremely complex and volatile interior lives, and breaking through to occasional moments of recognition, of which the most intimate, and unlikely, is the society lady and Tory MP's wife Clarissa Dalloway's understanding of Septimus Smith's life and death (though he knows nothing at all about hers).

Woolf's working title for the novel was 'The Hours' (which Cunningham takes as his title), and her notes to herself about the writing of 'The Hours' include this passage (which Cunningham uses as his epigraph):

> I should say a good deal about The Hours, & my discovery: how I dig out beautiful caves behind my characters; I think that gives exactly what I want: humanity, humour, depth. The idea is that the caves shall connect, & each comes to daylight at the present moment.[8]

As usual, when she was working on a new novel, it was issues of form which most concerned her. And she had set herself a challenging task for this modern novel: to write the story of an unremarkable woman in London, to link together two utterly different post-war lives with no apparent connection, and to set against each other, as she put it, 'the world seen by the sane and the insane side by side'.[9] In a deliberate allusion to Joyce's *Ulysses* (which Woolf disliked, but had read at least parts of with care and concentration), the novel takes place on a single day. On this day, a middle-aged, unemployed, married, wealthy upper-class woman who has just recovered from an illness, has an unexpected reunion with the man who wanted to marry her, and gives a party; a young married man of a lower class, who has fought in the war and is suffering from dementia, sees his doctors, and kills himself. The narrative weaves between the two without their ever meeting. The day's progress is marked by the striking and chiming of bells which sometimes seem to relate to or to embody the characters. (Hence the working title, 'The Hours'.) A variety of strategies are used – repeated images, quotations, lines shared between characters, recurring memories – to link the two main stories and to bind the characters' separate lives into a whole shape. Like Proust's long novel, *À la recherche du temps perdu* (which she admired), also much concerned with memory and time, it culminates in the giving of a party, at which the hostess hears the news of the young man's death, and some sense of conclusion is reached, even though the party is itself (as in Proust) a disappointment. As the hours go past and the story of the day unfolds, the characters continually go down into the 'caves' of their interior selves through memory, association, contemplation, vision, hallucination. A fluid, flexible narrative weaves between inner and outer time, immediate and imagined experiences, spaces, places and minds.

'Character' is as important to her as form. All Woolf's essays on modern fiction, written mostly in the years leading up to *Mrs Dalloway*, are about what new tools can be used by the 'modern' fiction writer to create character. She sees fiction as a form of life-writing. But she is at pains not to write autobiographical fiction, though many of her own emotions and experiences (including her breakdowns) are used for Clarissa Dalloway and Septimus Smith (and other characters in the novel, especially Clarissa's returning lover Peter Walsh, who feels a stranger to England and its establishment world). Clarissa Dalloway, a rather superficial, charming, poorly read, apolitical, conservative woman in her early fifties, with a teenage daughter and a smart house in Westminster, is nothing like Virginia Woolf, though she shares her intense memories of childhood, her sexual ambivalence and withdrawal (her strongest erotic emotions have been for her girlhood friend, Sally Seton), her need for both solitude and society, and her preoccupation with illness and mortality combined with a passionate love of the life of the city. Her interior life is at odds with the conventional establishment figure who is seen on the surface. We are made aware of this inner life (via the novel's 'tunnelling' methods) as Mrs Dalloway does the ordinary things a woman of her class and time would do – buying flowers, crossing the road, reading a message by the telephone pad, changing her clothes, mending her dress, getting ready for her party: the female domestic 'trivia' that, in *A Room of One's Own*, Woolf would wryly argue has been thought less 'important' as material for fiction than male subjects such as waging war or playing football.

Clarissa Dalloway has a vivid, strong, eager love of life, which has nothing to do with religious faith, but connects to her mystical sense of a form of immortality through memory and places. She detests coercion or bullying, those who want to force your soul or impose belief or obedience. This applies to the 'love and religion' of Doris Kilman, her daughter's companion, of whom she is scornful and jealous, the psychiatric methods of the mental doctor, Sir William Bradshaw, a guest at her party, and the demanding, infantile love once offered by Peter Walsh. She seems edge-on to the world she observes. This links her to the novel's other main character, Septimus.

'This late age of the world's experience had bred in them all a world of tears.'[10] Septimus, himself dry-eyed, is the victim of 'this late age of the world's experience'. An estate agent's clerk in his twenties, married to an Italian girl who makes hats, he went to war in 1914 and fought through till 1918, and saw his best friend, Evans, killed. Septimus comes back from the war suffering from shell-shock. He can't feel anything; he is hallucinating visions of the dead and has paranoid delusions that messages are being sent to him for him to broadcast. He feels he is in total isolation and cannot communicate. (So he could stand as an extreme version of the experimental, misunderstood artist.) He is threatening to kill himself, and the doctors are on to him. His single story embodies all the terrible deaths and losses of the Great War that underlie the surface of the novel.

Septimus, far out on the edge of the normal world, violently enacts the social critique which Woolf wanted her novel to contain. His presence exposes the social complacency, the class divisions, hypocrisy and exclusions of conservative post-war England – all sharply caricatured in the novel. These seem to crumble away in the light of Septimus's apocalyptic visions, triggered by the traumatic force of what he has witnessed in the trenches. Through the shimmer and glitter of 1920s party-going London pushes up all that terror, despair and grief.

Septimus's dementia, and its treatment, links him to Clarissa through the figure of Sir William Bradshaw, the eugenicist incarcerator of the mentally ill, who makes a tidy profit from his patients. When Sir William appears at Clarissa's party and mentions the suicide of one of his patients, Clarissa feels an inexplicable empathy. She perceives Septimus Smith's death as an act of free choice, as well as a thing of horror. In a sense he does it for her. The original plan for the novel was that she was 'to kill herself, or perhaps merely to die at the end of the party'.[11] (This is the authorial choice which will so interest Michael Cunningham.) Instead, Clarissa returns to her guests at the party, and is recognised as a living presence. The novel ends as if by claiming that it has achieved the job of fiction, of bringing her into being: 'For there she was.'

Mrs Dalloway is a 'modern' novel in several senses. It's published in 1925, in the middle of the decade of the greatest experiments in modernist writing. It's contemporaneous: written between 1922 and 1924, it is set on a Wednesday in June 1923.[12] It treats difficult and challenging subjects – madness, shell-shock, suicide, bisexuality, sexual repression, maternal jealousy, and the catastrophic effects of war – in a suggestive, ironical and unpolemical way. It makes bold experiments with a fictional form. It tells a whole history of a class and a society, even a country, on the basis of a single 'day in a life' – not the methods of a Victorian or Edwardian novel. And it uses the 'present moment' in the life of an ordinary woman, defined only by her married status and her surname in the title, as the centre for its meditation on life and death.

What does Michael Cunningham do with this contradiction in terms, a modernist classic, in his novel *The Hours?* First, and boldly, he sets it in America. Although Woolf never crossed the Atlantic, she once wrote a surreal, fascinated fantasy called 'America Which I Have Never Seen', and might well have made the journey, after the war, if she had lived. It was a brilliant stroke to move the story of *Mrs Dalloway* from London to New York, with all the excitement of city life transferred to the streets of Manhattan. Woolf's pleasure in 'the bellow and the uproar . . . the triumph and the jingle' of 'life; London; this moment of June' becomes Cunningham's stirring New York, 'the roil and shock of it', its 'racket' and 'intricacy'. Cunningham sees that *Mrs Dalloway* is a book in love with a city. It was written during the time when the Woolfs moved, in early 1924, into Bloomsbury from Richmond, the quiet suburb where they had been living since 1913 because of Virginia Woolf's breakdown and illness. London means life, the suburbs are a living death. The city is where the party is going on. She wrote rejoicingly in her diary: 'the whole of London . . . music, talk, friendship, city views, books, publishing, something central & inexplicable, all this is now within my reach, as it hasn't been since August 1913'.[13]

Woolf's novel begins: 'Mrs Dalloway said she would buy the flowers herself.' Cunningham's novel begins twice, once with Woolf's suicide, and once with Mrs Dalloway setting out to buy flowers. But in this case 'Mrs Dalloway' is a nickname given to a bisexual New Yorker, Clarissa Vaughan, by her friend and one-time lover, the writer Richard Brown, who is terminally ill with AIDS, at the end of the twentieth century. This Clarissa is fifty-two, like her namesake, but unlike her she is not married to Richard Dalloway; she lives with a woman called Sally, named after *Mrs Dalloway*'s Sally Seton. Like the original Mrs Dalloway, she is giving a party – a party for her dying friend, to celebrate his winning a literary prize for his novel, whose subject is a woman who commits suicide.

There are two other narratives in *The Hours*. One is the story of a suburban American housewife, Laura Brown, pregnant with her second child, who lives with her obtuse husband, just back from the war, and her anxious, over-dependent little boy, in a Los Angeles suburb, in 1949. Like *Mrs Dalloway*, this is a post-war story. (In a last twist in the novel, the little boy turns out to be the future writer, Richard Brown.) She is sleepwalking through her ordinary life which, on this day, consists in trying to make a cake for her husband's birthday party. But she is fighting against a strong sense of unreality, worthlessness and longing for death. And she is reading *Mrs Dalloway*. (The critic Michael Wood, in his review of *The Hours*, observed that the chief difference between *Mrs Dalloway* and *The Hours* is that 'no one in the first novel can have read the second, whereas almost everyone in the second seems to have read the first'.)[14] The fragile life of Laura Brown, trying to be a normal American wife and mother, is, I think, the most touching section of the book. We are left wondering to the end of the book whether, like the woman in her son's novel, she kills herself.

Cunningham's third story is that of Virginia Woolf, who is living in Richmond, married to Leonard, having her sister and her sister's children to a tea party in June 1923 – and writing *Mrs Dalloway*. She argues with her servants, is longing to move to London, feels jealous of her sister's family life, and is making her mind up whether or not to have Clarissa kill herself. In the end, she decides that 'sane Clarissa will go on, loving London, loving her life of ordinary pleasures, and someone else, a deranged poet, a visionary, will be the one to die'.[15] Framing that day in her life is the day of her suicide on 28 March 1941.

Cunningham's inventive, absorbing novel makes a sensitive re-invention of Woolf's inner life. He has a strong idea of what made Woolf's life heroic, of her dedication to her work in the teeth of illness, and her violent swings between moods of pleasure in life and abysses of depression. My reservations about his re-imagining of Woolf stem from a biographer's squeamish reluctance to see a real person made over into a fictional character, with made-up thoughts and speeches. I found it hard to accept the tone of voice of a Virginia Woolf who thinks to herself: 'Bless you, Quentin', or to her husband, 'If you send Nelly in to interrupt me I won't be responsible for my actions'. In these invented scenes and conversations, the class details don't always ring quite true. I can't hear Virginia Woolf wanting to rush and 'fix her hair', or Vanessa Bell commenting on 'a lovely coat for Angelica at Harrods'.[16] (Angelica would be much more likely to be wearing a cut-down jacket of Duncan Grant's, or a velvet cloak made out of old curtains.) But fiction, of course, is allowed to do this.

In the other two narratives, Woolfian echoes and parallels are woven in and out of Cunningham's American characters. Clarissa Vaughan's daughter Julia is, like Elizabeth Dalloway, in thrall to a woman who loathes Clarissa and makes her feel jealous. But this Doris Kilman is a militant feminist who resents Clarissa Vaughan's old-fashioned, bourgeois, domestic lesbianism. (This strand was cut in the film.) Septimus's hallucinations are re-enacted in Richard Brown's terminal illness: shellshock and the traumatic aftermath of the Great War are translated into the trauma of the AIDS epidemic and its effect on individuals. Woolf's own struggle against suicidal depression colours the story of Laura Brown. (Mrs Brown is the name Woolf gives, in her essay 'Mr Bennett and Mrs Brown', to the ordinary woman who sets a challenge to all novelists.) Clarissa Vaughan, like Clarissa Dalloway, is visited by an old friend, Louis, a past lover of Richard's, while she is getting ready for her party, an emotional visit in which he breaks down and weeps. More playfully, the lunch with a Mayfair hostess from which Mrs Dalloway feels excluded in Woolf's novel is turned into a lunch with a famous gay actor, nudgingly called Oliver St Ives. Royalty glimpsed in Bond Street by Mrs Dalloway becomes a film star – perhaps Meryl Streep? – spotted on the streets of Manhattan. (And, in the movie, there she is!)

Cunningham splits his story into three, Woolf splits her story into two: both strategies raise the question of how individual lives can connect to each other, and whether a single person has more than one self, one way of being. He is particularly interested in life as being, like writing, a kind of performance. Cunningham's Woolf pauses at the door of Hogarth House to pull herself together. 'She had learned over the years that sanity involves a certain measure of impersonation . . . She is the author; Leonard, Nelly, Ralph, and the others are the readers.'[17] Cunningham imagines Woolf impersonating an identity for the benefit of onlookers and 'readers', just as he is impersonating Woolf. He follows her interest, too, in the interior lives of ordinary women like 'Mrs Brown', and in the androgyny of authorship (here is a homosexual male writer impersonating a bisexual woman writer and writing about the lives of lesbians and homosexuals). Like Woolf, he is asking questions about how we value our lives. What is the value of 'a life of ordinary pleasures'?[18] Can a few outstanding moments provide consolation against the long beat of the hours? Do writing – and reading – make life bearable? Cunningham derives from Woolf, too, an idea of immortality which has nothing to do with religion. Clarissa Dalloway imagines that 'somehow in the streets of London, on the ebb and flow of things, she survived, Peter survived, lived in each other, she being part, she was positive, of the trees at home . . . part of people she had never met; being laid out like a mist between the people she knew best . . . but it spread ever so far, her life, herself'. Cunningham imagines Woolf, after her death, in the river, still a part of 'people she had never met': 'All this enters the bridge, resounds through its wood and stone, and enters Virginia's body. Her face, pressed sideways to the piling, absorbs it all: the truck and the soldiers, the mother and the child.'[19]

The Hours is not an imitation, or a pastiche, or exactly a rewriting; in fact this genre of book is hard to define. Michael Wood says that '*The Hours* is haunted by *Mrs Dalloway* . . . The relationship between the two novels goes beyond allusion, and even beyond the modernist habit of borrowing previous literary structures which T.S. Eliot called "the mythical method".' The critic Seymour Chatman, in a piece called '*Mrs Dalloway*'s Progeny: *The Hours* as Second-Degree Narrative', refers to Gerard Genette's *Palimpsests* in an attempt to define this brand of intertextuality. Is it a sequel, a variation on a theme, a pastiche, a parallel, an imitation, a rewriting, a plagiarism, a caricature, an homage or a transposition? Chatman argues that *The Hours* is 'an alternative version of *Mrs Dalloway*' in which the main project is to present the 'ordinariness' of gay life, to 'demonstrate that the gay world is not exotic, but populated by ordinary people'. His critique of *The Hours*, which he calls a 'post–closet reorientation', is that it 'excludes the rest of the world': its interest in gender politics downplays or sidesteps the wider social politics of its original.[20]

The rewriting of Woolf's life and work takes a different shape again in the translation of *The Hours* from novel into screenplay and film. If an uncertainty of social register, a narrowing of political focus to issues of gender, and a simplifying dramatisation of Woolf's creative processes were the weaknesses of Cunningham's otherwise persuasive and attractive novel, the film of *The Hours* – if treated as a biopic – is much more vulnerable to charges of vulgarisation, inaccuracy and sentimentalisation. Certainly its presentation of the social details of the Woolfs' lives was an irritant to this biographer. Hogarth House and Monk's House look too grand and elegant, more like Edith Wharton or Vita Sackville-West's house and garden than bohemian, messy, colourful Bloomsbury. The servants, in their matching uniforms, are too smartly turned out (though their ongoing battle with their difficult mistress is well done), and Vanessa, in a fine spiteful performance by Miranda Richardson, is absurdly posh, a high-society lady one couldn't possibly imagine picking up a paintbrush.

As for the Nose, Nicole Kidman, even with prosthetic addition and fixed scowl, doesn't look very like Virginia Woolf. She looks like Nicole Kidman wearing a nose.[21] She appears too young for the mid-forties author of *Mrs Dalloway*, let alone for the fifty-nine-year-old who kills herself. And she lacks charm. I wish something of Woolf's gleeful comedy, her hooting laughter, her allure, and her excited responses to people and gossip, had been caught. (It's a mark of Kidman's talent as an actress that those possibilities were so severely excluded: she could presumably have done all that if she'd been allowed to.)

David Hare's screenplay is more polemical than Michael Cunningham's novel. He makes much more of Woolf's rage with her doctors, and of the right to choose and proclaim one's sexuality. The three kisses that take place between women in film and novel – between Virginia and Vanessa, Laura Brown and her sick neighbour, Clarissa and her partner – are more deliberately emphasised than by Cunningham, who treats bisexuality as the normal condition of life. Everything is emphatic here. Virginia and Leonard (played with wonderful nervy intelligence by Stephen Dillane) hurl personal testimonies at each other on Richmond station: 'Only I can understand my own condition!' 'It was done out of love!' (Virginia's outburst in this scene – 'If I have to choose between Richmond and death, then I choose death!' played rather differently in the Richmond Odeon than anywhere else in Britain.) In a big scene for Meryl Streep, it is Clarissa Vaughan, not, as in the novel, the old friend who is visiting her, who breaks down in hysterical tears while she is getting ready for her party. This sentimental expressiveness is in strong contrast to Woolf's own fiction, one of whose most striking and alarming qualities is its inhibition. All the women in the film are on the edge of breakdown; all the emotional life is raging away on the surface (not, as in *Mrs Dalloway*, breaking through convention and guardedness). The acting and direction play up feelings for all they are worth. There are a great many scenes with long, emotional looks, tear-filled eyes, forgiving hugs and expressions of love. (It's refreshing to have a caustic cameo performance in the New York flower shop from Eileen Atkins, more usually seen as Virginia Woolf.)

For all its polemical earnestness about the mistreatment of mental illness and the constrictions imposed on Virginia Woolf after her breakdown, the film evacuates her life of political intelligence or social acumen, returning her to the position of doomed, fey, mad victim. I wish, for instance, that she could have been seen setting type at the Press alongside Leonard, as she so often did, instead of wandering off for gloomily creative walks on Richmond Hill. I wish that the idea of 'creativity' didn't consist in an inspirational flash of the first sentence leaping to the novelist's mind, shortly followed by a whole book. (Woolf took about three years, drafting and redrafting, to write *Mrs Dalloway*, and the first sentence she started with wasn't the first sentence she ended up with.) I wish that to the inattentive viewer it didn't look as if Virginia Woolf committed suicide just after finishing *Mrs Dalloway*. (Sure enough, one short review of the film, on a website called filmcritic.com, read: 'Mentally ill author Virginia Woolf (Nicole Kidman) is on suicide watch in 1920s England as she pens her novel *Mrs Dalloway*.')[22] Above all, I wish her suicide hadn't been transformed into a picturesque idyll. Woolf was no Ophelia: she drowned herself on a cold day in March in a dangerous, ugly river where the water runs so fast that nothing grows on the bare banks. She was wearing an old fur coat, wellington boots, and a hat held on by an elastic band. Whether she jumped or walked, dropped under or struggled, we don't know. When I challenged Stephen Daldry in an interview about his version of the suicide, he responded: 'We only had Kidman for four weeks in June, and we couldn't exactly strip the trees.'[23]

Where novel and film come together in an impressive tribute to Virginia Woolf, however, is in their eloquence about a subject which, so many years after *Mrs Dalloway*, and the death of its author, is still a highly problematic one. Can we choose whether to live or die? 'It is possible to die . . . She – or anyone – could make a choice like that. It is a reckless, vertiginous thought . . .' Laura Brown thinks, in the novel.[24] In all three narratives, a decision is being made about suicide. Why must someone die in her novel, Leonard Woolf asks Virginia, in the film. 'Someone has to die in order that the rest of us should value life more,' she replies. Laura Brown puts the 'vertiginous thought' behind her, and goes home, at least this time, to her family. Richard Brown, before he slides out of his top-floor window, tells Clarissa that he has stayed alive for her, but now she must let him go. How should we treat death? David Hare – perhaps too consolingly – imagines the voice of Virginia Woolf telling us, as she leaves us, that she has mastered this question, and understands what to do: 'to look life in the face and to know it for what it is; to love it for what it is, and then to put it away'.

The film of *The Hours* gained enormous publicity and won some prizes; and it sent readers back in droves, not only to Cunningham's novel but also to *Mrs Dalloway*, which for a short time became the number 1 paperback on Amazon's sales list, the first time the book had ever been a best-seller. There was even a poem called 'The Hours' written about the making of the film, by Mark Doty, who watched the filming of Clarissa going to buy flowers in a corner of New York sprayed with artificial snow. (One of the licences the film took was to set the Mrs Dalloway story in winter, not in June.)

Clarissa
buying the flowers herself.
I take it personally. As if,

no matter what, this emblem persists:
a woman went to buy flowers, years ago,
in a novel, and was entered

by the world . . .

Though they continue, shadow and replica,

copy and replay – adapted, reduced,
reframed – beautiful versions – a paper cone of asters,
golden dog nipping at a glove – fleeting,

and no more false than they are true.[25]

'No more false than they are true' would have been a useful line for some angry Woolfians, who were 'taking it personally', to bear in mind. *The Hours*, though a popular and widely enjoyed film, created considerable dismay in some circles. As always with Woolf's posthumous reputation, there were transatlantic differences. In Britain, the film brought Woolf's usual critics out from under their stones; the novelist Philip Hensher, always a vindictively anti-Woolfian voice, wrote a piece called 'Virginia Woolf Makes Me Want to Vomit', taking the opportunity to attack her 'truly terrible novels ... inept, ugly, fatuous, badly written and revoltingly self-indulgent'.[26] Some good fun was had at the expense of the Nose (one critic suggesting that in the scene where Virginia lays her head down on the grass next to the dead bird which her niece has left in the garden for burial, she is comparing beaks). In America, the film was mocked by some reviewers for pretentiousness and liberal pieties: for instance as 'a preposterous faux-feminist manifesto that blames the woes of the modern day female on her historical disconnectedness'. It also came under attack (Daldry told me in interview) from spokesmen for Catholic churches calling it 'an abomination' which 'should be banned ... There have been demonstrations outside cinemas, and suggestions that we're celebrating women who've abandoned their children.'[27]

Readers and viewers more sympathetic to feminism, gay culture and Woolf had other kinds of criticism (though the film had plenty of admirers, too). The family, in the voice of Vanessa Bell's granddaughter Virginia Nicholson, complained bitterly about Kidman's inappropriateness in the part, her gloom and lack of humour, and, particularly, about the absurd representation of Vanessa. But, as Nicholson admitted: 'How can I possibly look at the film objectively? From my angle, whatever they do is going to be wrong.' In a letter to me, she added sadly: 'This film will inform the perceptions of Virginia Woolf of a generation of cinema-goers.'[28]

Many Woolfians were no happier. Chat-rooms and Woolf email sites resounded with criticisms of the film. Here are two characteristic examples of the arguments, one more hostile than the other. The first is by Roberta Rubenstein, the second by Maria Alvarez:

> Like a copy of a copy, Woolf is diminished through replication ...
> Woolf is revealed ... as a very serious, rather abstracted woman whose

mind wanders from the details at hand to the details of the novel she's writing, who argues with servants, who causes her husband distress, who commits suicide by drowning. I'm afraid that too many film-goers will take from *The Hours* the impression of nothing more than a sad, eccentric writer – a figure far simpler than the intellectually robust and emotionally complex Virginia Woolf . . . I'm afraid for the real Woolf. I'm concerned that she has been made into Virginia Woolf lite.[29]

Woolf was a protean creature . . . *The Hours* sympathetically perpetuates one stereotype of Woolf – the restless, tortured, 'mad' artist in enforced exile from real life, and ultimately torn apart by this alienation. [But the film] will ensure that a new generation of young women will reinvent and reappraise her.[30]

These sorts of views were rounded up in a piece by Patricia Cohen in the *New York Times* for 15 February 2003, titled 'The Nose Was the Final Straw'. (The theme of the piece was trailed: 'A witty writer and activist has become a loser with an absurd proboscis, her devotees say'.)[31] Cohen commented: 'Many Woolfians are fuming, arguing that their idol has been turned into a pathetic, suicide-obsessed creature, her politics ignored, her personality distorted, and even her kisses inaccurately portrayed.' Various well-known American Woolf scholars were cited, Jane Marcus dismissing the novel (as well as the film) as 'a tiny, insignificant spin-off from a great book'; Brenda Silver advising, 'If you want to read Virginia Woolf, then read Virginia Woolf.' A Woolf doctoral student said 'What really put me off was the Nose', and added bemusedly: 'Were Woolf's contemporaries obsessed with her nose?' The Vice-President of the International Virginia Woolf Society, Vera Neverow, exclaimed: 'Oh my God, did they have to drown her twice?' And she spoke of 'having to defend my territory'. Michael Cunningham, writing to me about this debate, asked: 'How dare she, how dare anyone, consider Woolf his or her "territory"? I know of no other figure who inspires such ferocious possessiveness.'[32]

At the Virginia Woolf Conference at Smith College in June 2003, where the tone was predominantly feminist and pro-Woolfian, a panel chaired by Brenda Silver discussed the issue of possessiveness. This was a conversation about the struggle between authority and ownership on the one hand, and 'versioning', or 'appropriation', or 'translation', on the other. The film studies expert on the panel abandoned all notions of 'fidelity' in favour of an interest in 'transformation'. The English feminist critic Michèle Barrett dwelt (like Seymour Chatman) on the shift in 'political burden' from *Mrs Dalloway* to the film of *The Hours*. She had been irritated by David Hare's claim in his introduction to the published screenplay, that the devastation of AIDS provided a parallel to the devastation of the First World War. Barrett argued that there was really no parallel, but that the 'political centre or theme' of *Mrs Dalloway* had been dropped 'in favour of a different political scene, a meditation on the implications of sexual choice'. Daniel Mendelsohn, who had written a thoughtful piece on the different 'versionings' of Woolf by Cunningham, Hare and Daldry, in the *New York Review of Books*, argued that it is impossible not to think about 'a literary figure whom we all know' in relation to the film's version of her, impossible not to ask 'well, precisely *what* does this woman with this funny nose have to do with Virginia Woolf?' His reaction to the film was that it 'flattened her out', and 're-inscribed the popular cliché about female creators, that they walk around glowering all the time'. He minded that 'there are now fifty million American cinema-goers who think of Virginia Woolf as that dame who drowned herself and wore brown clothes'.[33] All agreed, more or less, that the film of *The Hours* was a kind of 'biopic', which had made up a version of Virginia Woolf's life-story.

Does it matter if the film's version of Virginia Woolf prevails for a time? There is no one answer. Yes, because it distorts and to a degree misrepresents her, and for any form of re-creation, of any significant life, in any medium, there is a responsibility to accuracy. No, because she continues to be re-invented – made up, and made over – with every new adapter, reader, editor, critic and biographer. There is no owning her, or the facts of her life. The Nose is her latest and most popular incarnation, but she won't stay fixed under it for ever. At the end of *Orlando*, Woolf's teasing spoof on conventional biography, her hero/heroine, reaching the present day, sniffing its smells and powdering her nose, calls all her various selves together. For 'a biography is considered complete if it merely accounts for six or seven selves, whereas a person may well have as many thousand'. James Ramsay realises, as he finally gets close 'to the lighthouse',[34] and finds it isn't a bit like he expected it to be, that 'nothing was simply one thing'.

Reading in Bed

When the biographer Richard Ellmann gave his inaugural lecture at Oxford, in 1971, on literary biography, he argued that biography is essentially a social narrative. 'For the biographer' (said Ellmann) 'who himself represents the social world, the social self is the real self; the self only comes to exist when juxtaposed with other people. The solitary self is a pressure upon the social self, or a repercussion of it, but it has no independent life.'[1] Changing 'himself' to 'herself', I want to explore the possibility of a biographical approach to the *solitary* self, in the person of the solitary reader. Though much has been written about the history of readers, there is still a lot to discover about the private reading habits of individuals. The historian Robert Darnton notes that 'The inner experience of ordinary readers may always elude us.'[2] But it may be possible to track the 'inner experience' of women writers as readers, and to look at the solitary space of reading which for many women writers has embodied one of the most formative pleasures of their lives – starting with some remarks by Virginia Woolf about women's reading:

> What a vast fertility of pleasure books hold for me! I went in & found the table laden with books. I looked in & sniffed them all. I could not resist carrying this one off & broaching it.[3]

> Sometimes I think heaven must be one continuous unexhausted reading. It's a disembodied trance-like intense rapture that used to seize me as a girl, and comes back now and again down here [i.e. in the country] with a violence that lays me low.[4]

And to Vita Sackville-West:

> Love is so physical, and so's reading.[5]

These are intensely erotic, bodily and pleasurable descriptions of reading. And they are, also, linked to feelings about girlhood and growing up. These clues laid by Virginia Woolf suggest the remarkable frequency with which women writers recall the vital formative pleasure of reading in girlhood, and how that pleasure is embodied both in a physical experience and also in a particular setting. Especially for women writers who grew up in the late nineteenth or early twentieth century – for instance Elizabeth Bowen, Edith Wharton and Virginia Woolf – and who may have been educated at home, the place of reading in the home, especially in its relation to the paternal library or study, is of lasting significance in their adult lives. How do some of these women writers transform or translate, make use of, their childhood place of reading in their adult writing life?

Woolf has a whole essay on the memory of youthful reading, which she calls, deliberately echoing her father Leslie Stephen, 'Hours in a Library'. It uses a strange physical image for childhood reading.

> With a little thought we can most of us recall the stages at least of our own initiation. The books we read in childhood, having purloined them from some shelf supposed to be inaccessible, have something of the unreality and awfulness of a stolen sight of the dawn coming over quiet fields when the household is asleep. Peeping between the curtains we see strange shapes of misty trees which we hardly recognise, though we may remember them all our lives; for children have a strange premonition of what is to come.[6]

This, by implication, is a passage about reading in bed, certainly about reading at night. And it is full of a language of the illicit – purloined, inaccessible, awfulness, stolen sight. It is about shame and secrecy, as well as about adventuring and remembering. Very often, the figure of the reading girl – a very familiar one to us all from fiction, painting, memoirs and autobiographies – is a figure whose pleasure has something hidden or illicit in it. Her books, and her time of reading, may be 'stolen'. And that sense of shameful reading has a history behind it.

The history of reading contains within it a conflict which recurs over and over again, in different formulations, between what one might call vertical and horizontal reading: the first regulated, supervised, orderly, canonical and productive, the second unlicensed, private, leisurely, disreputable, promiscuous and anarchic. The contrast between public and private, licensed and unlicensed, social and solitary reading has never been straightforward, and it has been interestingly complicated in books such as Kate Flint's *The Woman Reader* (1993).[7] But there are edicts and prohibitions galore to be found, over hundreds of years, warning against the danger of reading being done in the wrong way, of the wrong books, by the wrong people, and even in the wrong position. The splendid *Philobiblion* by Richard de Bury, Bishop of Durham, of 1344, defending his passionate love of books against charges of excess or profanity, has a great passage of invective against 'negligence' in reading, particularly against the kind of young scholar who, 'lazily lounging over his studies' on a cold winter's day, lets the snot from his nose drip down on to his book, or marks the page with the filth under his nails, or eats fruit or cheese over an open book, and then with his arms folded on the page falls into 'a profound nap', 'to the no small injury of the book'. This is a matter not only of not reading in the wrong way, but also of not letting the wrong people read: 'The laity, who look at a book turned upside down just as if it were open in the right way, are utterly unworthy of any communion with books. Let the clerk take care also that the smutty scullion reeking from his stewpot does not touch the lily leaves of books, all unwashed.'[8]

For a much later warning against indecorous or unlicensed reading we can turn from Richard de Bury to Jean-Baptiste de la Salle, the founder of the Brothers of the Christian Schools, warning young boys in 1703, in *The Rules of Christian Decorum and Civility*, against using their beds for reading, talking or playing. 'It is thought indecent and unmanly', he fulminates, 'to idly chit chat, gossip or sport in bed. Imitate not certain persons who busy themselves in reading and *other matters*; stay not in bed if it be not to sleep, and your virtue shall much profit from it.'[9] We can only imagine what he meant by 'other matters'.

Such examples, as Armando Petrucci noted in *A History of Reading in the West* (1999), point to a historical opposition between 'rigid, professional, ordered practices of reading' and 'free, relaxed, unregulated practices'. 'Certain rules' (Petrucci says) 'proclaimed that the reader must be seated in an erect position with his arms resting on a table and the book in front of him. Reading must be done with maximum attention, without moving, making noise, annoying others or taking up too much space . . . Reading is a serious and demanding activity requiring effort and attention. It often takes place in a group . . . Other modes of reading (alone, anywhere in the house, in total liberty) are . . . grudgingly tolerated, but felt to be potentially subversive.' In

Petrucci's survey of Italian reading habits, though some readers expressed a preference for reading in bed, most conformed to these ancient regulations for 'proper' reading – at a desk, in a library. Only one young woman in the sampling of eighty readers said that her favourite place and position for reading was 'lying flat on a rug'.[10]

Prohibitions against unlicensed reading obviously apply to male readers as well as to female readers. But edicts against unsupervised, unsuitable, dangerous reading have been particularly directed at women, especially in the eighteenth and nineteenth centuries. I don't go as far as the feminist critic Judith Fetterley who argues that, in a patriarchal and sexist culture, women's 'covert and hidden' reading of other women writers might be thought of as a secret erotic pleasure analogous to 'the gratifications of masturbation'.[11] But it is certainly the case that women's secret reading has been thought – probably rightly – to be a dangerous habit.

Everyone knows a story of a girl whose intense reading separates her from the family, is disapproved of as unhealthy or unfeminine, may lead on to a great career, but can also be the source of late disappointments and tragedy. In biographies and memoirs of women's reading lives, there are persistent examples of a struggle not only over what women are allowed to read, but over the *place* allowed for young women's reading. The rarity, until the twentieth century, of a woman's having her own reading room or separate space is attested to over and over again. How far back this goes is fascinatingly described in Dora Thornton's 1996 book on the study in Renaissance Italy, *The Scholar and his Study*. There were very few women, such as Isabella D'Este, who could afford to have a study of their own, and not just (as in many representations of the Virgin Mary) books by their bed or in their place for prayer. 'Women very rarely owned studies,' Thornton notes, 'a fact which has much to do with the perceived dignity of women, their education, and the problematic status of learned women ... The freedom to read and study was questionable, since a woman alone – and therefore in some measure outside society – was suspect and sometimes feared.'[12]

From Tudor to eighteenth-century England, there are many instances of women writers with no place or room of their own. The life-story of the playwright Elizabeth Cary, Lady Falkland (1585–1639) gives us a dramatic and, lately, much-studied example. In the hagiographical *The*

Lady Falkland: Her Life, written by one of her daughters, we hear how the prodigious Elizabeth

> learnt to read very soon and loved it much . . . Without a teacher, whilst she was a child, she learnt French, Spanish, Italian [and] Latin . . . She having neither brother nor sister, nor other companion of her age, spent her whole time in reading; to which she gave herself so much that she frequently read all night; so as her mother was fain to forbid her servants to let her have candles, which command they turned to their own profit, and let themselves be hired by her to let her have them, selling them to her at half a crown apiece, so was she bent to reading; and she not having money so free, was to owe it them, and in this fashion was she in debt a hundred pound afore she was twelve year old.

At the age of seventeen, Elizabeth was married to Sir Henry Cary, who left her in his mother's home shortly after the marriage. Her mother-in-law 'used her very hardly, so far, as at last, to confine her to her chamber; which seeing she little cared for, but entertained herself with reading, the mother-in-law took away all her books, with command to have no more brought her; then she set herself to make verses'. Lady Cary became known for her play *The Tragedy of Mariam the fair Queene of Jewry* (written between 1603 and 1612, published 1613). She had eleven surviving children, converted to Catholicism, was repudiated by her husband, continued to write, and died in poverty. Her story has been described, by Barbara Kiefer Lewalski, as 'an inner conflict between domestic subservience and intellectual independence'.[13]

The dubiousness, even the threat, of the solitary woman reader is well attested to in later periods. Jacqueline Pearson's book on women's reading in the eighteenth century has a great deal to say about what one novel of the time (Charlotte Dacre's *The Confessions of the Nun of St Omer*) calls 'Dangerous Reading'. Women reading could be identified with seduction, inflammation, corruption, abnormality, sloth, selfishness and unfeminine anti-social habits. Reading in the carriage, reading while having your hair done, and, above all, reading in bed, were targets of criticism. So women readers were often secret readers, concealing their habit, or else they made reading acceptable by reading communally, reading aloud. But as long as the household's library belonged to the father, there were few parents who would say, as Dr Johnson recommended to a friend, 'Turn your daughter loose in your library!' More often, fathers locked up their books against their wives and daughters.[14] And the nineteenth-century history of reading is rich in advice manuals on the importance of right methods in reading, recommendations for reading aloud in groups to counteract the dangerous delights of *solitary* reading, warnings against the corrupting and over-exciting influence of novels, and testimonies to the conflict for women between domestic duties and reading time.[15]

No more elegant and ironical fictional illustration exists of the woman reader secreting unlicensed and dangerous reading in her bedroom than in Stendhal's *Le Rouge et le noir* of 1830, where Julien detects that certain books – Voltaire, for instance, and anything 'hostile to the interests of Throne and Altar' – in the *risqué* library of his employer, the marquis de la Mole, are going missing, since Mademoiselle de la Mole, who looks so prim and pious in church, has 'the secret habit of stealing books from her father's library' and taking them off to her room.[16]

The story of the woman writer with no place to call her own goes on for a surprisingly long time. An anthology of 1992 called *The Pleasure of Reading*, with essays by forty writers on their childhood reading, reiterated over and over again (for men as well as women, it must be said) the importance of the place of early reading. Three other ingredients were often mentioned: the association of childhood reading and secrecy, the importance of being read to, and, in some households, a settled hostility to 'the reading girl'. For some, the parents' bookshelves were very important. Doris Lessing, born in 1919 and brought up in what is now Zimbabwe, says: 'I began reading at seven, off a cigarette packet, and almost at once progressed to the books in my parents' bookcase, which would be found in any middle-class household then . . . sets of Dickens, Walter Scott, Stevenson, Kipling. Some Hardy and Meredith. The Brontës. George Eliot.' But many of these women writers remembered reading as a secret activity. A.S. Byatt says that because she was a sick child with asthma she spent 'much of her childhood in bed, reading'. Margaret Atwood remembered that she 'used to drag the really dubious books off into corners, like dogs with bones, where no one would see me reading them. I resorted to flashlights under the covers.' These writers vividly remember – as I imagine we all do – the *place* of their early reading. Sally Beauman, for example: 'I can remember the day I learned to read; I can remember the room in which I did so.' Emma Tennant, growing up in a huge Victorian Gothic castle in Scotland, 'read up and down the house', in attics and basements: 'Reading for me is tied inextricably to place.' And Germaine Greer, in a distant echo of Elizabeth Cary, remembered reading secretly at night in the face of implacable opposition from her mother: 'So the light would not show under the door I read under the sheets but not by the light of a battery torch, which I had no money to buy. I pinched candle ends from the parish church and burned them in bed ... My front hair still stands up in a crinkly quiff from being regularly singed.'[17]

In fiction, we can all think of examples of the solitary, impassioned, absorbed reading girl. There is Jo in the attic in *Little Women*, eating apples and crying over *The Heir of Redclyffe*. (Clearly this was a common American girlish habit, since among the heroine's few bedside books in Ellen Glasgow's 1913 novel of provincial post-war Southern life, *Virginia*, there is 'a conspicuously tear-stained volume of "The Heir of Redclyffe"'.) There is Maggie Tulliver being reprimanded for reading too much in *The Mill on the Floss*, or Jane Eyre hiding behind the curtain in Mrs Read's house with her copy of Bewick.

In many memoirs by women writers, or in fictional versions of their own experiences, private, obsessive, addictive girlhood reading is very often described as a secret experience intensely embodied and couched in a highly physical language. The formative act of reading, carried out both in response to and in opposition to the life of the family, was for a large number of women one of the most crucial and determining features of their early lives. And the physical *place* of their childhood reading is very often set in contrast to the 'official' reading space in the house: the father's library, study or office.

The Anglo-Irish writer Elizabeth Bowen (1899–1973) is extremely eloquent on this subject of reading 'deeply, ravenously, unthinkingly, sensuously, as a child', as in her 1946 essay on childhood reading, 'Out of a Book' (where for 'he', I think, read 'she', or 'me'):

The child lives in the book ... he flings into the story the whole of his sensuous experience which from being limited is the more intense. Book dishes draw saliva to the mouth; book fears raise gooseflesh and make the palms clammy; book suspense makes the cheeks burn and the heart thump. Still more, at the very touch of a phrase there is a surge of brilliant visual images: the child rushes up the scenery for the story.[18]

She often makes the point that any place or scene in real life which the child may associate with a scene or description in a book will keep that association for ever: 'It has not only given body to fiction, it has partaken of fiction's body.' 'Fiction's body' is a concept that interests Bowen very much. The physical world of the book permeates the child reader, who is giving all his – or her – body to the act of reading. Something read and imagined in childhood – for instance, for the Irish Bowen, London – has an extraordinarily powerful physical impact: 'This envisaged London gained on me something of the obsessive hold of a daydream; it invested itself with a sensuous reality – sounds, smells, motes of physical atmosphere – so powerful as to have been equalled since by almost no experience of so-called reality.'[19]

This fascination with the obsessive physical hold a place in a book can have on a child's imagination is also found in her broadcast of 1947 on her childhood reading of Rider Haggard's *She*, which led her to find the Thames Embankment, when she at last saw it, a 'disappointment, being far, far less wide than Horace Holly had led me to expect'.[20] But what she did carry into adult life from her childhood reading of *She*, Bowen says, was the idea of 'obstination, triumphant obstination': 'Want any one thing hard enough, long enough, and it must come your way. This did strike deep: it came up like a reinforcement, because in my day, my childhood, all polite education was against the will – which was something to be subdued, or put out of sight as though it did not exist. Up to now, I had always expected books to be on the side of politeness.'[21] It is a good example of the child finding her own form of secret education in her books. Bowen went to school, and wrote eloquently about her schooldays in her essay 'The Mulberry Tree' and in a number of fictional versions. But the education she received at school seems to have been much more to do with social behaviour and manners than with reading. That was her own, private discovery.

Bowen is a writer much concerned with memory (Proust is very important to her) and the necessary disillusion involved in growing up. The point she keeps making in her essays on childhood reading is that, however much we would like to return to it, the experience is irrecoverable: 'It is not only our fate but our business to lose innocence,

and once we have lost that it is futile to attempt to picnic in Eden.'[22]
The experience of reading as a girl is a kind of secret, a private place,
constructed and only inhabitable at the time before domestic or sexual
or social demands have pressed in on it. Yet, though it can't be re-
enacted as an experience, the 'forgotten books' of childhood leave an
ineradicable trace on the writer's adult life.

> The imagination, which may appear to bear such individual fruit, is
> rooted in a compost of forgotten books. The apparent choices of art are
> nothing but addictions, pre-dispositions: where did these come from,
> how were they formed? The aesthetic is nothing but a return to images
> that will allow nothing to take their place ... the imaginative writer was
> the imaginative child.[23]

The imaginative child reading alone in her private space is an image that
recurs in many memoirs and fictions of the American women writers
who grew up between the 1870s and the 1910s. These can be images of
painful isolation as well as addictive pleasure. So Willa Cather
(1873–1947) growing up in a small house in Red Cloud, Nebraska,
conflicted and unhappy in her sexuality, culturally ambitious, unconfi-
dent, in revolt against her mother and the provincial life of the town,
spent much of her girlhood reading, 'sitting in her father's office at
night or hidden away upstairs in the attic, reading *Huckleberry Finn* and
Swiss Family Robinson, *The Pilgrim's Progress*, Dumas and Stevenson,
mixed up with *Paradise Lost* and the *Iliad, Sartor Resartus* and *Anna
Karenina*.'[24]

The novelist Ellen Glasgow (1873–1945), growing up isolated in an
unhappy Virginian family (I tell her full story later in this book), taught
herself to read, and reading became, she said, in her memoir *The Woman
Within*, 'the greatest consolation of my life'. Her books were derived,
initially, from her father's library, and, in early childhood, from his
reading aloud. Later, in her teens, Glasgow's addiction to reading
alienated her from friends and family. She would sneak out of bed at
night to read until two in the morning in her father's study. She
remembered: 'I begrudged the hours I spent asleep or talking to my
acquaintances, who regarded books as not only unnecessary in well bred
circles, but as an unwarranted extravagance. Besides, did not everybody
know what happened to blue-stockings?'[25]

Glasgow stayed on as an adult in the family home, but she was only allotted her own official space for working after she had published her first book at the age of twenty-four. As with Willa Cather, her reading and writing put her in confrontation with her environment. A more benign version of the reading daughter is found in the memoir of Eudora Welty (1909–2001), whose story I will also come back to. In *One Writer's Beginnings* (1984), Welty recalled her childhood in Jackson, Mississippi as having a great deal to do with books. Her parents' living-room was always called 'their library' and her parents valued their books, which her mother read aloud to her as a child and which she then began, very young, to read for herself. One of her powerful childhood memories was of being taken out of school at six or seven with a 'fast-beating heart' and having to rest in her parents' bed. In the evening, they would sit and talk in the room where she was half sleeping, and she would hear 'the murmur of their voices, the back-and-forth'.[26] In her partly autobiographical novel, *The Optimist's Daughter* (1912) the heroine, Laurel, also remembers lying in bed and hearing 'the rhythmic, nighttime sound of the two beloved reading voices'. In the novel, Laurel's father has just died. She is left alone in her parents' house, and goes into what was her father's 'library'. Although her father remarried, disastrously, after her mother's death, nothing has been changed in the study. She sits at her father's desk and looks at his books – which provide a revealing and endearing brief insight into a Southern American lawyer's reading for relaxation in the first half of this century, a mixture of popular travel books, British classics, Rider Haggard and P.G. Wodehouse:

> She saw at once that nothing had happened to the books. *Flush Times in Alabama and Mississippi*, the title running catercornered in gold across its narrow green spine, was in exactly the same place as ever, next to Tennyson's Poetical Works, Illustrated, and that next to Hogg's *Confessions of a Justified Sinner*. She ran her finger in a loving track across *Eric Brighteyes* and *Jane Eyre*, *The Last Days of Pompeii* and *Carry On, Jeeves*. Shoulder to shoulder, they had long since made their own family. For every book here she had heard their voices, father's and mother's. And perhaps it didn't matter to them, not always, what they read aloud; it was the breath of life flowing between them, and the words of the moment riding on it that held them in delight.[27]

The daughter's protected, tender memory of her parents' voices, reading or talking out loud, found in both the memoir and the novel, is connected to the privileged, sacrosanct space of the father's study, which is now for the daughter to inhabit, just as it is for the adult woman writer to read and to recreate the story of her parents' marriage.

That tender link between the dead father and the living daughter is echoed with almost alarming intensity by the American novelist Mary Gordon, who has written a great deal about her Jewish, Catholic-convert father, and who, in an anthology called *A Passion for Books*, describes being taught to read very early by her father, and reading *with* her father as a child, in a perpetual present tense of pleasure and love:

> When my father and I are reading, we lounge and sprawl. He is on his green chair and I am on the floor near his feet. Or we are on the rose-coloured couch with its upholstered flowers, or sitting up together on my bed. We are in a place where the people we live among don't go. They aren't readers. *We* are almost nothing else.
>
> Reading with my father, I am always safe and he is always handsome . . . Reading, we're removed from anything that can accuse or harm us. If there's anything in a book I don't like, he makes it go away. Because I'm scared when we read 'Peter Pan', he takes a scissors and cuts out every reference to Captain Hook. He reads to me from a book full of holes, full of spaces, spaces he fills in with something he invents, something that will bring me joy.[28]

How often, in these examples, is girlhood reading associated with reading in bed, or at night-time, or sneaking out of bed to read, or listening to parents' voices reading in bed. The child reader – female or male – with the torch under the blankets is one of the most pleasurable images of secret prohibition-breaking, secret discovery. And of course it isn't just children who read in bed. There is a whole section on 'Reading in Bed' in that curious, addictive, pseudo-Burtonian compilation, Holbrook Jackson's *The Anatomy of Bibliomania*, with such delectable examples as that of Diana of Poitiers, who 'rose at six, bathed in rain-water, rode a league or so and returned to bed, where she lay reading until midday'. Jackson even manages to find a recommendation for reading in bed as good for the health, quoting the Oxford Regius Professor of Medicine, and great bibliophile, Sir William Osler

(1849–1919): 'With half an hour's reading in bed every night as a steady practice, the busiest man can get a fair education before the plasma sets in the periganglionic spaces of his grey cortex.'[29]

Alberto Manguel, in *A History of Reading*, has a delicious chapter called 'Private Reading', which begins with the story of Colette reading Victor Hugo's *Les Misérables* in bed at the age of eight, describes his own luxurious childhood experience of reading in bed, and goes on to talk about the 'particular quality of privacy' of reading in bed: 'a self-centred act, immobile, free from ordinary social conventions, invisible to the world, and one that, because it takes place between the sheets, in the realm of lust and sinful idleness, has something of the thrill of things forbidden'.[30] That complete privacy of the bedroom was hard to come by until the late nineteenth/early twentieth century, his reading history tells us, but for his two major examples of women writers who were bed-readers, their bedroom, he argues, was their only refuge from society and their only place of freedom as reader and writer. Colette, his first example, began and ended her life reading in bed, spending her last ten years, as her biographer Judith Thurman tells us, working, reading, sleeping and socialising in what she called her 'raft', her day-bed.

Manguel's other example of a famous reader – and writer – in bed is Edith Wharton (1862–1937). He cites Cynthia Ozick's description of Wharton's using her bedroom as her workplace: 'Out of bed, she would have had to be, according to her code, properly dressed, and this meant stays. In bed, her body was free, and freed her pen.'[31] When Percy Lubbock came to collect anecdotes from Wharton's friends, in the late 1930s, for his rather spiteful memoir of her, he was given many accounts of Wharton's settled habit of working in her bedroom early in the morning, before she dedicated the rest of the day to her guests or her business. (Though she would find time in her early morning writing hours to send little notes to her house-guests to arrive with their breakfast trays, telling them the plans for the day.) Wharton's friend Vivienne de Watteville, writing to Lubbock in 1938, said that Wharton wrote between bath and breakfast, never for more than two hours and never less. She would let the sheets of foolscap fall to the floor as they were written, and they would be gathered up and typed out by her secretary for revision later.

Characteristically, there is nothing idle, wasteful or unproductive about Edith Wharton's use of books in bed. But the manuscript of an unpublished, undated story, probably from the 1920s, suggests that she took pleasure, too, in night-time reading in bed, as well as in early morning writing-in-bed. In this story, 'The Great Miss Netherby', a young American girl, Penelope Pride from Organ City, goes to visit her aunt, Alexa Netherby, who has made a great hit in New York and Paris as a house decorator, has moved (like Wharton) to live in the South of France, and (like Wharton) has a magical garden full of irises. Penelope, who is not as naïve and uncultivated as she is pretending to be, arrives for her visit, and niece and aunt size each other up. Aunt Alexa shows Penelope her bedroom, which has a luxurious big bed. The girl expresses surprise.

> Miss Netherby smiled. 'You expected the usual sleeping-car shelf – the kind of thing that house-decorators consider *jeune fille*? I always thought Carpaccio's St Ursula must have inspired the first *wagon-lits* designer. But why shouldn't a virgin want to stretch and turn over now and then? I like a bed like a swimming-pool myself.'
>
> 'I'm sure I shall too – . . .' her guest acquiesced.
>
> 'Do you [ever] read in bed?' Miss Netherby pursued. 'Because here's the switch. But no, of course you don't.'
>
> 'Well, I hadn't thought of it,' Penelope confessed brightly.
>
> 'You just sleep and sleep, you fortunate child?'
>
> 'Well, what's a bed for?'
>
> 'Ah – what indeed,' murmured her aunt.[32]

But Edith Wharton didn't confine her books to her bedroom. Her private library was one of the greatest pleasures of her life, and had its roots in her childhood reading. She had a curious habit, before she could actually read, of doing what she called 'making up'. This began for her as an extremely young American in Paris, that is, when she was about four or five and her family had just moved, temporarily, to Europe. She had begun inventing stories before then – from the moment she could remember, in fact – but now she 'found the necessary formula'. She had to have a book in her hands, preferably with lots of thick black type, and she would walk rapidly up and down in an 'ecstasy' of invention, turning the pages as if reading, regardless of whether the book was upside down or not, and improvising out loud, and very fast, an imaginary story, a kind of dream narrative. 'Making up' then overlapped with learning to read: at that stage, she would use the books partly to improvise with and partly to read from.

In her autobiography, *A Backward Glance* (1934), Wharton describes this activity as ecstatic and compulsive, and sets it comically against her mother's demands for her to socialise with other children. 'Mother' (she would say, urgently) 'you must go and entertain that little girl for me. *I've got to make up.*' Maternal disapproval is implied in the word 'deplorable', which Wharton applies, as in her mother's voice, to such incidents. She describes her parents spying on their child's peculiar activity through half-closed doors, 'distressed' and 'alarmed' by her need for solitude in which to pursue her obsession, and trying to distract her with toys and playmates. In the unpublished version of her autobiography, 'Life and I', she gives an even more physical account of her passion for story-telling, and her relief when released into it from social obligations, 'the rapture of finding myself again in my own rich world of dreams'. Her account of 'the ecstasy which transported my little body' is extremely, perhaps deliberately, erotic: there's evidently something masturbatory and orgasmic about these 'enraptured sessions', and the anxious spying parents treat them as dangerous and unhealthy. In an unpublished, unfinished, semi-autobiographical novel called 'Literature', she gives this experience to a boy, Richard Thaxter (who will grow up to be a writer). He is described as being so 'excited' by the act of 'making up' that he has to pace up and down, almost running, and becomes hot and feverish with the 'thrill and stimulus'. Almost like an emission or discharge, the story he's inventing seems to 'curl up from the page like a silver mist'. Wharton also gives Dicky Thaxter her own early addiction to the sound of words. He gets his first inspiration for reading and writing from his father's recitation, in his pulpit, of David's lament for Absalom, and is then mocked at by obtuse relations for his attempts to write it down phonetically.[33]

Wharton links her ritualised, solitary, physical act of 'making up' with a later phase, after the family's return from Europe to America, when she was ten or eleven, and would 'steal away' to read for hours, lying on the rug in her father's library. She uses the same words in her memoirs for her addiction to reading in the 'kingdom' of her father's library, as for her earlier 'making up': 'secret ecstasy', 'enraptured sessions'. 'Whenever I try to recall my childhood it is in my father's library that it comes to life. I am squatting on the thick Turkey rug, pulling open one after another the glass doors of the low bookcases, and dragging out book after book in a secret ecstasy of communication.'[34]

Though she was in many ways to react against her genteel, conventional 1860s and 1870s New York upbringing, her idea of a 'private library' grew from what she described in *A Backward Glance* as 'the background of books which was an essential part of the old New York household'.

Wharton read her way through childhood. From a very early age, she felt that through the possession of books she could escape 'being that helpless blundering thing, a mere "little girl".'[35] Though her mother censored her reading of fiction ('a fact hardly to be wondered at', Wharton notes, 'since her own mother had forbidden her to read any of Scott's novels, except *Waverley*, till after she was married'), Wharton looked back on this prohibition as an advantage, for it 'threw me back on the great classics, and thereby helped to give my mind a temper which too-easy studies could not have produced'.[36]

As a young adult, Wharton took refuge from a difficult marriage in books. Reading, as well as writing, was one of the most central, essential emotional experiences of her life. She built her friendships on conversations about, and exchanges of, books. By the end of her life Wharton had written forty-five books and owned two houses in France, each with its perfectly designed library, where she had accumulated about four thousand books.

There are 'private libraries' in many of her novels and stories, and very often these are feminised versions of the male library – the patriarchal inheritance, the male dilettante bachelor collector's preserve. There *are* women characters in Wharton who envy the male library and think of it as a man's preserve, like Lily Bart with Lawrence Selden, in the first chapter of *The House of Mirth* (1905):

> He ushered her into a slip of a hall hung with old prints . . . Then she found herself in a small library, dark but cheerful, with its walls of books, a pleasantly faded Turkish rug, a littered desk, and, as he had foretold, a tea-tray on a low table near the window . . . Lily sank with a sigh into one of the shabby leather chairs.
>
> 'How delicious to have a place like this all to one's self! What a miserable thing it is to be a woman.' She leaned back in a luxury of discontent.

But very often the closed-off library seeps out into the drawing-room, and becomes an important bookish space for women. Far from being a secret, private space, the library, in Wharton's adult appropriation of it, is a comfortable, social, domesticated space. (One of Wharton's friends remembered her saying, when complimented on how well she had set up the desk in the guest-room, with a light and writing-paper, flowers, envelopes and stamps: 'I am rather a housekeeperish person.') The woman's reading space in Wharton's fiction is less cut off from the house, and more decorative, than the patriarchal library. It's associated with flowers, pictures, comfort and hospitality – with human sympathy. It's a social as well as a reading space. Justine Brent, in *The Fruit of the Tree* (1907, Chapter 32), sits in a drawing-room transformed 'into a warm yet sober setting for books, for scattered flowers, for deep chairs and shaded lamps in pleasant nearness to each other'. Mrs Hazeldean in *Old New York* (1924, Chapter 7), achieves in her library/drawing-room, an 'enchanting' atmosphere created by a woman who can somehow see to it that 'the flowers grow differently in their vases, the lamps and easy-chairs have found a cleverer way of coming together, and the books on the table are the very ones one is longing to get hold of'.

The woman's library as an expression of female power and seductiveness is a vital part of the plot of Wharton's novel *Hudson River Bracketed* (1929), of which 'Literature' was an early version. (The title refers to an East Coast architectural style.) The hero, Vance Weston (short for 'Advance'), comes East from a philistine and provincial environment in the Midwest, Euphoria in Illinois (Wharton had never been to the Midwest herself). He discovers culture and becomes a writer. The source of his inspiration is the private library of a dead woman, Miss Lorburn. He is introduced to this library by the woman he is going to fall in love with, the wonderfully named Halo Spear. To the naïve uncultured Vance, the nineteenth-century private library is a place of wonder:

> Vance stood alone in Miss Lorburn's library. He had never been in a private library before; he hardly knew that collections of books existed as personal possessions, outside of colleges and other public institutions. And all these books had been a woman's, had been this Miss Lorburn's, and she had sat among them, lived among them, died reading them – reading the very one on the table at his elbow!

The 'very one' is Miss Lorburn's copy of Coleridge, open at 'Kubla Khan'.

Vance sets out on his career as a writer in New York, but he is drawn back to Miss Lorburn's private library. Eventually the story of the lonely woman who was 'kept warm' by her books, as an image of a more valuable, richer literary culture than the one he is trying to succeed in in present-day New York, becomes the subject of his own successful novel. So Edith Wharton, a woman writer with her own 'private library', invents a male writer re-imagining a woman reader in her library.[37]

For Virginia Woolf (1882–1941), who famously did not go to school or university, and who did all her addictive childhood reading at home, the appropriation of the father's library, and the translating of the woman writer's room from a space of limitation and deprivation to one of power and freedom, is the central story of her writing life. The night nursery at 22 Hyde Park Gate, which in the 1890s became Virginia Stephen's bed-sitting-room, and where above her head she could hear Leslie groaning, rocking in his chair as he wrote and dropping his books with a thump on the floor, is the room, she says in her memoir of 1939–40, which 'explains a great deal' about her work.[38] The reading she was doing in that room – very often in bed – was of books taken from her father's library, reading willingly done under his orders and surveillance. In 1897, when she was fifteen, she listed in her diary the books he was giving her to read: Froude's *Carlyle*, Creighton's *Queen Elizabeth*, Lockhart's *Life of Scott*, Carlyle's *Reminiscences*, James Stephen's *Essays in Ecclesiastical Biography*, her godfather James Russell Lowell's *Poems*, Campbell's *Life of Coleridge*, Carlyle's *Life of Sterling*, Pepys's *Diary*, Macaulay's *History*, Carlyle's *French Revolution*, Carlyle's *Cromwell*, Arnold's *History of Rome*, Froude's *History of England*, Leslie Stephen's *Life of Fawcett*.

Reading under orders and surveillance was done willingly at the time: 'I am to reread all the books father has lent me'.[39] But from the age of fifteen she was, also, forming her own taste – like a private passion for the Elizabethan writer Richard Hakluyt's narratives of travel and adventure – from the run of Leslie's library. And mixed up with all that historical prose went an addictive reading of novels, often out loud to her sister Vanessa: *Felix Holt*, *John Halifax, Gentleman*, *North and South*, *Wives and Daughters*, *Barchester Towers*, *The Scarlet Letter*,

Shirley, *Villette*, *Alton Locke*, *Adam Bede*: all this in 1897. 'Reading four books at once,' she noted frequently.

It was now that she developed her feelings about reading at random, reading as a 'common', not a specialist, academic reader, that would form the backbone of her essays on self-education. Virginia Woolf is one of the great advocates of disreputable reading, junk reading, serendipitous reading, dream-reading, reading while looking out of the window, reading while running a high fever: as in 'On Being Ill', one of the best accounts there is of horizontal reading.

How Virginia Woolf forged her intellectual history *against* the example of her father (as well as the domestic and marital example of her mother) is the story of – among others of her books – *A Room of One's Own*, *To the Lighthouse*, *The Years* and *Three Guineas*. In her argument over the legacy for twentieth-century women of oppression and lack of privilege or of formal education, she thinks of women overwhelmingly as 'the daughters of educated men'. In most of her writing about women readers and writers she gives examples of exclusion, deprivation, limitations and anxiety. Much of her writing stems from resistance and opposition. So, in her formulation of Victorianism, she resists and satirises the patriarchal despot embodied in Leslie Stephen; and in her lifelong thinking about biography, she set herself against the kind of official memorial of public men summed up by her father's great work, the *Dictionary of National Biography*.

All this is very well known. But there is another story going alongside it, too, which has tended recently to be discredited, the story of what the reading girl, as writing adult, *derived* from her father's intellectual example. Just as, in *Three Guineas*, Woolf urges twentieth-century professional women not to forget, but to make use of in their working lives, what they have inherited from their mothers' poverty and discouragement, so she finds it possible to make good use of what she first learned from her father, his energetic, eclectic, dedicated passion for reading. One example of this switches the image of the woman reader from the horizontal to the vertical, from indoors to outdoors, from secrecy to boldness, and from the woman writer as daughter to the woman writer as adult.

In his essay on 'The Study of English Literature' (1887) Leslie Stephen resists the authority of critics and argues for self-confidence and spontaneity in reading: 'This I may say, Take hold anywhere, read what you really like and not what someone tells you that you ought to like; let your reading be part of your lives.'[40] Woolf remembered this in her 1932 essay, 'Leslie Stephen': '"Read what you like", he said . . . To read what one liked because one liked it, never to pretend to admire what one did not – that was his only lesson in the art of reading.' And she came back to it in one of her last essays, 'The Leaning Tower', written in wartime, in 1940. Here Leslie Stephen is cited, unnamed, as 'an eminent Victorian who was also an eminent pedestrian advising walkers: "Whenever you see a board up with 'Trespassers will be prosecuted', trespass at once." ' She goes on in turn to recommend 'trespassing' as the best kind of literary self-education: 'Let us trespass at once. Literature is no one's private ground; literature is common ground. It is not cut up into nations; there are no wars there. Let us trespass freely and fearlessly and find our own way for ourselves.'

Jane Austen Faints

Jane Austen's novels are kinds of life-writing, much concerned with family plots, gossip, stories, guesswork, knowledge, assessments of human behaviour, and the importance of reading people right: their histories, their motives, their secrets and desires. There's an intriguing demonstration of this in the scenes between Anne Elliot and Mrs Smith in Austen's last finished novel, *Persuasion*. These scenes have been criticised for awkwardness and clumsy plotting, and it's assumed she would have revised them if she had not fallen ill. But the rough edges of an author's work can be very revealing, especially an author usually as polished and meticulous as this one.

The situation is this. Mrs Smith, once Miss Hamilton, was kind to Anne when, aged fourteen, she went 'unhappy to school' after her mother's death. But she is now, twelve years later, an impoverished widow, crippled with rheumatism, living in confined lodgings in Bath. Anne visits her (much to the scorn of her snobbish father, Sir Walter the baronet) and admires Mrs Smith's capacity for making so much of the diminished thing that her life is. Mrs Smith tells Anne about her landlady's sister, Nurse Rooke, who visits Mrs Smith and reports to her something of what's going on in the town. Mrs Smith says of this offstage character: 'Hers is a line for seeing human nature ... She is sure to have something to relate that is entertaining and profitable, something that makes one know one's species better. One likes to hear what is going on.' Anne observes that she must have many sickroom stories of heroism and fortitude; Mrs Smith looks doubtful, and says that they are more often stories of weakness, 'selfishness and impatience'. This 'line for seeing human nature', then, is realistic and uncensored.

It turns out, in the second long scene between Anne and Mrs Smith, that Mrs Smith also gets her local information from 'a laundress and a waiter'. Through her sources, Mrs Smith has heard a rumour that Anne is likely to be soon engaged to her cousin, Mr Elliot. Only when Anne disabuses her of this idea does Mrs Smith expose to her Mr Elliot's 'real' character; he is a heartless, designing, 'wary cold blooded being', set on advancing himself financially and socially through marriage, and plotting to inherit the baronetcy through marrying Anne. As proof of this, Mrs Smith shows Anne a ten-year-old letter, dated 1803, which is very rude about Anne's father. Anne is shocked by this, but also feels that she shouldn't be reading 'private correspondence'. Mrs Smith explains how she has heard about Mr Elliot's plots via Nurse Rooke – whom she calls 'my historian' – who has got it from the wife of a Colonel Wallis, who is Mr Elliot's friend. 'The stream is as good as at first; the little rubbish it collects in the turnings, is easily moved away.' Once Anne accepts this 'representation of Mr Elliot', Mrs Smith provides even more dramatic evidence of his past villainy: he was responsible for ruining Mrs Smith's late husband, and she has letters to prove it.

Awkwardly as this slab of information is bumped into the novel, it makes a vivid version of biography. Following the trail of the story and clearing away the rubbish that's accrued to it through gossip and rumour, using written evidence to prove a point, drawing on whatever sources of information you can get, building up a 'representation' of the character: these are the biographer's jobs. These scenes invoke, too, the moral reservations so often attached to biography – dislike of gossip, distrust of 'low' sources of information, squeamishness about reading private correspondence, suspecting witnesses of having a private agenda. So the 'Mrs Smith' episode in *Persuasion*[1] makes a good entry-point for some thoughts about the telling of Jane Austen's life-story, which has had to negotiate a number of 'turnings' in the stream and a fair amount of accumulated 'rubbish'.

The best-known fact about Jane Austen's posthumous life is that her story was guarded and shaped by her family. The legacy of that guardianship is seen on the covers of the last six biographies of Jane Austen, published between 1984 and 2001: they all have the same picture of her, because that's the only one there is: Cassandra Austen's 1811 pen and watercolour drawing of her sister, with the cap, the curls, the beady brown eyes, the crossed arms, and the wry (even 'caustic') sideways look. It is the only front-face portrait of Jane Austen (the original image was touched up and prettified for the family memoir) and it's a symbol of how, for many years, the family kept control of her image. As Marilyn Butler put it in a review of some of those recent biographies, 'for the first century at least [after her death], the main qualification for the task [of being Jane Austen's biographer] was to be a relative.'[2]

First there was her brother Henry Austen's 'Biographical Notice', published in the posthumous 1818 edition of *Northanger Abbey* and *Persuasion*. Then there was her niece Anna Lefroy's 'Recollections of Aunt Jane' of 1864, and her other niece Caroline Austen's memoir ('My Aunt Jane Austen') of 1867, unpublished until 1952 (followed by her 'Reminiscences', written in the 1870s). Then there was her nephew James Edward Austen-Leigh's *A Memoir of Jane Austen*, of 1870, and her great-niece (daughter of her niece Anna) Fanny Lefroy's 'Family History', from the 1880s. Then there was the 1884 selection of her letters by Lord Brabourne, son of Austen's niece Fanny Knight, carelessly edited, with an effusive commentary, and dedicated to Queen Victoria. Early in the twentieth century, there was her great-nephew and great-great-nephew William and Richard Austen-Leigh's *The Life and Letters: A Family Record*, of 1913, on which the Austen scholar and editor Deirdre Le Faye would base her *Jane Austen: A Family Record*, first published in 1989 and revised in 2004. These family versions are revealingly compared by Kathryn Sutherland in her 2002 edition of some of these memoirs, in which she notes that there are rival claims, within them, to 'the more authentic portrait' of Jane Austen.[3]

Deirdre Le Faye edited a fine new collection of Jane Austen's letters in 1995. But one feature of the family's lingering control over Austen's body of work is that numerous letters, or parts of letters – the sort of evidence Mrs Smith was able to flourish in front of Anne Elliot – were destroyed by Cassandra. Austen's sister obliterated the evidence of her responses to the crucial events in her life, such as the sudden death of Cassandra's fiancé in 1797, the family's move from Steventon, and Austen's possible romantic involvements. It's long been argued that the effect of this 'culling' of Cassandra's is, as one of Austen's biographers, Claire Tomalin, puts it, to leave the impression that 'her sister was dedicated to trivia. The letters rattle on, sometimes almost like a comedian's patter. Not much feeling, warmth or sorrow has been allowed through ... You have to keep reminding yourself how little they represent of her real life, how much they are an edited and contrived version.' A more recent counter-argument is that the letters, rather than being disparaged by comparison with the novels, should be attended to for what they do reveal, and for the 'texture of domestic life' they present. Or, perhaps, as Sutherland suggests, there 'was never a confiding correspondence to hold back': it's just that biographers are suspicious of 'gaps and silences'.[4]

Apart from the letters, most of the evidence biographers have to draw on is family anecdote and memoir, some written long after the event. If only Austen had kept a journal, as Mr Tilney in *Northanger Abbey* assumes Catherine Morland must certainly do, like all other young ladies of her class! Instead of which, her biographers have had to make do with stories and legends handed down and repeated: certainly a muddied stream. Take the mysterious story of Jane Austen's failed romance with a handsome clergyman in Devonshire. This hazy episode is the only candidate for a serious love-affair, apart from her flirtation, at twenty, with Tom Lefroy, which was put an end to by family pressures. It's a family legend which originated in a remark said to have been made by Cassandra.

> There is a family tradition that during one of these seaside holidays between 1801 and 1804 Jane met the only man whom she could seriously have wished to marry, had fortune been kinder to her. Cassandra knew the details of this brief episode, but in her later life passed on to her niece Caroline Austen merely the barest outline of what had happened years before. In 1870 Caroline wrote out the account, for her brother's use in preparing the second edition of the *Memoir*.[5]

Caroline's story was that her Aunt Cassandra (whose own fiancé had died tragically when she was twenty-four), on meeting a good-looking man in 1828, said he reminded her of the clergyman in Devonshire who was 'greatly attracted' by Caroline's Aunt Jane, and who said he would come back to see her. But news then followed that he had died. Deirdre Le Faye comments that 'in the absence of any further evidence from outside sources . . . Jane's stillborn romance can only remain "nameless and dateless".' But the very fact that the story was so hazy attracted biographers to it. One Austen devotee, Constance Pilgrim, even made up a whole book about the romance, *Dear Jane: A Biographical Study*. Joan Rees, in *Jane Austen: Woman and Writer* (1976) wrote: 'According to family tradition . . . Jane Austen fell deeply in love *more or less at first sight* [my italics], with an extremely charming young clergyman who has never been satisfactorily identified. Although he returned her feelings ... [she] received the tragic news that, just like Cassandra's fiancé, the man she loved had suddenly died.' Rees continues: '*What is hard to doubt* [my italics] is that she had been able to draw on experience as well as imagination for her descriptions of the states of falling and being in love.' The biographer John Halperin, following this line, exclaims, with no provisos: 'This time she had *loved!*' (his italics.) The legend satisfies conventional habits of explaining the life of a spinster or old maid as one of thwarted love; and it provides ammunition for romantic readings (as in the film *Shakespeare in Love*) which want to link a personal experience of lifelong, hopeless longing with the plots of the novels, so that Fanny Price or Anne Elliot can be read as standing in for a lovelorn Jane Austen. But the legend of thwarted love can also fuel a negative view of a resentful, bitter, caustic Jane Austen, which reads her irony as 'pathological, a problem any good husband could relieve ... All social criticism written by women is born of disappointment in love.' More recent biographies have chosen to dismiss the mysterious Devonshire clergyman as an invention of Cassandra's or as 'mistily romantic' as the Devon coast itself.[6]

In the matter of the lost clergyman, biographers are responding, according to their different agendas, to the family's construction – a very successful one – of a version of Jane Austen which held sway for many years. In Marilyn Butler's words, this was 'that the author was a very domestic woman, and that outside her family she had no profound attachments or interests'. 'Immediately after Jane Austen's death', notes the novelist Carol Shields in her sympathetic short life of Austen, 'she was entombed in veneration.' The Austen family's Jane Austen was not a professional writer, but a home-loving daughter, sister and aunt, and above all a good Christian. Her gravestone inscription, prepared by her brothers, remarked on 'the benevolence of her heart, the sweetness of her temperament, the extraordinary endowment of her mind', but did not mention her books. Her brother Henry's 'Biographical Notice' of 1818 emphasised that she wrote with 'no hope of fame nor profit' and that 'in public she turned away from any allusion to the character of an authoress'. Henry Austen drew attention to her 'perfect placidity of temper', the kindness of her wit, her tranquillity, her complete lack of interest in fame and money, her reading of 'moral' writers, and her being 'thoroughly religious and devout'. This has been well described as an attempt 'to project an image of a ladylike, unmercenary, unprofessional, private, delicate and domestic author'.[7]

Though the 1870 *Memoir* by her nephew James Austen-Leigh gave a livelier impression, and allowed that Austen could be funny about her neighbours, her nephew (by then an elderly clergyman) was at pains to add that 'she was as far as possible from being censorious or satirical'. It's often been noted that Jane Austen was becoming 'Victorianised', and the *Memoir* characterises her above all as a shining light in her own home – 'a comfortable, approachable figure who put down her needlework to pick up her pen' – rather like a later Victorian heroine, Dickens's Esther Summerson, in *Bleak House*.

> Underneath [Jane Austen's bright qualities] lay the strong foundations of sound sense and judgement, rectitude of principle, and delicacy of feeling, qualifying her equally to advise, assist, or amuse. She was, in fact, as ready to comfort the unhappy, or to nurse the sick, as she was to laugh and jest with the light-hearted ... [Her nieces] know what a sympathising friend and judicious adviser they found her to be in the many little difficulties and doubts of early womanhood ...
>
> She was a humble, believing Christian. Her life had been passed in the performance of home duties, and the cultivation of domestic affections, without any self-seeking or craving after applause.

Whatever it was made her a writer seems quite separate from the rest of her life:

> Hers was a mind well balanced on a basis of good sense, sweetened by an affectionate heart, and regulated by fixed principles; so that she was to be distinguished from many other amiable and sensible women only by that peculiar genius which shines out clearly enough in her works, but of which a biographer can make little use.

When illness struck her, she patiently readied herself for death. Austen's illness has been variously diagnosed as Bright's disease, Addison's disease, a lymphoma such as Hodgkin's disease, or breast cancer; the 1870 memoir does not go into unpleasant details. As with the fewness of portraits or the haziness of love-affairs, whatever had most to do with her bodily life is hardest to track down.

One Victorian reviewer of the *Memoir* asked: 'Might not we . . . recognise her officially as "dear Aunt Jane"?' A recent feminist critic comments grimly: 'We might and we did.'[8] The family story fed into versions of Jane Austen which have been in contention for well over a hundred years. Austen studies – editing, criticism, biography, social history – are now as conflicted and oppositional as the original accounts of her were tranquil and benign. As Deidre Lynch observes – a critic who specialises in the Austen wars, with all their 'passionate acrimony' and 'vehemence of partisanship' – 'a customary method of establishing one's credentials as a reader of Austen has been to suggest that others simply will insist on liking her in inappropriate ways'.[9] But the peculiarity of the Austen wars is that although the different versions of her can be seen to be very much of their time – a late-Victorian Jane Austen, a wartime Jane Austen, a post-sixties feminist Jane Austen – they don't supersede one another, but coexist and jostle for position. It's as though the body of this author – which her relatives tried so hard to sanctify – is continually being torn into parts and put back together again.

The family version lent itself easily to an 'English Heritage' Jane Austen, benign heroine of an idyllic, rural, golden age England, the saintly and serene maiden aunt making the most of her sheltered uneventful life, her wit and wisdom always on the side of morality, restraint and good sense. This Tory Jane Austen, beloved of the Janeites and the Jane Austen Society, and cherished by nineteenth- and early twentieth-century admirers such as Kipling, Macaulay and Lord David Cecil, has been ferociously attacked, but it hasn't gone away. It gets into the Austen tourist industry and the hugely popular Jane Austen movies, even though rural England of the late eighteenth century has long ceased to be described by historians as the clean, green, pastoral of the nostalgic film adaptations, all bonnets and carriages and parks and starched pinnies, and Colin Firth and Alan Rickman striding about in ruffled shirts and shiny boots.

Recent critics and biographers are more likely to describe Austen's landscape and social context in terms of instability, exploitation, provincial discontent, rural crime, social climbing and imperial profit-eering, and the Austen family as, in Marilyn Butler's phrase, 'a family of meritocrats struggling to get ahead in a competitive, money-driven society'.[10] Ever since the psychologist D.W. Harding's crucial *Scrutiny* essay of 1940 on Austen's 'regulated hatred', and the American critic Marvin Mudrick's 1952 book on her defensive use of irony, she has been read (by some) as expressing anger and resentment in her fiction against a life of constriction and repression.[11] That idea of a resentful double life, kept down by a family censorship in which Austen was herself complicit, has done a great deal to demolish the benign Jane Austen of the Janeites. So has a quite different, severe historical account of Austen (pioneered by Marilyn Butler in the 1970s), not as a secretly resentful misfit, but as a hard-line Tory purveyor of establishment values, summarised (by critics who disagree with Butler) as providing 'arms for the bourgeois thought police' and endorsing 'a repressive middle-class ideology of manners': 'an anti-Jacobin novelist writing in defence of patriarchal authority and the country house which provided one of its most potent symbols'.[12]

Yet the English Heritage Jane Austen still lives on, as in Nigel Nicolson's *The World of Jane Austen* ('she loved the luxury of Godmersham . . . above all she loved its countryside . . . where everyone seemed perennially at peace with each other and the external world'), or in the glossy pages of Susan Watkins's 1996 Thames & Hudson picture book *Jane Austen in Style*, the cover of which shows a grand country house in Kent, and, in an inset medallion, the dance scene, starring Jennifer Ehle, from the BBC film of *Pride and Prejudice*. Watkins's introduction promises that 'in these pages, from the vantage point of a particular English country gentlewoman, a journey is made through the society and surroundings of a group of people of unsurpassed elegance and refinement'. 'Here we will see *how* the country gentry lived – in an ambience of cultural politeness, with a keen though delicate sensibility, well balanced by common sense.' That's the long-established Jane Austen of the Janeites, purveying nostalgia for 'a golden age of the English gentry'. That version of Austen was at its peak in the early twentieth century, when 'images of the late eighteenth century countryside . . . connoted a harmonious refuge from the modern world between 1918 and 1945'. But the remarkable thing about the genteel, nostalgic, benign version of Austen is its persistence, not only in picture books but also in literary criticism. It creeps in, for instance, to a critical book of 1987, which concludes that 'in the poignancy of the secular situations she sets before us, and of the human inadequacies they reveal, we may find the angelic dismay, sorrow and compassion'.[13]

Critics wanting to construct a more robust, less sanctified Austen have to push hard against the genteel, nostalgic version. At the same time that 'Austenmania' – movies, coffee-table books and mugs, T-shirts, guided tours of Chawton – has vigorously persisted, there's an equally vigorous, ongoing proliferation of rival critical, bibliographical and historical readings.[14] Editors of her work are starting to undo the received shape of the *oeuvre*, established by R.W. Chapman from the 1920s onwards in his editions of the novels, the letters and the 'minor works'. Feminist critics of Austen (Margaret Kirkham, Mary Poovey, Nancy Armstrong, Claudia Johnson) have for some time been questioning the 'gendered public–private ascription of spheres of activity' which commits Austen to the realm of domestic minutiae and to a local, apolitical treatment of the 'little bit (two inches wide) of ivory', her much-quoted description of her own scope and materials. It has long been argued that 'Jane Austen was deeply involved in, and cognisant of, the major ideological debates of her time.' One social historian looking at Austen in the context of Regency England has argued with the persistence of the 'polite' version of Jane Austen which 'still attempts to deny that she ever wrote about fleas, naked cupids and bad breath'. A Marxist critic of her work, following the example of Raymond Williams, claims that 'far from endorsing the given, and emergent values of late-eighteenth-century capitalism she was in many ways deeply critical of them'. An influential feminist critic, Terry Castle, dared to suggest in 1995 that Jane Austen's closest and most passionate relationship was with her sister Cassandra ('Was Jane Austen Gay?') and was greeted with a storm of abuse from Jane's devotees, as though Castle had somehow 'polluted the shrine'. Post-colonial critics of Austen, beginning with Edward Said on 'Jane Austen and Empire' in 1989, observe that, now she has been thoroughly politicised, studies of Austen involve an interrogation of the concept of 'English' and of the classical canon of English Literature. It's argued by such critics that Austen's function has been 'as an entropic model of the backward look to the green core', and that she has stood in the canon of English literature as 'the benign female signature of nostalgic agrarian Romanticism'.[15]

Biography tends to lag behind critical debate, but these hotly contested readings of Jane Austen – many of which, like Terry Castle's, involve biographical disputes – have begun to make their way into the telling of

Jane Austen's life-story. That story, and its versions, demonstrate very vividly the argument of the American feminist critic Carolyn Heilbrun, that, until recently, biographies of women who don't fit into the standard models have been difficult to write, and have been written 'under the constraints of acceptable discussion'. Even if the family version of Jane Austen's life is resisted or demolished, her story raises particular challenges for the biographer. Heilbrun noted (in 1988) that it was still difficult to find a way of writing about 'the choices and pain of the women who did not make a man the centre of their lives'.[16] If the virtuous and benign – or thwarted and bitter – maiden aunt is refused as the working model, what other shapes can this story take?

Since the 1960s, biographies of Austen have placed the emphasis on the frustrations of her familial position of dependency, her long servitude to her hypochondriacal mother, her cloistered relationship with Cassandra, the loneliness, even desperation, of her middle age, her realism and misanthropy. The gap between the pious self-effacement of the family version, and the mordant wit and energetic, worldly-wise brilliance of the novels, is frequently noted. And the idealised 'dear Aunt Jane' is undermined by pointing to the notable eruptions of viciousness or grimness in the letters – notoriously on Mrs Hall of Sherbourn who 'was brought to bed yesterday of a dead child, some weeks before she expected, owing to a fright. – I suppose she happened unawares to look at her husband.'[17]

One of the most dramatic moments in the life, and one of the places where all Austen's biographers have to decide what to do with the handed-down family versions, is the scene in which Jane Austen faints. The story is told, sticking closely to the family reports (and without much questioning of them), by Deirdre Le Faye, in *Jane Austen: A Family Record*. Le Faye's sources are Fanny Lefroy's unpublished family history of the early 1880s (citing her mother Anna's report), a letter from Caroline Austen to James Edward Austen-Leigh of 1869 (which was reprinted in R.W. Chapman's *Jane Austen: Facts and Problems* in 1948), the 1870 *Memoir*, the 1913 *Life*, and the letters from Jane to Cassandra early in 1801.

Jane (as Le Faye calls her) had been away from home (the rectory at Steventon in Hampshire where she was born and had lived all her twenty-five years), staying at Ibthorpe with her friend Martha Lloyd (whose sister Mary was married to one Austen brother, James, and who would later marry another Austen brother, Frank.) Cassandra was also away from home, staying at Godmersham Park in Kent, home of their distant cousins, the wealthy Knights, who had adopted Jane's brother Edward. (Any one moment in Austen's life immediately brings in such thick swathes of family connections.) The story, as pieced together by Le Faye, is as follows:

> While Jane was away, the latent strain of impetuosity in the Austens suddenly manifested itself in her father; and family tradition says that as she and Martha arrived from Ibthorpe early in December [1800] they were met in the rectory hall by Mrs Austen, who greeted them with: 'Well, girls, it is all settled, we have decided to leave Steventon in such a week and go to Bath' – and to Jane the shock of this intelligence was so great that she fainted away. Mary Lloyd, who was also present to greet her sister, remembered that Jane was 'greatly distressed'.
>
> No letters to Cassandra survive for the month of December 1800, which suggests that she destroyed those in which Jane gave vent to feelings of grief and perhaps even resentment at being so suddenly uprooted from her childhood home without any prior consultation by her parents as to her own opinions in the matter – Cassandra too had presumably been left in ignorance of this decision. 'My Aunt was very sorry to leave her native home, as I have heard my Mother relate' . . . To exchange permanently the homely but comfortable rectory and the fields and woodlands of Hampshire for a tall narrow terrace house in one of Bath's stone-paved streets must have been [a] dismaying . . . prospect to Jane . . . So hasty, indeed, did Mr Austen's decision appear to the Leigh-Perrots [Austen's maternal uncle and his wife] that they suspected the reason to be a growing attachment between Jane and William Digweed, one of the four brothers at Steventon manor house. There is not the slightest evidence of this supposition in Jane's letters . . . It seems most probable that Mr Austen's age and Mrs Austen's continuing ill health were the deciding factors for retirement . . .
>
> By January 1801 Jane had recovered her composure, and the six letters written in the New Year are in her usual style of cheerful irony . . . The plans for the retirement to Bath naturally figure largely in these letters . . . 'I get more & more reconciled to the idea of our removal . . . It must not be generally known however that I am not sacrificing a great deal in

quitting the Country – or I can expect to inspire no tenderness, no interest in those we leave behind.'[18]

Jane Austen's faint seems to provide a clue to many aspects of her life, and not surprisingly it has been a test case for biographers. 'Why' (asks Kathryn Sutherland, who looks closely at the family versions of this scene) 'does this one distressing moment matter, and why do subsequent biographers embellish it so enthusiastically?' It exposes her dependent position, as a woman of twenty-five unable to make her own choices. It has implications for her relations with her mother, who could be read, in this anecdote, as bludgeoning and insensitive. It suggests the kind of quick, intense and sensitive responses which we may want to identify as a mark of genius. It provides a rare sight of her emotions expressing themselves in a physical gesture. It may imply that the habits of a rooted, settled life made the decision to move a great shock. Beyond that, it makes us aware of the family circle, especially women, who were her witnesses and interpreters, and of the difficulty of piecing together the story from the gaps and silences in the letters and from the handed-down evidence. And it seems to offer an intimate moment for biographers to make the most of, since – as John Wiltshire puts it, writing on biographers' desires to get close up to Jane Austen – 'biography's appeal to readers is inseparable from the dream of possession of, and union with, the subject'.[19]

The faint is a challenge for readers of Austen's life and works who see her as a rational, ironic, conservative, Johnsonian satirist.[20] Fainting, after all, is one of many symptoms of extreme, even alarming sensibility (or of affectation of sensibility) which Austen, if read as an ironist, was so concerned to satirise or regulate in her fiction. John Mullan, writing on 'the language of feeling' in the eighteenth century, notes how women are represented as 'inherently liable to internal disorder', and how feminine sensibility 'exists on the edge of an abyss', where an extreme of sensibility becomes – as for Marianne Dashwood – 'dangerous affliction'. Fainting was one of the much-noted symptoms of such dangerous extremes of hysteria and hypochondria. Devotees who praise Austen for her Augustan wit and wisdom express some anxieties over the faint. The granddaughter of the author of the *Memoir*, Emma Austen-Leigh, writing in 1939 on *Jane Austen in Bath*, thinks it was unlike her: 'Tradition says Jane fainted away from the shock, and although this sensibility is not quite in keeping with what we know of her character, there is little doubt that for a time she was very unhappy.' A leading academic 'Janeite' of the early twentieth century, A.C. Bradley, takes a more gallant, protective tone (often used by her male admirers in this period), but also sees the faint as uncharacteristic: 'We learn that, when suddenly told of her father's decision to leave Steventon, their home in the country, and reside in Bath, she fainted away; a fact which I mention with some compunctions, for she would have been horrified by the idea that this proof of her "sensibility" would some day be made public.'[21] Note that both these apologists use the phrase 'fainted away', which they have taken from the 1913 *Life*, somehow more elegant and less brutal than 'fainted'.

That rational, controlled Jane Austen, who would have been embarrassed by showing her sensibility in public, has been countered by writers who have become interested in the bodily life in her writings. John Wiltshire's first book on Austen, *Jane Austen and the Body*, argues that Austen uses the 'unhealthy body' as a source of events in her fiction, and that bodies (especially in distress or ill health) are 'sites in which cultural meanings are inscribed'. Extreme emotions – grief, rage, despair, loneliness – which are socially repressed or censored, find their expression as physical symptoms. Wiltshire is drawing on Arthur Kleinman's theory of 'somatisation', in which illness is thought of as a language for what is being repressed: 'emotions are deposited in the body and there reproduced as illness symptoms'. For Austen's female characters illness may be their only way of getting their emotions 'legitimised and respected' – like Jane Fairfax in *Emma*, who seems at one point to be having a severe physical breakdown or episode of 'neurasthenia', and who can only express her concealed distress in this fashion. Wiltshire doesn't mention Jane Austen's faint, but it could be the perfect example of a repressed or restricted emotional life finding its only possible outlet in a dramatic act of bodily weakness.[22]

The interpretation of the faint will depend on what kind of Austen is being purveyed. Obviously, readers who identify Austen with the 'green core', with the rural, secluded heartland of England, and who read her life and character as quiet, static, regional and domestic, will assume that enforced removal to town life would come as an unpleasant shock, and they point to evidence from the novels (particularly *Persuasion*) for her dislike of Bath. Critics who want to shift this family-derived version of the 'timid Austen trapped within a regard for the local and familiar', resist the story of the faint. Deidre Lynch pours scorn on those inter-war commentators who maintained as 'an article of faith' 'Austen's home-loving attachment to a green nook' and 'who told and retold the story of how Jane swooned when Reverend Austen announced his intention to move the family to Bath'. Clara Tuite, in her treatment of the 'commodification' of Austen, notes that Bath's use of Austen for its tourist industry has been 'a sore point for many Austen devotees, particularly given the fact that Austen made some beautifully disparaging remarks about Bath, and was rumoured in the family history to have fainted at the shock of the news that she and her family were about to move there'. Margaret Kirkham, writing a revisionary feminist account of Austen in the 1980s, turns the whole story on its head. It is important, she says, 'because it illustrates the way in which the life of the legendary Jane Austen has been created'. She notes that the 1913 *Life* tells us that 'Tradition says that ... Jane Austen fainted away' when she heard the news. But when Austen's niece Caroline Austen, daughter of James, wrote her 1869 letter describing the event, she inaccurately said that Cassandra was present, and she didn't mention the faint. Her account reads: 'My Mother [Mary Austen, née Lloyd] who was present said my Aunt was greatly distressed.' It was the *Memoir*, followed by the Austen editor R.W. Chapman in 1948, that piled on the emotion: 'We cannot doubt that the loss of her native country and of the multitude of associations which made up her girlish experience was exquisitely painful. Her feelings cannot have been less acute than Marianne's on leaving Norland, or Anne's on leaving Kellynch.' But Kirkham, having unpicked the evidence, goes on to argue that Austen's silence after she got to Bath could have meant, not that she was depressed, but that she was busy enjoying herself.[23]

No biographer of Jane Austen leaves out the faint, but all of them have to decide what to do with the story. John Halperin, whose 1984 *Jane Austen* has been described as 'consumed by smouldering resentment at her lot, incapable of love, and cynical about personal relationships', and whose biography was certainly setting out to disrupt previous readings of her life, makes the most of the drama, and writes as if with inside knowledge of her feelings, drawn from her novels:

Jane fainted. She was not a fainter; the emotional disturbance must have been acute. Beneath her celebrated composure she was high-strung. And she was upset. It is significant that for December 1800 . . . there are no letters extant – bearing silent testimony, perhaps, to the novelist's agitated state of mind . . . Did her feelings resemble those of Marianne Dashwood upon leaving Norland – or those of Anne Elliot upon leaving Kellynch? We shall never know. What we do know is that Steventon had been everything to Jane Austen, and she never liked Bath; Anne Elliot . . . 'persisted in a very determined, though silent, disinclination for Bath.' All Jane's roots were at Steventon . . . The novelist was 'exceedingly unhappy' upon hearing the news, says the author of the *Memoir*, a man not given to exaggeration. There can be no doubt that she was unhappy. Indeed, she was to remain dissatisfied for a good many years. A decade of rootlessness was about to begin; this was a watershed event in her life.

Note the biographer's strategic uses of 'must have' and 'perhaps' and of rhetorical questions, the setting of unprovable hypotheses ('we shall never know') against resounding conclusions ('there can be no doubt' . . . 'Indeed'), the ease with which evidence is adduced from the novels, and the tendency to trust the family version, as put together by R.W. Chapman and, later, Deirdre le Faye – though Halperin goes on to dismiss the rumour that the Austen parents were trying to get her away from William Digweed. This passage comes in a chapter called 'The Treacherous Years', in which Halperin argues that bitterness and dislocations clouded the 'dark' years of 1801 to 1804 for which no letters remain, and that 'adversity blanketed energy and inspiration'. So he adopts the standard view that Jane Austen was acting out the feelings she gave to her heroines, and that to be uprooted from home was to be stopped in her creative flow. Readings of Austen's authorial career (such as Kathryn Sutherland's) which dispute the chronology of two bursts of creativity with a long fallow gap in between, arguing rather for a long period of literary experimentation, will not accept this version.

Park Honan's 1987 *Jane Austen*, which places her more thoroughly in her social and political context, uses the sources more carefully, but comes to similar conclusions:

At this news Jane Austen fainted, so Anna Lefroy heard . . . Cassandra was absent when the decision was made, and Mary Austen found Jane quite alone and 'greatly distressed' – but a younger daughter's tears were insignificant. Aunt Perrot knew or imagined why Jane was 'distressed'. The family *had* to move, that lady felt, because of a romantic attachment between Jane and a Digweed man. What could one expect? But dear Jane would forget her suitor when she was living at Axford Buildings in Bath . . . In leaving Steventon she was being uprooted and crushed . . . She was being taken from a small community, which she knew well . . . There could be no compensation in a jangling crowded town. Her sense of place was part of her confidence, and *that* was being torn from her. One could be sad in leaving a place because connections are cut *too* easily: other people part from one too readily, and friendships are exposed as less significant than one had hoped and perhaps as insignificant as they really are. But the precious intimacy of talk and feeling she had with Martha [Lloyd] or Catherine [Bigg] or Mrs Lefroy was rare, and it was cruel to leave. A loss may be a gain, but how does one happily endure without love, friendship, peace and delight? . . . She meant to be cheerful but until well into January 1801 she found little to allay what Mary called her 'distress' . . .

The tactic here seems to be a pretence at writing an eighteenth-century novel, perhaps a novel by Jane Austen, in which some of the facts are given to us from the imagined viewpoint of Aunt Perrot, and the events provide an excuse for a general meditation on uprootings.[24]

Two British lives of Jane Austen came out in 1997, one by Claire Tomalin and one by David Nokes. Both give us a troubling and troubled Austen, placed in a discordant and dangerous late eighteenth-century English landscape, and belonging to a family with some dubious secrets and connections. Yet their treatment of her life – and of her faint – could hardly be more different, though they are using much the same materials and evidence.

Claire Tomalin's biography is interested in the story of a woman's life, and how to tell it. What effect would being fostered by a wet-nurse have on a baby girl? Might it create a lifelong defensiveness and an emotional distance between mother and child? What would be the toughening results of being sent away to school very young? What would it feel like to be a teenage girl starting to menstruate surrounded by young boys 'thundering about the house'? Is it anachronistic to feel pity for young wives pregnant immediately after marriage, and then every year, and often dying in childbirth? (Austen did: 'Poor Animal, she will be worn out before she is thirty,' she wrote of her niece Anna Lefroy, pregnant again in 1816 immediately after the birth of her first child.) Women's feelings – about the pleasures of dancing or the imprisoning effects of bad weather – are constantly conjectured. Tomalin sees, as others have, conflict and exasperation with the strong, stubborn mother. She casts some shadow over the quasi-marital closeness with Cassandra, who is viewed as sombre, prim and responsible for hurrying them both into middle age. (Tomalin finds the story of their wearing identical bonnets in their mid-twenties 'depressing'.) The key word in this biography (there always is one) is *tough*. This Austen is a witty, ebullient girl taking a series of knocks. The brief youthful flirtation with Tom Lefroy is dealt with tenderly, as is her painful change of mind over a later proposal. This is not, though, the standard male version of the embittered old maid who longed above all else to be married. Here Jane Austen is imagined as discovering that 'spinsterhood . . . could be a form of freedom'. The worst pressures are those of family life: lack of independence and privacy, endless domestic commitments, and feeling like an 'awkward parcel' at the grander homes of her wealthier brothers.

Tomalin's version of the faint deals carefully with the possible motives of the Austen parents and with the sources: 'This is Mary Austen's account, who was there; and although she misremembered the presence of Cassandra, there is no reason to doubt the truth of it . . . James's daughter Anna was told her Aunt Jane fainted. Whether she did or not, it can hardly be doubted that the whole thing was a shock, and a painful one.' There follows an account of the arrangements for the move, and a suggestion that the letters Cassandra destroyed immediately after the event may have been 'too full of raw feeling and even anger'.

> She strained to keep up the easy, gossipy note . . . but the jokes to Cass often feel forced: '. . . It must not be generally known however that I am not sacrificing a great deal in quitting the Country – or I can expect to inspire no tenderness, no interest in those we leave behind.' . . . There is a briskness and brightness in Jane's letters at this time, much keeping up of spirits, but no enthusiasm. She is doing what she has to do, making the best of a situation over which she has no control, watching the breaking up of everything familiar . . . fitting in with plans in which she

has no say, losing what she loves for the prospect of an urban life . . . no centre, no peace, and the loss of an infinite number of things hard to list, impossible to explain.

Looking ahead over the silence that followed, Tomalin constructs a whole theory of depression:

The ejection from Steventon made severe practical difficulties for her; it also depressed her deeply enough to disable her as a writer. Depression may be set off when a bad experience is repeated, and it seems likely that this is what happened here. First as an infant, then as a child of seven, Jane had been sent away from home, frightening and unpleasant experiences over which she had no control . . . Through her writing, she was developing a world of imagination in which she controlled everything that happened. She went on to create young women somewhat like herself, but whose perceptions and judgements were shown to matter; who were able to influence their own fates significantly . . . To remove her from Steventon would destroy the delicate balance she had worked out . . . So there was both a perfectly good rational basis for wanting to be at home, and a residue of the terrors of infancy and childhood about banishment and exile, ready to spring out when they threatened again. That this new exile was brought about by the same people as before, her parents, against whom she could neither rebel nor complain, must have made it worse . . . Her account of Fanny's permanent low spirits after a childhood trauma, and her very different account (in *Sense and Sensibility*) of Marianne unable to combat her misery and willing herself into serious illness, show how well she understood depression. And however she dealt with and controlled her own, it struck at the core of her being: it interfered directly with her power to write.[25]

It is a highly plausible version, made all the more so by the sympathetic narrative of a woman's life that surrounds it, and by cunning little touches like the use of 'Cass' and 'Jane' to suggest inwardness, the biographical hooks for plausibility ('seems likely', 'must have'), and the reasonable demonstration of links between the work and the life. All the same, it is entirely constructed and hypothetical, just as much of a figment as the 'dear Jane' of the family *Memoir*, but this one – like many other twentieth-century biographies – dependent on our accepting post-Freudian psychoanalytical terms (loss of control, the repeating of 'childhood trauma', willing oneself into illness) for an eighteenth-century writer.

Tomalin's version was influential on the novelist Carol Shields, who pays close attention in her short biography to the bodily features and body parts in Austen's work. She argues that there are so few references to bodily acts or images in the novels that 'the rarity of such allusions sometimes gives them power, as though minor physical allusions are code words for larger sensations'. All the same, she is dubious about the faint: 'Can she really have fainted, she who in her earliest work mocked extravagant emotional responses, especially those assigned to women?' She draws attention to the unreliability of the evidence ('not securely embedded in eyewitness reports . . . the story is muddled and riddled with inconsistencies'), and notes that unanswered questions remain: 'Did other choices occur to her? Were other possibilities offered?' Still, her main line agrees with Tomalin's, that this was a painful uprooting which 'would have required extraordinary feats of adjustment'. She imagines Jane Austen 'swallowing hard' and trying to make that adjustment; she thinks the letters to Cassandra sound 'merry and expectant and feverishly false', and she agrees with Tomalin that 'there can be little question that Jane Austen's rather fragile frame of creativity was disturbed following the move to Bath'.[26]

Almost all biographies, when the subject undergoes pain or suffering, look for someone to blame, and David Nokes, whose combative life came out in the same year as Claire Tomalin's, puts the blame firmly on the Austens, whom he vilifies as a crew of snobbish, greedy, competitive entrepreneurs. Their 'habit of suppressing awkward or embarrassing facts' (such as Jane's 'mad' brother George, sent away from home as an infant and never afterwards referred to, or Jane's aunt, Mrs Leigh-Perrot, standing trial for grand larceny), and their 'idealisation of Jane Austen's posthumous reputation', 'has had its inevitable effect on subsequent biographies', says Nokes. He sets out to undercut this 'policy of censorship' and to present a more alarming Austen. He sees her as deeply unromantic: malevolently resentful of the privations of her life, pleasure-loving and malicious. The mysterious Devonshire clergyman, according to Nokes, was probably an invention of Cassandra's. (Possibly, he argues, Cassandra and Jane didn't get on as well as is generally thought: there may have been 'rivalry – even treachery' between them.) This Jane Austen is more interested in amusement and self-advancement than romance. Far from contentedly living a quiet rural life, she couldn't wait to get away from it, and longed for wealth, luxury and amusement. She was Mary Crawford, rather than Fanny Price. But Nokes also wants us to see her as a complicated and challenging human being, torn between self-punishment and self-conceit, and dangerously subversive of the pieties and moralities of her time. When she began to be known as an author and visited London, Austen expressed anxiety at the thought of being shown off as an exhibit. 'If I *am* a wild beast, I cannot help it,' she wrote to Cassandra from London in 1813. Nokes, who loves this quotation and frequently cites it out of context, calls her 'rebellious, satirical and wild'.

As all literary biographers must, he has to find a way of understanding the work's relation to the life, and his is to argue that Austen used the fiction as a form of punishment. So she invents a self-mortifying heroine, Fanny Price, as a way of rebuking her own desire for fame, success and entertainment. Or else the novels work as 'vicarious gratification'. For all Nokes's robust iconoclasm, his desire to rival Austen in empathy and imaginativeness leads him into some riskily fictional, even surprisingly sentimental and old-fashioned passages, as here, imagining Austen writing *Persuasion* at night and thinking back on the time when she gave in to family persuasion not to marry Tom Lefroy: 'That night, as she lay on her bed, listening to the sound of the rain on the window pane, and feeling still the dull ache in her back, Jane allowed herself to imagine how it might have been. It was, at least, a kind of vicarious gratification to confer on her heroine the consummation that had always been denied to her.'

If Nokes allows himself, here and there, a few moments of 'Janeite' tenderness, he makes up for it by being very fierce and sardonic about the faint, which he uses as a weapon to beat all previous Austen biographers round the head with. 'Jane Austen's fainting fit appears as a crucial traumatic event in all the traditional accounts of her life. Yet the authority for this story is not strong, and we might pause to query why it has found such widespread acceptance.' He goes on to doubt the reliability of Caroline Austen's account, written at second hand so long after the event, and its embellishment, many years later, in the *Memoir*, where the faint is introduced. And he notes how eager 'subsequent biographers' have been to accept this account:

> Austen's biographers have been happy to repeat a story which accords so well with their own views of how she *ought* to have felt. Imagine her anguish! To be torn away from the native Hampshire village that she loved and dragged away, against her will, to Bath, that fashionably soulless resort of quacks, hacks, thieves, conspirators and hypochondriacs. There is a tendency for them to wax indignant on her behalf at such a forced removal.

He quotes Deirdre Le Faye, Park Honan and R.W. Chapman on her distress. 'All these biographers', he adds, 'note a significant gap in the sequence of letters between Jane and Cassandra at this time, and draw similar conclusions from it.' But he has a different interpretation of the gap (very like Margaret Kirkham's, though he doesn't cite her): 'Quite possibly the inadmissible sentiments which Cassandra chose to suppress were those of an unseemly excitement.' He quotes the letter to Cassandra of January 1801 which Le Faye and Tomalin and others quote: 'It must not be generally known that I am not sacrificing a great deal in quitting the country – or I can expect to inspire no tenderness, no interest in those we leave behind.' But Nokes reads it differently: 'This is not the language of someone who feels crushed, grief-stricken or incarcerated . . . For years Jane had dreamt of a larger world, where she might savour the luxury of well-proportioned rooms, or indulge a taste for wild coach-rides. On her visit to Bath two summers earlier, she had thrown herself with some energy into the excitement of gala concerts, fireworks, shopping and scandal.' Perhaps the silence of the Bath and Southampton years, which biographers have used 'to confirm their sense of the feelings of unhappiness and displacement which she must have experienced in these busy cities', was actually due to the fact that this Jane Austen, a good-time girl, was having such a busy and social urban life that she had no time for writing: 'Happiness may be just as destructive of literary dedication as unhappiness. And it is equally possible to suggest that it was an abundance of amusements, rather than the absence of inspiration, that prevented her from writing.'[27]

This is more exciting, but just as hypothetical, as the versions which construct depression from the gaps and silences. It provides an intriguing example of quite contrary interpretations of a life from much the same data. Read alongside each other, and set in the context of the long and continuing battles for possession of the posthumous body of Jane Austen, these two biographies provide a riveting example of biography as a relativist process of conjecture, invention, intuition, and manipulation of the evidence. They also point to the mystery of lives, which Austen, for all her penetrating analytical abilities and comic control, often invokes. John Wiltshire notes drily: 'We actually know much less about Jane Austen than her biographers would have us believe.'[28] And that resistance to being known is something the novelist herself was interested in. Mrs Smith can produce the evidence (even from dubious lower-class sources) of Mr Elliot's villainy, and can confirm Anne's doubts about him: proof, witness, demonstration, seem incontrovertible. But what isn't so clearly explained is, for instance, why she takes so long to give Anne this information, or what her motives are, or what kind of pleasure Anne gets out of visiting her. One of the things Austen's novels do is to make us understand how difficult it is to know other people right through. As Fanny Price exclaims to Mary Crawford in the shrubbery in *Mansfield Park*[29] (though she isn't really listening), how incomprehensible the human mind is, and how 'peculiarly past finding out'!

On Being Ill

The story of the body's life, and the part the body has to play in our lives, is one of Virginia Woolf's great subjects. Far from being an ethereal, chill, disembodied writer, lacking in sensuality or physicality, she is always transforming thoughts and feelings and ideas into bodily metaphors. She writes with acute – often extremely troubling – precision about how the body mediates and controls our life-stories. Body parts – whether as erogenous zones or location of symptoms or figures of speech – are strewn all over her pages. Rage and embarrassment are felt in the thighs; a headache can turn into a whole autobiography; dressing up the body is an epic ordeal; and a clenched fist, feet in a pair of boots, the flash of a dress or the fingertip feel of a creature in a salt-water pool, can speak volumes.

Nowhere is her attention to body parts more eloquent and intense than in the essay 'On Being Ill'. It is one of Virginia Woolf's most daring, strange and original short pieces of writing, and it has more subjects than its title suggests. Like the clouds which its sick watcher, 'lying recumbent', sees changing shapes and ringing curtains up and down, this is a shape-changing essay, unpredictably metamorphosing through different performances. It 'treats' not only illness, but language, religion, sympathy, solitude and reading. Close to its surface are thoughts on madness, suicide and the afterlife. For good measure, it throws in dentists, American literature, electricity, an organ grinder and a giant tortoise, the cinema, the coming ice age, worms, snakes and mice, Chinese readers of Shakespeare, housemaids' brooms swimming down the River Solent, and the entire life-story of the third Marchioness of Waterford. And, hiding behind the essay, is a love-affair, a literary quarrel, and a great novel in the making. This net or web (one of the key images here) of subjects comes together in an essay which is at once autobiography, social satire, literary analysis, and an experiment in image-making. By its sleight of hand and playfulness, and its appearance of having all the 'space and leisure' in the world for allusion and deviation, it gallantly makes light of dark and painful experiences.

Illness is one of the main stories of Virginia Woolf's life.[1] The breakdowns and suicide attempts in her early years, which can be read as evidence of manic depression (though that diagnosis has also been hotly contested) led, in the thirty years of her adult writing life, to persistent, periodical illnesses, in which mental and physical symptoms seemed inextricably entwined. In her fictional versions of illness, there is an overlap between her accounts of the delirium of raging fever (Rachel in *The Voyage Out*), the terrors of deep depression (Rhoda in *The Waves*) and the hallucinations and euphoria of suicidal mania (Septimus in *Mrs Dalloway*). All her life, severe physical symptoms – fevers, faints, headaches, jumping pulse, insomnia – signalled and accompanied phases of agitation or depression. In her most severe phases, she hardly ate, and shed weight frighteningly. Terrible headaches marked the onset of illness or exhaustion. The link she makes in the essay between 'fever' and 'melancholia' was well known to her. Her jumping pulse and high temperatures, which could last for weeks, were diagnosed as 'influenza'; in 1923 the presence of 'pneumonia microbes' was detected. At the beginning of 1922 these symptoms got so bad that she consulted a heart specialist who diagnosed a 'tired' heart or heart murmur. Teeth-pulling (unbelievably) was recommended as a cure for persistent high temperature – and also for 'neurasthenia'. (There is a hallucinatory visit to the dentist in 'On Being Ill'.) It seems possible, though unprovable, that she might have had some chronic febrile or tubercular illness. It may also be possible that the drugs she was taking, for both her physical and mental symptoms, exacerbated her poor health. 'That mighty Prince' 'Chloral' is one of the ruling powers in 'On Being Ill'. Chloral was among the sedatives she was regularly given, alongside digitalis and veronal, sometimes mixed with potassium bromide – which could have affected her mental state adversely. With the drugs went a regime of restraint: avoidance of 'over-excitement', rest cures, milk and meat diets, no work allowed. All her life, she had to do battle with tormenting, terrifying mental states, agonising and debilitating physical symptoms and infuriating restrictions. But, in her writings about illness there is a repeated emphasis on its creative and liberating effects. 'I believe these illnesses are in my case – how shall I express it? partly mystical. Something happens in my mind.'[2] 'On Being Ill' tracks that 'something' in the 'undiscovered countries', the 'virgin forest', of the experience of the solitary invalid.

The immediate story behind the writing of 'On Being Ill' begins with Virginia Woolf falling down in a faint at a party at her sister's house in Charleston on 19 August 1925. The summer had been going swimmingly up till then. *Mrs Dalloway* and *The Common Reader* were published earlier in the year, and whenever she 'registered' her books' 'temperature' they seemed to be doing well. She was full of ideas for starting her next novel, *To the Lighthouse*, and she was at the most intimate stage of her absorbing, seductive relationship with Vita Sackville-West. But then, 'why couldn't I see or feel that all this time I was getting a little used up & riding on a flat tire?'[3] The faint led to months and months of illness, and her letters and diary, from September till the New Year (when no sooner did she start to get better than she contracted German measles) are full of frustration and distress. 'Have lain about here, in that odd amphibious life of headache . . .' 'I can't talk yet without getting these infernal pains in my head, or astonishingly incongruous dreams.' 'I am writing this partly to test my poor bunch of nerves at the back of my neck . . .' 'Comatose with headaches. Can't write (with a whole novel in my head too – its damnable).' 'The Dr has sent me to bed: all writing forbidden.' 'Can't make the Dr say when I can get up, when go away, or anything.' 'I feel as if a vulture sat on a bough above my head, threatening to descend & peck at my spine, but by blandishments I turn him into a kind red cock.' 'Not very happy; too much discomfort; sickness . . . a good deal of rat-gnawing at the back of my head; one or two terrors; then the tiredness of the body – it lay like a workman's coat.'[4]

During these slow months, two friendships were changing shape. Vita Sackville-West was tender and affectionate to Virginia Woolf in her illness, and making herself more valuable by the threat of absence: her husband, Harold Nicolson, was being posted by the Foreign Office to Persia; Vita would be off, from Kent to Teheran. (The 1926 version of 'On Being Ill' made a private joke – later cut out – about how, in an imaginary heaven, we can choose to live quite different lives, 'in Teheran and Tunbridge Wells'.) Their letters became more intimate, and Woolf noted in her diary that 'the best of these illnesses is that they loosen the earth about the roots. They make changes. People express their affections.'[5] Just so, in 'On Being Ill', 'illness often takes on the disguise of love . . . wreathing the faces of the absent with a new significance' and creating 'a childish outspokenness'. That longing for the absent loved one, and the desire to call out for her, would make its way into *To the Lighthouse*. 'On Being Ill' anticipates the novel in other ways too: her joke about the mind in its 'philosopher's turret' prepares for Mr Ramsay, and the essay's frequent images of water, waves and sea journeys spill over into the novel. In illness, she says in the essay, 'the whole landscape of life lies remote and fair, like the shore seen from a ship far out at sea'. Cam, in the boat going to the lighthouse, will echo this: 'All looked distant and peaceful and strange. The shore seemed refined, far away, unreal. Already the little distance they had sailed had put them far from it and given it the changed look, the composed look, of something receding in which one has no longer any part.' Absence and distance are themes in both essay and novel.

The other changing friendship of 1925 was more of an irritant; but the essay would not have been written without it. In the 1920s, the Woolfs and their Hogarth Press had become closely involved with T.S. Eliot. They published each other between 1919 and 1924, and she tried to help him get the literary editorship of the *Nation* (which in the end Leonard Woolf took on instead). All this literary reciprocity ran into difficulties when in 1925 Eliot became a rival publisher at Faber & Gwyer, stole one of the Woolfs' authors, and reprinted *The Waste Land* (which the Woolfs had published in 1922) without warning them. 'Tom has treated us scurvily'.[6] It was a difficult moment for him to be commissioning an essay from her for his literary magazine, an invitation which she accepted in flattering terms ('I should think it an honour to figure in your first number').[7] But she was late in sending her piece ('Dear Sir', she wrote half-jokingly, 'I am sending my essay tomorrow. Sorry to have delayed, but I have been working under difficulties.')[8] His response to 'On Being Ill' was unenthusiastic: not surprisingly, when its quirky musings are set against his much more authoritative, impersonal style of essay-writing. Typically, this threw her into a state of depression and anxiety: 'I saw wordiness, feebleness, & all the vices in it. This increases my distaste for my own writing, & dejection at the thought of beginning another novel.'[9] Perhaps Lily Briscoe's anger at Charles Tansley's criticism in *To the Lighthouse* ('Women can't paint, can't write') partly finds its inspiration here.

Eliot's publication of 'On Being Ill' in his high-minded quarterly, the *New Criterion*, for January 1926 was the first of several outings for the essay. In April 1926, a shortened version was published in a middlebrow

New York magazine, the *Forum*, under the title 'Illness: An Unexploited Mine'. In July 1930, Virginia Woolf typeset a new edition of 250 copies of 'On Being Ill' for a Hogarth Press pamphlet, again making some cuts and changes. She signed each copy, exaggerating in her diary the labour of sitting in front of 'the handmade paper on wh. I have to sign my name 600 times'.[10] Vanessa Bell designed an appealing new jacket. It was an attractive, if flawed, publication, as this letter of Woolf's to an unidentified correspondent suggests:

> As one of the guilty parties I bow to your strictures upon the printing of 'On Being Ill'. I agree that the colour is uneven, the letters not always clear, the spacing inaccurate, and the word 'campion' should read 'companion'. All I have to urge in excuse is that printing is a hobby carried on in the basement of a London house, that as amateurs all instruction in the art was denied us; that we have picked up what we know for ourselves; and that we practice printing in the intervals of lives that are otherwise engaged. In spite of all this, I believe that you can already sell your copy for more than the guineas you gave, as the edition is largely oversubscribed. So that though we have not satisfied your taste, we hope that we have not robbed your purse.[11]

After her death, Leonard Woolf reprinted the 1930 version of the essay twice, giving that as its first publication date, perhaps as a way of wiping out Eliot's earlier connection to the essay altogether.[12] In recent years, 'On Being Ill' has gained new recognition in a burgeoning literature of pathography, cited on medical websites alongside books like Anne Hawkins's *Reconstructing Illness: Studies in Pathography* (1993), Arthur Frank's *The Wounded Storyteller* (1995), Thomas Couser's *Recovering Bodies: Illness, Disability, and Life-Writing* (1997) and Oliver Sacks's *A Leg to Stand On* (1994).

'I am very glad you liked my article', Woolf wrote to a friend about 'On Being Ill' in February 1926. 'I was afraid that, writing in bed, & forced to write quickly by the inexorable Tom Eliot, I had used too many words.'[13] 'Writing in bed' has produced an idiosyncratic, prolix, recumbent literature – the opposite of 'inexorable' – at once romantic and modern, with a point of view derived from gazing up at the clouds and looking sideways on to the world. Illness and writing are netted together from the very start of the essay.

Why has illness not been as popular a subject for literature as love, she asks? (This question could not be asked now.) Why has the 'daily drama of the body' not been recognised, the 'great wars of the body' always neglected? Why does literature always insist on separating the mind, or the soul, from the body? Perhaps because the public would never accept illness as a subject for fiction; perhaps because illness requires a new language – 'primitive, subtle, sensual, obscene'. (In the manuscript of the essay she had 'brutal' for 'primitive'.) But illness is almost impossible to communicate. The invalid's demand for sympathy can never be met. People at once start complaining about their own condition. And, apart from a few (female) eccentrics and misfits (whom she colourfully and rapidly invoked), the world can't afford regular sympathy: it would take up the whole working day. Besides, illness really prefers solitude. 'Here we go alone, and like it better so.' The ill have dropped out of the army of workers and become deserters. This gives them time to do things normal people can't do, like looking at the clouds or the flowers. And what they find comforting about clouds and flowers is not their sympathy, but their indifference. The ill, unlike the 'army of the upright', recognise Nature's indifference; they know Nature is going to win in the end, when ice will bury the world. What consolation is there for that thought, she goes on to ask? Organised religion? The idea of heaven? An alternative, secular idea of heaven, as invented by the poets? And poets (she jumps lightly on) are what we need when ill, not prose writers. 'In illness words seem to preserve a mystic quality.' We are attracted to intense lines and phrases, to the incomprehensible, to the texture of sounds. We make rash readings without critical intermediaries, for instance of Shakespeare. And if we have had enough of him, we can read some trash like Augustus Hare's life of two nineteenth-century aristocratic ladies, which gives us a rush of scenes and stories, with which the essay ends.

This loose improvisation is netted together by a complex pattern of images, drawing on water, air, earth and fire, desert wastes and mountain peaks, deep forests and vast seas, clouds, birds, leaves and flowers, as though through illness a whole alternative universe is created. Intensely physical, the writing insists on the body, like a pane of glass, as the transmitter of all experience. The body is monster and hero, animal and mystic, above all actor, in an essay so much about play-acting and scene-making.

As the images cohere, a satire on conformity begins to emerge. The ill are the deserters, the refuseniks. They won't accept the 'co-operative' conventions. They blurt things out. They turn sympathisers away. They won't go to work. They lie down. They waste time. They fantasise. They don't go to church or believe in heaven. They refuse to read responsibly or to make sense of what they read. They are attracted to nonsense, sensation and rashness. On the other side of the glass is 'the army of the upright', harnessing energy, driving motor cars, going to work and to church, 'with the heroism of the ant or the bee', writing letters to *The Times*, communicating and civilising. Her prototypes for these good citizens, snatched rather wildly from the newspapers she happens to be reading at the time, are the Bishop of Lichfield, and Samuel Insull, who, before his collapse and disgrace in the Depression years, was co-founder, with Edison, of the General Electric Company, head of the Chicago empire of utility and transportation companies, and the bringer of electrification to 'the cities of the Middle West': a wonderful embodiment of productive energy. There is a faint suggestion that in separating themselves from the army of workers, the ill are like pacifists or non-combatants, unconscientious objectors who nevertheless have their own battles to fight.

Reading in bed, reading when ill – like 'writing in bed' – is, it's suggested, a form of deviancy. The theme of rash reading, making one's own 'notes in the margin', seems also to allow for rash writing, writing with the apparent wilful inconsequentiality and inconclusiveness of this essay. 'On Being Ill' is as much about reading and writing as it is about illness: in fact it's about reading and desire, as though our erotic longings for absent lovers as we lie in bed with a high temperature get translated into longings for language. At the centre of the essay there is a description of what it feels like to be lying on our back looking upwards. What do we see?

Ordinarily to look at the sky for any length of time is impossible . . .
Now, lying recumbent, staring straight up, the sky is discovered to be something so different . . . that really it is a little shocking. This then has been going on all the time without our knowing it! – this incessant making up of shapes and casting them down, this buffeting of clouds

together, and drawing vast trains of ships and wagons from North to South, this incessant ringing up and down of curtains of light and shade, this interminable experiment with gold shafts and blue shadows, with veiling the sun and unveiling it, with making rock ramparts and wafting them away – this endless activity, with the waste of Heaven knows how many million horse power of energy, has been left to work its own will year in year out. The fact seems to call for comment and indeed for censure. Ought not some one to write to *The Times*? Use should be made of it. One should not let this gigantic cinema play perpetually to an empty house. But watch a little longer and another emotion drowns the stirrings of civic ardour. Divinely beautiful it is also divinely heartless. Immeasurable resources are used for some purpose which has nothing to do with human pleasure or human profit.[14]

Woolf's vision of clouds is a modern, technological vision, a 'gigantic cinema', anticipating her fascinated essay on 'The Cinema', which she published not long after. It is also a theatrical spectacle, ringing up and down its curtains of light and shade. And it is closely connected to the theme of reading that runs through the essay. A few paragraphs later, these insubstantial structures – 'rock ramparts' being created and wafted away – are implicitly contrasted with the solid structure of long prose works – 'arches, towers, and battlements' standing firm on their foundations – which are not, she says, what we want to read in illness. What we might want to read is Shakespeare, if we can shake the 'flyblown' dust of criticism off him and read him fresh. Shakespeare runs strongly under that cloudscape; it's hard to read it and not to think of Hamlet's wilful, nonsensical play with clouds ('Very like a whale'), or of Prospero's vanishing enchantments: 'And, like the baseless fabric of this vision,/The cloud-capp'd Towers, the gorgeous Palaces,/The solemn Temples, the great Globe itself,/ Yea, all which it inherit, shall dissolve,/And, like this insubstantial Pageant faded/Leave not a Rack behind.'[15]

Most of all, Antony's speech to Eros, before he chooses to die, about the changing shape of clouds, is invoked: 'That which is now a Horse, even with a Thought/The Rack dislimns, and makes it indistinct/As water is in water.'[16] Antony goes on to tell Eros that he cannot hold his own 'visible shape': he has lost his sense of himself. In all these Shakespearian cloudscapes, so present to her mind in this essay, the 'insubstantial pageant' of the clouds is closely linked to sleep and dreams, and it also embodies a sense of confusion, or anguish, or crisis. For both Prospero and Antony, there is a faint suggestion that 'rack' (meaning a drift of wind-blown clouds) might also invoke 'rack', meaning an instrument of torture on which one is stretched out in agony (like a sick-bed), as Lear is stretched on 'the rack of this tough world'.

The Shakespearian allusions in 'On Being Ill' all have to do with suicide. 'I read *Hamlet* last night,' she wrote to Vita Sackville-West on 23 September 1925, three weeks after agreeing to write 'On Being Ill'.[17] *Hamlet* is in the essay from the beginning, in her reference to the 'undiscovered countries' of illness, and in her use of the phrase 'shuffled off'. 'To be or not to be', Hamlet's meditation on suicide and whether we should make our own way into that 'undiscovered country from whose bourn no traveller returns', is lurking, like Antony's speech to Eros, in the margins of the essay.

Would the Christian faith, she asks suddenly in the middle of the essay, give its believers enough conviction 'to leap into Heaven off Beachy Head?' (a well-known suicide spot). Under its playful surface, there is a muffled, anguished debate going on about whether illness can take one so far out to sea, so high up the mountain peak (like Septimus in *Mrs Dalloway*), so apart from 'normality', that suicide might seem the only escape.

The last section of the essay (cut from the *Forum*'s version) seems, at first sight, a peculiar coda. We are suddenly treated to a potted version of a minor nineteenth-century historian's life of two unknown aristocratic ladies, jumbled comically together in the manner Woolf favours for her essays on 'eccentrics' and 'obscure lives'. Like many of her essays on women, this tells the story of a gifted woman suppressed and imprisoned by her circumstances. Yet it seems a rather random example of desultory reading, until we get to the last image, of the widowed Lady Waterford, who 'crushed together' the plush curtain 'in her agony' as she watches her husband's body being taken to his grave.[18] This makes a startling echo of the sick person who, earlier in the essay, has to take his pain in one hand and 'a lump of pure sound' in the other and 'crush them together' to produce a 'brand new word'.

'Crushing together' is an action produced by agony. And, both for the invalid mastering illness through language, and the 'great lady' mastering her grief, it is an image of fierce courage. 'To look these things squarely in the face would need the courage of a lion tamer.' ('Of ten thousand lion tamers – for these lions are within us not without'.) Virginia Woolf does not write explicitly about herself; as in almost all her essays, she does not say 'I', but 'we', 'one', 'us'. Yet the essay is a demonstration of her heroic powers of endurance and courage, her lack of self-pity, and the use she made of her bodily and mental suffering, every bit as productive as Mr Insull: how she put them to work, and transformed them into imaginative writing.

That process of imaginative transformation isn't only inspired by reading Shakespeare. There's a strong presence in the essay, too, of the Romantic writers Virginia Woolf read throughout her life – who themselves were steeped in Shakespeare.[19] Her title is like one of Hazlitt's, who called his essays 'On Going a Journey', or 'On the Fear of Death'. Shelley, Keats and Coleridge are mentioned or quoted; De Quincey, Charles Lamb and Wordsworth are all in play. That cloudscape of Woolf's, with its 'incessant making up of shapes', shows how deeply absorbed she was at this time in reading De Quincey. She published an essay on his work, called 'Impassioned Prose', in the same year as 'On Being Ill'. De Quincey had been one of Julia Stephen's favourite writers. He comes into *To the Lighthouse*, with echoes of his autobiographical essay 'Suspiria de Profundis', in which he contemplates – as Mrs Ramsay does, and as Woolf does in 'On Being Ill' – 'that side of the mind which is exposed in solitude'. (The phrase is Woolf's, from 'Impassioned Prose'.)[20] In 'Suspiria', too, De Quincey talks of the human brain as a palimpsest, in which all the layers of our feelings and memories coexist: this explains why our whole life flashes before our eyes at the moment of death (he gives an example of a near-death by drowning) or why, in illness or fever or under drugs, our deepest experiences and feelings can be exposed.

Yes, reader, countless are the mysterious handwritings of grief or joy which have inscribed themselves successively upon the palimpsest of your brain – and like the annual leaves of aboriginal forests, or the undissolving snows on the Himalayas, or light falling upon light, the endless strata have covered up each other in forgetfulness. But by the

hour of death, but by fever, but by the searchings of opium, all these can
revive in strength. They are not dead, but sleeping.[21]

These thoughts lie under Woolf's adventure, in 'On Being Ill', into the
'undiscovered countries' we reach as the 'waters of annihilation' close
over us, or as we make our way alone into the 'virgin forests', the
'snowfields', of illness.

De Quincey often writes about cloudscapes, or invokes Shakespeare's
cloud-language. In an extraordinary passage in 'Suspiria', he writes
about himself as child, in deep grief after the death of his sister, sitting
in church and looking out of the window. The 'white fleecy clouds' that
he sees shape themselves, in his 'sorrow-haunted eye', into 'a vision of
beds' full of sick and dying children, 'tossing in anguish, and weeping
clamorously for death'. In *Confessions of an English Opium Eater*, he
describes the terrifying and stupendous architecture of his dreams
under the effects of opium, and compares these architectural dreams to
cloudscapes. He illustrates his meaning with a passage from Wordsworth's *The Excursion*, which describes clouds forming 'towers' and
'battlements that on their restless front/Bore stars'.[22] Woolf faintly
echoes this passage, when she uses the phrase 'arches, towers and
battlements', talking of the effect solid prose has on us. De Quincey's
opium dreams of cloud-like, architectural visions in his dreams are
accompanied by what he calls a 'deep-seated anxiety and gloomy
melancholy', and by terrifying headaches – both of which Woolf knew
about all too well.

Like Wordsworth, whom she often read, Woolf finds no consolation
for the human condition in her cloudscapes. Wordsworth wrote in a
sonnet of 1807 ('Those words were uttered as in pensive mood') on the
changing beauties of cloudscapes as 'unstable as a dream of night'. They
'find in the heart of man no natural home'.[23] It's the same idea, in
different words, as Woolf's on the 'divine heartlessness' of that
spectacular vision of clouds in 'On Being Ill', which has 'nothing to do
with human pleasure or human profit'. Woolf, like Wordsworth, is
asking that most serious question under the light surface of her essay:
where do human beings find consolation or sympathy for their anguish?
Not in the sky: and not, according to her, in any idea of anything
beyond the sky, any 'undiscovered country' of immortality or afterlife.
What consolation or freedom or escape we have is going to be found

here, in language and writing and the work of the imagination. The shifting clouds in the sky are alien to us, ultimately no use to us (and she makes a joke about their uselessness – ought it not to be censured?) They just go on playing to an empty house. But what the imagination can do with them – especially when released by the reckless, anarchic permission that illness seems to provide – is of immense use to us.

In 'Impassioned Prose', Woolf describes De Quincey making 'scenes' in his writing: 'Scenes come together under his hand like congregations of clouds which gently join and slowly disperse or hang solemnly still.'[24] One of the 'scenes' of De Quincey's that she cites is of 'Lamb asleep in his chair'. In this touchingly evocative reminiscence, De Quincey remembers how his friend Charles Lamb – the essayist, poet and dramatist – would always fall asleep in his chair after dinner, with a seraphic expression on his face, 'a repose affectingly contrasted with the calamities and internal storms of his life'.[25] Charles Lamb's history, so full of 'calamities and internal storms', is one of the stories of anguish invoked in 'On Being Ill'. The most peculiar and painful quotation in the essay is from Lamb. (I take it as a planted clue to Lamb's presence in 'On Being Ill' that one of the sets of initials Woolf gives to the sympathetic visitors who visit the sick is 'C.L.') And Charles Lamb's essays and letters were also in her mind at this time: she wrote a letter on 18 September 1925 to her friend Janet Case, praising Lamb's dashing and brilliant style. The letter of Lamb's she quotes in 'On Being Ill' is an agonised meditation on how the mind can prey on itself without enough work to do. Woolf writes:

> We dip in Lamb's letters – some prose writers are to be read as poets – and find 'I am a sanguinary murderer of time, and would kill him inchmeal just now. But the snake is vital' – and who shall explain the delight?

She is quoting a letter from Lamb to the Quaker poet Bernard Barton, written on 25 July 1829, in great despondency. Lamb's sister Mary – as she intermittently had to be, after she killed their mother in a fit of mania – was confined in an asylum. He was staying in London, not at his country home in Enfield, and was feeling a terrible sense of solitude. He had given up the dull, routine, rather oppressive job he had done for over thirty years, as a clerk in East India House, three years before. At first he had felt a great sense of relief; now he felt – as he often did – a terminal depression. This is the letter Woolf quotes from:

> I pity you for overwork, but I assure you no-work is worse. The mind preys on itself, the most unwholesome food. I brag'd formerly that I could not have too much time. I have a surfeit. With few years to come, the days are wearisome. But weariness is not eternal. Something will shine out to take the load off, that flags me, which is at present intolerable. I have killed an hour or two in this poor scrawl. I am a sanguinary murderer of time, and would kill him inchmeal just now. But the snake is vital.[26]

Lamb's essays, most of which he wrote under the pen-name 'Elia', were some of Woolf's favourite Romantic writings; she found him very 'congenial'.[27] Two of his essays are echoed in 'On Being Ill'. One is a piece called 'The Convalescent', in *Last Essays of Elia*, where Lamb describes, just as she does, the peculiar state of mind that comes over the sick person who has a 'nervous fever'. Like her, he writes on the 'supreme selfishness' and self-absorption of the sick person, on how he becomes 'a world unto himself – his own theatre', how the outside world seems to fall away from him, and on how 'sympathy' is limited by sickness.

> How sickness enlarges the dimensions of a man's self to himself! He is his own exclusive object . . . What passes out of doors, or within them . . . affects him not . . . He has put on his strong armour of sickness, he is wrapped in the callous hide of suffering . . . He is his own sympathiser; and instinctively feels that none can so well perform that office for him.

The other essay she must have had in mind is called 'Popular Fallacies: That We Should Rise with the Lark', which is close to Woolf's satire on 'the army of the upright'. Much better to stay in bed, says Lamb, just like Woolf: 'While the busy part of mankind are fast huddling on their clothes, are already up and about their occupation, content to have swallowed their sleep by wholesale; we chose to linger a-bed, and digest our dreams.'[28] After all, why should we get up? 'We have nothing here to expect, but in a short time a sick-bed, and a dismissal.'

It's his profound melancholia and terror of insanity which is part of

Lamb's attraction for Woolf, and which explains his presence in 'On Being Ill'. But what she admires him for, above all, is the imaginative energy with which he transforms himself from melancholic depressive into dazzlingly playful and inventive essayist. In 'On Being Ill' there is a passage on the possibility of living out the lives which in childhood we think we might have, until we settle into the confines of the one life we *are* going to lead. It's a passage which anticipates *Orlando*, the next novel she will write after *To the Lighthouse*, and after that *The Waves*, in which Bernard ends the novel thinking of all the un-lived selves he might have been: 'those old half-articulate ghosts who keep up their hauntings by day and by night; who turn over in their sleep, who utter their confused cries, who put out their phantom fingers and clutch at me as I try to escape – shadows of people one might have been; unborn selves.'[29] In 'On Being Ill', she writes: 'There is no harm in choosing, to live over and over, now as a man, now as a woman, as sea-captain, or court lady, as Emperor or farmer's wife, in splendid cities and on remote moors, at the time of Pericles or Arthur, Charlemagne, or George the Fourth – to live and live till we have lived out those embryo lives which attend about us in early youth until "I" suppressed them.'[30] For Woolf, as for some of the great writers she reads and makes use of on her sick-bed, writing – and reading – can shape and keep those possibilities of alternative, imaginary lives, which otherwise are lost to us for ever, like dreams, or clouds.

Father and Son:
Philip and Edmund Gosse

The term 'life-writing' is sometimes used when the distinction between biography and autobiography is being deliberately blurred, or when different ways of telling a life-story – memoir, autobiography, biography, diary, letters, autobiographical fiction – are being discussed together. Virginia Woolf used the term 'life-writing' in her memoir of her own life, 'Sketch of the Past', when she was talking about the importance of placing the individual life in the context of family, inheritance, influences, environment and 'invisible presences': putting 'the fish in the stream'.[1] 'Life-writing' seems a useful formula for a book like Edmund Gosse's *Father and Son*, a memoir which is also an autobiography, and a biography which is also, to some extent, a fiction. Gosse's subversive and poignant account of his relationship with his father anticipates many, much more outspoken twentieth-century versions of this genre, such as Philip Roth's *Patrimony*, or Blake Morrison's *And When Did You Last See Your Father?*, or Mary Gordon's *The Shadow Man*. One thing these rewritings of parents by children have in common is an intense physicality. The body of the father hangs over these pages like a 'shadow man'.

In the case of Edmund and Philip Gosse, the story is a particularly interesting one because it marks the turn from Victorian to modern 'life-writing' (*Father and Son* matches Samuel Butler's *The Way of All Flesh* and Lytton Strachey's *Eminent Victorians* in irreverence and irony), and because father and son are equally gifted in their different fields.

When Edmund Gosse published *Father and Son* in 1907 (anonymously, but everyone knew it was him), his friend Henry James wrote to him at once, effusively, telling him he had read the book with 'deep entrancement', and praising it as 'the very best thing you have ever written', full of 'vivacity & intensity', its 'frankness & objectivity' carried through 'with rare audacity'. He had one reservation, that there were a few places where 'I feel it go too far; not too far, I mean, for truth, but too far for filiality, or at least for tenderness'.[2] A few days later

Gosse received a letter from George Moore, who always said he was the initiator of *Father and Son*, since he had told Gosse, when he published his *Life* of his father in 1890, that he should follow it with 'a great psychological work [on] your father's influence on you'. Don't tell it as a biography, he had urged him; 'tell it in the first person'.[3] Moore, in his own autobiographies, prided himself on his 'perfect candour and complete shamelessness'. When he read *Father and Son* he thought it not candid enough. He wrote to Gosse: 'That sense of decency, *which as a writer you should not have,* you could not overcome.'[4]

The two letters illustrate the two sides of an acute late-Victorian disagreement over life-writing. Should it respect privacy, dignity, 'decency' and family feeling, or should it tear down censorship, hypocrisy and convention? *Father and Son* made one of the crucial interventions in that debate, and changed the terms of the genre. In its time it was praised for its wonderful candour, humour and humanity, but also dispraised for 'going too far'. (The *TLS* reviewer, for instance, wondered if the author had 'settled with his conscience how far . . . it is legitimate to expose the weaknesses . . . of a good man who is also one's father'.)[5] But it was also seen, then and since, as a key moment in the deconstruction of 'Victorian' life-writing, a process which began with Froude's scandalous exposure of Carlyle in the 1880s, and culminated, after the war, with Lytton Strachey's *Eminent Victorians* – much admired by Edmund Gosse. Like Samuel Butler's savage fictional account of mid-nineteenth-century Evangelicism, *The Way of All Flesh* (1903), *Father and Son*, as Ann Thwaite says in her biography of Gosse, 'feels modern'.[6]

Gosse invented a new kind of book which, as he said firmly, was not a biography of his parents, nor an autobiography, but 'a study of two temperaments' and a 'diagnosis of a dying Puritanism'.[7] There was no real precedent for it, unless you count Mark Rutherford's *Autobiography* or George Moore's narcissistic *Confessions of a Young Man*. It resists definition (not biography or autobiography, not quite memoir or fiction) and sustains an unusual, and compelling, mixture of involvement and detachment. Gosse describes, with tenderness and comedy, understanding and resentment, his solitary, peculiar childhood, in the 1850s and 1860s, as the late, only child of two 'extreme Calvinists' (*FS*, Ch. 1). Philip and Emily Gosse were members of a small group of 'Brethren' who believed that they could be elected to the company of Christ's saints through conversion and through the blood of the Lamb, that there need be no intermediaries ('no priest, no ritual, no festivals, no ornament of any kind') between them and God, that Holy Scripture was literally true, that they had 'direct access to the word of God', that they should keep themselves apart from unbelievers, heathens and Papists, breaking bread and taking communion together, but should work to convert all those they met on their travels. Those who had been converted and baptised as 'saints' had to watch perpetually, live soberly, avoid temptation and keep themselves 'righteous and godly' in anticipation of the Second Coming, which they believed was imminent. 'Washed in the Blood of the Lamb, they would never taste of death, but would enter into Christ's joy and sit down on his throne.' Edmund Gosse would write later of 'Dissenters . . . who don't know whether to take in the washing or not, since the Lord may come while the clothes are in the suds'.[8]

Both these intransigent believers were people of exceptional gifts. Philip Gosse was an outstanding naturalist – zoologist, entomologist, botanist, lepidopterist, ornithologist and marine biologist, the pioneer of the marine aquarium, the renowned collector, classifier and illustrator of sea-anemones and corals, elected Fellow of the Royal Society for his expertise in 'microscopic zoology' (his main passion was for rotifera, 'those minute aquatic animals found in the floccose sediment in ponds, lakes, ditches and tidepools') (*PG*, p. 316). His wife was an extremely imaginative, intelligent and strong-willed person, who channelled her powers into religious writing. (A pious memorial to Emily Gosse, *Tell Jesus*, by another 'saint', Anna Shipton, spoke of her 'peculiar faculty of illustrating her subject in conversation', and listed sixty 'Gospel Narrative Tracts' by Mr and Mrs P.H. Gosse.)[9] One of the saddest details in *Father and Son* – and one of the many places where nature, temperament and desire are set against religion – is of Emily Gosse's suppression of her natural story-telling talents, which she feared must be wicked and ungodly: 'This is, surely, a very painful instance of the repression of an instinct . . . Was my mother intended by nature to be a novelist?' (*FS*, Ch. 2). After her excruciating death from cancer, the seven-year-old Edmund was left in the care of 'the father', whose threefold dedication – to his work, to bringing up his little boy as a 'saint', and to his fixed, dogmatic system of belief – had powerful and lasting effects on the life and character of 'the son'.

Edmund Gosse treats his father's life-story, retrospectively, as both admirable and ridiculous. He sees the crucial fractures in it, the cracks in the system, coming at two points. One was the notorious publication of *Omphalos: An Attempt to untie the Geological Knot* (1857), which painfully attempted to reconcile his belief in the literal truth of the Bible with the mounting evidence for evolution, natural selection, and the mutability of species. When Edmund Gosse describes his father's position in 'this period of intellectual ferment', he describes (as with his mother's sacrifice to God of a potential career as a novelist) an agonising clash between 'every instinct in' his father's 'intelligence', which 'went out at first to greet the new light', and his need to maintain an unshaken belief in 'the law of the fixity of species'. This led him to develop a theory 'to justify geology to godly readers of Genesis'. 'It was . . . that when the catastrophic act of creation took place, the world presented, instantly, the structural appearance of a planet on which life had long existed.' The 'Law of Prochronism' was meant, as Thwaite comments, to 'settle once and for all the conflict between religion and science'. But unsympathetic commentators read it, crudely, as an attempt to prove that 'God hid the fossils in the rocks in order to tempt geologists into infidelity' (*EG*, p. 36; *FS*, Ch. 5; *PG*, p. 222). The book, as Edmund Gosse noted in his first life of his father, 'was received with scorn by the world of science and with neglect by the general public'.[10] Such widespread derision was extremely painful to its author – a situation which would be re-enacted in Edmund Gosse's own professional life.

The other key struggle, also characterised by the repression of instinct in the interests of fixed beliefs, was the father's battle to keep the son on the straight and narrow path to heaven. The scenes in *Father and Son* where the son begins to have doubts about the father's infallibility are done with a wonderfully rueful re-enactment of his youthful sense of gravity. The boy's experiment with an 'act of idolatry', praying to the morning-room chair ('O Chair!'), as a fearful test of God's wrath ('but nothing happened . . . God did not care'); the 'spiritual anguish' of having secretly had a mouthful of the plum pudding smuggled in by the servants on Christmas Day ('Oh! Papa, Papa, I have eaten of flesh offered to idols!'), and the father's hurling of the sacrilegious pudding on to the fire; and the piercing shriek that interrupts the father's long bedside prayers, as a huge beetle 'with more legs than a self-respecting insect ought to have', makes its way inexorably up the counterpane towards the boy – these famous moments brilliantly apply a light touch to a world in which nothing could be taken lightly (*FS*, Chs 2, 5, 7). (Peter Carey gave them a second life in the childhood scenes in *Oscar and Lucinda*.)

Just as Philip Gosse was for many years only remembered as the natural scientist who tried to defend creationism, so Edmund Gosse has come to be read and acclaimed almost exclusively as the author of *Father and Son*, though, in his lifetime, he was *the* pre-eminent, prolific, established and influential late-Victorian man of letters. What has not been so much remembered, and it's one of the virtues of Ann Thwaite's work on Edmund Gosse that she reminds us of it, was that even without *Father and Son*, he was an important figure in the development of Victorian biography.

Most readers of *Father and Son* aren't aware that this was Gosse's second version of his father's life. He published *The Life of Philip Henry Gosse, FRS*, soon after his father's death, in 1890. Though, as friends like George Moore and John Addington Symonds told him, this first 'official' life didn't have enough of *him* in it – 'Only', Symonds added plaintively, 'how can we do veracious psychological self-portraiture?' (*EG*, p. 319) – it did set the terms for his treatment of Philip Gosse in the later book. 'My only endeavour', he wrote, 'has been to present my father as he was ... He utterly despised that species of modern biography which depicts what was a human being as though transformed into the tinted wax of a hairdresser's block ... I have taken it to be the truest piety to represent him exactly as I knew him and have found him.' Edmund Gosse's own first biographer, his friend Evan Charteris, noted: 'He brushed aside the tradition of Victorian biography [and] looked at his father objectively, studying the incongruities and the complex psychology of his character, and presenting a portrait which satisfies the reader that he has been shown the truth.'[11]

That claim to truth-telling – however dubious it may have turned out to be – does point to one strand in Gosse's writing of Victorian *Lives*. When he was a child, he produced elaborate 'Zoological Sketches' in imitation of his father's work; when he was an adult, he was known as a very good mimic. There is an element of mimicry or imitation within the writing of biography, as the biographer uses the subject's own words and actions to 'bring them alive'. The kind of writing Gosse most enjoyed doing was the anecdotal portrait: profiles of famous writers in collections like *Critical Kit-Kats*, *Portraits and Sketches*, *Aspects and Impressions* or *Silhouettes*. He admired Boswell, and wanted biography to be free, truthful, lively and candid. 'If biographers would only see', he wrote in 1897, 'how much they enhance the qualities of their subjects by admitting peculiarities and even failings' (*EG*, p. 3). In his 1902 essay on Biography for the *Dictionary of National Biography*, he complained (like Carlyle) about the Victorian tendency in biography towards 'a certain false and timid excess of refinement'. The 'true conception' of biography, he argued, 'as the faithful portrait of a soul in its adventures through life, is very modern'. The biographer should not 'gloss over frailties or obscure irregularities'; biography is not 'an opportunity for panegyric or invective' or for 'vanity and sentiment'.[12] He admired French literature enormously, and was drawn to the French literary art of the short, witty portrait, like the *Historiettes* of Tallemant des Réaux, a gossipy seventeenth-century biographer of his life and times, a French John Aubrey much enjoyed by Gosse: 'His *Historiettes* threw a beam of disconcerting light into the closed and scented chamber of the Grande Siècle'; he resisted the encroaching seventeenth-century convention that biography should 'produce a grandiose moral effect'.[13]

Gosse's own literary biographies, mainly written for short-length series of 'Men of Letters' or 'English Worthies' – of Jeremy Taylor, Coventry Patmore, Sir Thomas Browne, Congreve, Gray, Raleigh, Ibsen – were compressed and vivid (*EG*, pp. 413–14). His bold attempt as a child to test God's wrath by worshipping a wooden chair came in useful when he published a questioning piece on Queen Victoria, soon after her death, in the April 1901 issue of the *Quarterly*. Was the Queen 'a human being at all?' he asked. 'How much of the worship was paid to a woman and how much to a fetish?' The article caused a sensation, and it paved the way for Lytton Strachey's later debunking of Victoria and Victorians. Writing on *Eminent Victorians*, Gosse said that 'in this country the majority have always enjoyed seeing noses knocked off statues'.[14] Of Strachey's *Queen Victoria*, in 1921, Gosse said, generously: 'He is the earliest of the biographers to insist that a cat, and still more a careful student of the whimsicalities of life, may look steadily at a queen' (*EG*, p. 410). But he had done it first.

For all this, and in spite of *Father and Son*, it's hard to think of Edmund Gosse as a pioneering life-writer, well ahead of his time. In some ways he was deeply embedded in the conventions he criticised.

His 1917 life of Swinburne (whose close friend he had been) was disappointingly guarded and decorous. Gosse explained to his friends that he had been working under difficulties, including 'the embargo laid on any mention of drunkenness' and 'a still heavier sexual embargo'.[15] But the next generation – in the voice of Ezra Pound – complained: 'We do not wish a Swinburne coated with a veneer of British officialdom and decked out for a psalm-singing audience' (*EG*, p. 478). Gosse disapproved of Wilde, and backed off from his friend Robbie Ross, who was supporting Wilde, during the scandal of Wilde's trial (*EG*, p. 359). He thought Forster's *Howards End* was *risqué* and crude. He was involved in the censoring of J.A. Symonds's posthumous reputation, one of the most notorious examples of the suppressions that surrounded nineteenth-century life-writing. After Horatio Brown's euphemistic *Life* of Symonds, which translated all his self-tortured homosexuality into religious crises, Gosse, who had exchanged many painful letters on sexuality with Symonds, and was his executor, burnt most of Symonds's most revealing papers, and put his memoirs under a fifty-year ban – not even allowing it to be broken by Symonds's daughter, Janet Vaughan, who walked out of Gosse's house in disgust at his censorship (*EG*, p. 321).

It is ironic that the tolerant, sympathetic friend of Swinburne and Symonds and Gide, the advocate of Ibsen, and the author of a pioneering, candid memoir, should have come to seem, for the next generation, the paradigmatic hypocritical Victorian conservative, ruling over the national taste from the pages of the *Sunday Times*. Sir Edmund Gosse's snobbery, clubbishness, love of Mayfair dowagers, stately homes and patronage, made him look revoltingly smug in his late years. For Bloomsbury in the 1920s, he stood for all the establishment stuffiness and hypocrisy they wanted to challenge. Strachey, whom he so admired, despised him. Virginia Woolf turned him into Sir Nicholas Greene, the archetypal literary hanger-on and operator, in *Orlando*, her parody of Victorian biography.

There were flaws, too, in his smooth surface. Like his father, Gosse went through a period of professional disrepute, in 1886, when his Clark lectures at Cambridge were the subject of a jealous but devastating attack on their accuracy, leading to 'a veritable vendetta of criticism' (*EG*, p. 270). There was a posthumous scandal, too, over the extent to which Gosse was complicit with the literary forgeries of Thomas Wise, many of whose frauds Gosse bought for his library and helped – perhaps innocently – to authenticate (*EG*, pp. 389–90).

When the lives of Victorian writers began to be reassessed in the twentieth century, Gosse thus seemed a perfect target for disparagement. Charteris's bland 1930s *Life and Letters* – the sort of biography Gosse himself would have disliked – left every stone unturned. But if hypocrisy, smugness, professional inaccuracy and bibliographical fraud were the obvious charges, what else might there be to uncover? Gosse was 'outed' as a closet homosexual in Phyllis Grosskurth's 1964 biography of Symonds: his passionate attachment to the sculptor Hamo Thornycroft (Gosse isn't a homosexual, he's Hamo-sexual, Strachey is supposed to have said) (*EG*, p. 194) has since then been read as the 'real' story of the life, hidden behind the husband and father and much honoured, influential man of letters.

Ann Thwaite's thorough and professional resuscitation of Edmund Gosse in 1984 set out neither to attack nor to inflate him, but to look at the paradoxes and peculiarities of this 'establishment' life. It's a good example of how Victorian life-stories can begin to be retold, after successive phases of panegyric, criticism and exposure. She wanted to find out how the anxious little boy of *Father and Son* become the self-satisfied fat cat Sir Edmund Gosse. In her desire to be fair and balanced, she makes the childhood look less traumatic and plays down Gosse's homosexuality. What interests her most is the ambition, competitiveness and fallibility in Gosse's professional life; she is especially good on what Henry James called 'his genius for inaccuracy'.

Thwaite resists one way of making a modern story out of a Victorian life, which is to psychoanalyse it. She doesn't make the connection – though it is a fascinating one – between Gosse's anxiety about pleasing his father and being a perfect child 'saint', and his thin-skinned reactions to criticism as an adult. And though she discusses Gosse's confused letters about his sexuality, written to Symonds in the 1890s, after the most intense phase of his relationship with Hamo Thornycroft is over, she doesn't link them to the writing of *Father and Son*. Yet it is tempting to think that repressed sexual feeling may have been translated into that story of natural instincts repressed by a system of rigid laws and codes, and that *Father and Son* was much more of an autobiography than Gosse admitted.

Thwaite sees that Edmund Gosse's resistance to Philip Gosse was also based on likeness, and that father and son were very similar in some ways. The figure of Philip Gosse stayed in her mind long after her book on Edmund Gosse, as a much more endearing one than *Father and Son* allowed. In the twenty years between Ann Thwaite's biography of Edmund Gosse and her book on Philip Henry Gosse, there have been many developments in the writing of Victorian life-stories. Much work has been done on the construction of Victorian masculinity, by critics such as Trev Broughton, Joseph Bristow, Michael Tosh and David Amigoni.[16] Most of the central figures of Victorian intellectual life, among them Ruskin, Newman, Hopkins, Darwin, Matthew Arnold, G.H. Lewes, Henry James, William Morris, George Moore and the Brontës, have been the subject of large-scale, revisionary biographies. Studies of minor or neglected figures (like Claire Tomalin's book on Ellen Ternan or Ann Thwaite's own biography of Emily Tennyson) have switched the emphasis away from the Lives of Great Men; group biographies or lives of friends, such as Norma Clarke's *Ambitious Heights* (on the Jewsbury sisters, Felicia Hemans and Jane Welsh Carlyle) have changed our sense of biography as, above all, the pursuit of towering individuals. Nineteenth-century science has been the object of intense interest and reassessment. A life of Philip Henry Gosse was timely in 2002.

And his story, set free from the gloomy image of him in *Father and Son*, is a remarkable one. Thwaite describes a more passionate, imaginative, adventurous and influential person than we might have expected. She sees the combination in him of dedicated naturalist and fundamentalist Christian as leading, not to an absurd rigidity of mind, but, on the contrary, to a 'state of excited anticipation as he enjoyed the glimpses of the wonderful here on earth' (*PG*, p. 2). The young Henry Gosse (as she calls him, since his wife used his middle name) travelled from Poole to Newfoundland, where he worked as a clerk and studied butterflies and other insects; then to Canada, where he tried to farm, and developed his talents as a field naturalist; then to Alabama, as a teacher, where he discovered more plants and animals and – to his horror – slavery; and later to Jamaica, where he worked as a collector and illustrator of insects and other species. Gosse's middle and later years with Emily and Edmund in Devon, the years of *Father and Son*, look much less parochial, set in the context of those early adventures.

At every point, Thwaite gives examples (accompanied by Gosse's appealing illustrations) of his informed, curious, impassioned attention to detail. Some of these are lyrical and poetic – a flock of wild parrots in Alabama looks like 'an immense shawl of green satin on which someone had worked an elaborate pattern in scarlet and gold and azure' (*PG*, p. 89). In some he is tenderly careful – training a humming-bird to take sugar from his lips, or mourning the death of his cat in childbirth. Some show his excitement in the mysterious possibilities of nature, like his fascination with the possibility of sea serpents. And always there is the excitement and dedication of that peculiar species, the religious scientist. Gosse speaks of his microscope as a tool of visionary delight, which unlocks 'a world of wonder and beauty before invisible, which one who has once gazed upon it can never forget, and never cease to admire' (*PG*, p. 156). What he sees through it – particularly the rotifera or 'wheel-animalcules' – were objects of endless amazement to him. These 'animated specks' were 'creatures that swim with their hair, that have ruby eyes blazing deep in their necks', 'who creep without feet, seize without hands and eat without mouths' (*PG*, p. 317). Thwaite sees Henry Gosse's struggle to reconcile belief and science as touching rather than absurd. And she gives a sympathetic account of his appalled realisation, at the last, that his life's whole conviction – that he would not see death, but be taken up to be with Christ and his saints at the second coming – was false. God had betrayed him: like every other animal, he was going to die.

The essential argument of this biography is that Edmund Gosse grotesquely distorted his picture of his father, with his usual 'genius for inaccuracy'. Thwaite doesn't go quite as far as to call *Father and Son* an act of cruelty or revenge. But she reads what, in its time, was seen as a welcome reaction against extreme Victorian pieties as a travesty of an admirable Victorian life, in all its energy, idiosyncrasy and humanity. In returning us to the father's story, and reconstructing him as a tender, loving, humane and admirable character, she has to come down rather hard on Edmund Gosse (harder here than in her earlier biography of him). She continually corrects the false accounts he gives. She finds no evidence for his having been, as he asserts, an unwanted child. The family was much less hard-up than he suggests, and his life as a child was, she deduces, much more gregarious and enjoyable than he remembered, or presented, it as being. After Emily's death, Philip Henry Gosse had friends, successes, published books, gave classes, and was not the lonely morbid figure of his son's book. They were not locked together as a claustrophobic pair, but had Edmund's grand-mother living with them for several years. The letters of exhortation and the appeals to his conscience which followed Edmund to London, and which he so much complained of, were letters which he himself needed and invited. And so the evidence mounts up, to prove 'how highly selective the son's account' is (*PG*, p. 189). In her eagerness to rehabilitate Gosse Senior, Thwaite is, necessarily, rather dogged and grudging towards the enchanting bitter comedy which Edmund Gosse makes of his childhood.

Analogies between the writing of biography, and the examination of species in an aquarium, or under a microscope, are irresistible. Virginia Woolf uses the image in a witty and eloquent passage about the reductive effects of biography:

> Here is the past and all its inhabitants miraculously sealed as in a magic tank; all we have to do is to look and to listen and to listen and to look and soon the little figures – for they are rather under life size – will begin to move and to speak, and as they move we shall arrange them in all sorts of patterns of which they were ignorant, for they thought when they were alive that they could go where they liked; and as they speak we shall read into their sayings all kinds of meanings which never struck them, for they believed when they were alive that they said straight off whatever came into their heads. But once you are in a biography all is different.[17]

Both Gosses draw analogies between the scientific study of species and the art of biography. Philip Henry Gosse speaks of his delight in 'the minute details of habits, the *biography* of animals' (*PG*, p. 142). Edmund Gosse, in his lecture on Tallemant des Réaux, says that he slowly built up his life-stories 'with the patience of a coral insect . . . With regard to human character he was like a zoologist or a botanist, collecting specimens and amassing observations.'[18] Which Gosse you prefer may depend on whether you are more interested in creatures, or people. When Edmund Gosse, as a child, is imitating his father's zoological studies, he draws a picture of a 'man', with the annotation: 'It is to many hard to believe that a Man is an animal, however, he is.' 'Philip Henry

Gosse never drew a man in his life,' Thwaite comments (*PG*, p. 245). Gosse tells the story in his first life of his father:

> When I was a child, I was for ever begging him to draw me 'a man', but he could never be tempted to do it. 'No!' he would say, 'a humming-bird is much nicer, or a shark, or a zebra. I will draw you a zebra' . . . Man was the animal he studied less than any other, understood most imperfectly, and, on the whole, was least interested in . . . He would have cheerfully given a wilderness of strangers for a new rotifer.[19]

Father and Son ends with the son freeing himself from the father. The terms in which he does so demonstrate why it is that life-writing so fascinates us, as we watch the evolution of an individual, setting nature, temperament and desire against rules and precedents. But the terms he uses for the son's self-enfranchisement also echo the father's delight in the wondrous particularity of each different species. 'He took a human being's privilege to fashion his inner life for himself.'

An Appetite for Writing:
Thurman's Colette

Judith Thurman's fine *Life* of Colette isn't one of those biographies where the author strolls (or lumbers) on stage as a character, but one of its pleasing qualities is Thurman's taste for wry, dashing interventions. She allows herself to step forward now and then with stylish, witty strokes of opinion: 'French intellectual life is, in its way . . . a provincial village – rivalrous, gossipy, and homogeneous.' 'A marriage may be sustained by a deep complicity between two spouses long after the extinction of desire.' 'Every divorce forces a triage of the ex-couple's friendships.' 'It was love, it was France, so everybody was lying.'[1] My favourite of these is her image for Colette's solid capacity for survival when all around her, at the *fin-de-siècle*, were self-destructing on opium, ennui, and ever-more competitively exotic vices: 'On every storm-tossed vessel filled with retching bodies, there is usually one passenger, freakishly sound, who strolls the pitching deck on steady feet while insolently eating a ham sandwich' (*C*, pp. 83–4).

Thurman perfectly sums up there what she wants to emphasise in Colette's extraordinary character: her bravura, her pragmatism, her insouciance, her finger raised to the conventions (including the conventions of unconventionality), and, above all, her appetite. This book is all about bodily needs, greed and hunger. Gide famously praised Colette for revealing in *Chéri* (which he has 'devoured it in a single breath') those 'least admitted secrets of the flesh'. Thurman takes the phrase as her appropriately, 'louche' title (*C*, pp. 300, xiii).

Colette's life, and its manifold translations into the performance art of her writing, are poised in this biography between starvation and 'voluptuous' repletion. She was born, we are told to imagine, with 'an insatiable appetite', identifying from the first moments of her life 'feeding and seduction'. Her 'appetite for work' was prodigious. Her gourmandise, gluttony and bingeing became notorious. She despised anorexia, a frequent affliction among her *fin-de-siècle* women friends. Getting fat at fifty made her even more sensual. Love is a sort of 'alimentary canal', she wrote. She bullied her daughter and her stepchildren over their eating habits; she was always fattening up the stepson with whom she was also having a passionate affair. She 'denied death' in wartime by eating, making sure of a regular supply of onions and potatoes (*C*, pp. 22, 71, 318, 546, 328, 442).

Two incidents show up the greedy peasant in Colette. She describes herself, at the dress rehearsal for *La Chair*, the pantomime of 1907 in which she aroused outrage and desire by baring her left breast in the role of a Hungarian smuggler's mistress, 'cold and tired' and 'yearning from the depths of her soul for a ham sandwich, or two – or three – with mustard'. On meeting the young Proust at a Paris dinner party, where the 'pretty-boy of letters', distracting her from her cassoulet with his flattery, tells her her soul is filled with the day-dream of Narcissus, she retorts that 'her soul is filled with nothing but red beans and bacon rinds' (*C*, pp. 182, 87).

Colette's greediness is placed in its context: the turn of the century in which she came to fame as a writer, a theatrical performer, a notorious character and a sexual icon, was 'an era of gourmandise', of the flesh trade, of the consumption of 'casual pleasures' and of women served up as a 'grande bouffe' on the stage and in magazines. Gourmandise was a national virtue as well as a mark of the times: Colette belonged to a country which 'respected sexual appetite', as opposed to Anglo-Saxon abstinence (*C*, pp. 111, 517, 317).

But Thurman's reading of Colette's appetite goes much deeper than that. She bases her whole interpretation of Colette's life and work on the oscillation between appetite and self-starvation. Everything fits the pattern (and if this biography is to be criticised, as well as praised, it is for its masterful forcing of all Colette's work and behaviour into a patterned synthesis). For instance, Colette's early fictional heroines are voracious for love in the form of sexual domination, but they know that 'some forms of greed are toxic'. The 'pattern' for the characters in 'the erotic underworld' of *The Pure and the Impure* (1941) is that they find all kinds of ways to 'master their voracity': with 'defensive self-starvation', celibacy, sadism, asceticism – however they can control their sense of helpless hunger (*C*, pp. 121, 339–40).

Why should this be Colette's recurrent theme? Because, Thurman shows us, she was neglected by her father and over-protected by her mother (nevertheless a fine, noble, stoic figure in this book), and fell prey as a very young, greedy adventurer to the sexual and emotional dominance of Willy Gauthier-Villars. So, for her, 'there was no middle ground between her terror of abandonment and her fear of being consumed'. Because of this, Thurman argues, she could never transcend the 'scenario of domination and submission' in her sexual relationships, though she broke free of her abjection by writing. 'Eat and thrive', was her motto. But this was 'a symptom of her intolerable anxiety about all forms of hunger. She utterly abhors a vacuum, and her famous insatiability is proportional to her exaggerated terror of any vital insufficiency – of love, nourishment, or money' (*C*, pp. 108, 275–6).

Because appetite – for love, sex, work, fame, adventure, money, vagabondage, homes, creature comforts and control, as well as for food – is the key to this story, 'naturally' the body fills the text. Colette's vigorous shapely long-haired teenage allure, her physical energy and robustness, her pioneering commitment to gymnastics, for developing an athletic, muscular and 'self-supporting' body, so disturbingly in contrast with her sexual subjection to 'the pudgy erotomane' Willy; her daring physical exhibitionism on stage, the grand sensuality of her 'corpulent and secure' middle years as a great writer who had 'consolidated her flesh and her power', and her striking looks in old age, with the frizzed mauve hair and dramatic make-up, leap out at us from these pages. This was a writer whose 'sense of self' was vested not in her mind but her body (*C*, pp. 135, 52, 214, 189).

But, as Thurman warns us, the words 'naturally' and 'nature' are to be used gingerly here. Colette was often cried up (for instance by Montherlant) as France's 'child of nature'. But 'beware when the French admire something as natural'. For all her peasant energies, love of the country, spontaneous exhibitionism and outspokenness, Colette was a cunningly self-constructed creature, nowhere more so than in her writing. Her most 'natural' qualities – her rewriting of herself as an unbookish child, the apparent transparency of her literary self-revelations, her vivid sensual prose – were carefully devised and maintained. 'She is never as transparent or as spontaneous as she seems,' Thurman writes wisely, placing her in the company of Proust, Wilde or Huysmans, rather than Rousseau. The slow labour of her writing, the heavily worked-over manuscripts, give the lie to 'the illusion of naturalness'. One of the phrases Thurman likes and often quotes is Colette's description of herself to her lover Missy, an aristocratic lesbian transvestite, as 'your insufferable fake child' (*C*, pp. xviii, xix, 211, 409, 186, 196, 282, 385). She was a fixer, a faker, and a performer.

Thurman is at her very best where the biographer's job is most difficult, in disentangling the fact from the fiction, and in pinning down the self-contradictions and the paradoxes in Colette's behaviour. This heroine of female independence constructed herself, after the subjection of her early years, as a free agent, while struggling not to give up her femininity. Her 'cult of the self' set itself against the accepted conventions of female behaviour. Yet, for all her bisexuality, lesbian friendships, encouragement of women writers, reckless physical exhibitionism, creation of dynamic and redoubtable female characters, and close female relationships, Colette was also anti-feminist. Thurman argues that in her writing she takes on the voice of the 'Old Man' of the misogynist *fin-de-siècle*. The price of triumph for Colette's 'New Woman' is 'her female form. She devours man and incorporates his powers' (*C*, pp. 114, 351).

In her politics, she is at once 'an iconoclast' and 'a conservative'. Here was a woman (light years ahead of her time as well as profoundly embedded *in* her times) who committed acts of tremendous daring provocation – or 'immodest innocence' – displaying herself in sexually deviant theatrical performances while divorcing her husband and taking up with a lesbian lover, or flaunting her erotic liaison with her young stepson while her second marriage to Henri de Jouvenel was breaking up. Yet 'she saw no contradiction, and never would, between supporting conservative positions and living her life in revolt against them'. Her personal history of 'radical non-conformity' didn't prevent her from expressing 'casually anti-semitic' views or from knuckling under in passive denial and complicity during the German occupation of France, even though her third husband, Maurice Goudeket, was a Jew and was briefly interned by the Gestapo (*C*, pp. 368, 330, 102, 256, 133). Thurman surveys this discreditable section of Colette's life with admirably stringent judiciousness.

Colette's public bravura was also a mode of evasion and concealment. Even more surprising, the apparent freedom and candour of self-expression in her fiction was combined with a high degree of public reticence, for instance about the publication of her correspondence. And, looked at as closely and interrogatively as they are by Thurman, it becomes apparent that her writings are transformations rather than confessions. Even though she 'channels her life into fiction almost as fast as she lived it', the fictions manipulate the life with craft and deliberation. Her early *Claudine* novels of childhood, school and teenage life, 'authored' by Willy, were acts of 'literary transvestism', 'a woman writing as a man who poses as a boyish girl'. The years with Willy were turned into 'highly selective' memories, coloured with vengeful rancour, in *My Apprenticeships* and *The Vagabond*. Her mother was made over into a less ordinary, and less humane, figure, in *Sido* and *My Mother's House*, where 'Sido should not be confused with the real Madame Sidonie Colette' (*C*, pp. 330, 126, 85, 65, 201, 156, xvii). 'In the opening pages of *Break of Day*, a narrator who calls herself Colette defines herself as the daughter of a woman named Sido . . . At the same time, she is careful to remind us that . . . we are not to seek the real Colette either here or elsewhere in her novels.' She gives her 'famous caution': 'Am I portraying myself? Have patience, this is only my model.' Thurman sees her writing as poised between two (somewhat Philip Rothian) impulses: 'To lie, to confess'. Colette learned the art of self-dramatisation from her years in the theatre, and her whole life is described by one witness (in one of the many new pieces of information Thurman has unearthed) as 'a theatre piece' (*C*, pp. 367, 492, 40, 297).

And what a piece it was! We are taken confidently, knowledgeably and entertainingly through all its stages: the country childhood and the 'family romance' (with the possible trace of Martinique Creole in her mother's ancestry), the erotic bondage to Willy, Colette as a sulky unknown provincial girl in *belle époque* Paris, the long, painful, public marital separation, the plunge into Lesbos with poor sad Missy, and the vagabondage years of theatrical touring. Then, the wild sexual charge of her second marriage to the unfaithful Henri, Colette's refusal to come to terms with the death of her mother, her growing fame and professionalism, the birth and lamentably inadequate upbringing of her daughter 'Bel-Gazou', the shocking replacement of Henri by his stepson, the comfort and stability of her last marriage (very well imagined), and her grand progress into a national monument and sacred monster – and into years of courageous battle with illness and age.

In all her dealings with Colette's varied professions (including journalism, real estate, and a spell as a beautician who sent people out of her parlour looking 'twice as old' as when they came in) (*C*, p. 396), and in her coverage of the huge span of time Colette lived through in French society, culture and politics, Thurman is lucid and interesting. She has a very big cast of characters to handle (I would have liked a family tree) and sometimes we have to be rather artificially reminded of their histories when they reappear. But they are always vividly individualised, especially Colette's remarkable women friends – the beautiful, witty actress Marguerite Moreno, the morbid freakish neurasthenic Renée Vivien, the writer Annie de Pene, tough and truthful, the reclusive poet Hélène Picard. My favourite letter (which should be in the text, not a footnote) is Colette's advice to Moreno about her writing, brutal, funny, and helpful: 'You lose most of your expressiveness when you write . . . Stick in a description of the décor, the guests, even the food . . . And try, oh my darling, to conceal from us that it bores the shit out of you to write! . . . I love you, I embrace you, I want you to write "prestigious" stuff, you understand me? Ta Colette' (*C*, p. 543).

The woman who makes things hardest for this biographer is Colette's daughter. Thurman has acknowledged (for instance in a *New York Times* interview with Jean Strouse) that 'overcoming the severity of my judgement of Colette as a mother' was one of the most difficult things she had to do.[2] Colette's ruthless resistance to motherhood was explicitly voiced by Claudine long before Colette had a child. ('A child? Me? What end do you pick it up by?') And 'the mother's denial would never waver in its resolve'. Her refusal to re-enact her own mother's protective intimacy with her, and her fear of letting herself have strong feelings for her child, created, inevitably, a relationship of terrible destructive inadequacy for Bel-Gazou. This is a chilling story, and Thurman tells it squarely, for instance demonstrating coolly how Colette 'took moral credit for her absence' from her daughter's (disastrous) wedding. It's one of the many amazing facts in this narrative that Bel-Gazou became, in later years, her mother's 'priestess' and devoted defender (*C*, pp. 96, 251, 413, 488).

There are times, reading this life, when I wanted to join sides with Martha Gellhorn, who, as a young journalist in her twenties, having an affair with Colette's ex-lover and stepson, and meeting her in 1935 when Colette was sixty-two, described her as 'a terrible woman. Absolute, utter hell . . . evil.' But Judith Thurman's great achievement is to have been sufficiently intelligent, subtle and flexible to present her notorious subject quite freshly, without sainting her or monstering her.

Cocteau, Colette's confidant and admirer, said of her: 'Monsters need their tamers, and without them, they figure out their power and eat us' (*C*, pp. 411, 469). If Colette was a monster, then Thurman has succeeded in taming her without being eaten.

The Sheltered Life: Ellen Glasgow

One of Ellen Glasgow's early novels, *The Deliverance* (published in 1904, when she was thirty-one, and set in the 1880s) has a remarkable minor character called Mrs Blake. She is the widow of a man who went mad and died after the Civil War, when his land and house, handed down through two hundred years, were bought by the coarse and corrupt Bill Fletcher, who used to oversee his slaves. The Blake family have had to move into the overseer's house and make their living farming his tobacco fields. There is a bitter feud between Blake's degraded, illiterate son Christopher – a Heathcliffian noble savage – and the overseer's family. (Deliverance from the feud comes at last through Christopher's love for Fletcher's daughter.) But Mrs Blake knows nothing of all this. She is blind and paralysed from a stroke, and for fifteen years has been kept in blissful ignorance by her son and daughters of what has happened to the family – or the country. She thinks that the South won the war, and that they are still living in 'Blake Hall'. The faithful house servants who stayed on with the Blakes, but who gained their freedom after the war, she still thinks of and refers to as her 'darkeys'. And her children expend a great deal of ingenuity in maintaining her illusions for the sake of 'her terrible pride'.[1]

> She lived upon lies . . . and thrived upon the sweetness she extracted from them . . . It was as if she had fallen asleep with the great blow that had wrecked her body, and had dreamed on steadily throughout the years.[2]

She dies, at last, because she is brutally undeceived by the wicked Bill Fletcher. One of her daughters complains that she misses the pretence she has had to sustain for her mother:

> 'I don't know how it is, but the thing I miss most . . . is the lying I had to do. It gave me something to think about, somehow. I used to stay awake at night and plan all sorts of pleasant lies that I could tell about the house and the garden, and the way the war ended, and the Presidents

of the Confederacy – I made up all their names – and the fuss with which each one was inaugurated, and the dresses their wives and daughters wore. It's all so dull when you have to stop pretending and begin to face things just as they are.'[3]

This strange invention gives us the quintessence of Glasgow. The paralysed, blinded old Southern belle, locked into her romance of the past, dreaming it still in the middle of grim realities of which she is quite unaware, is the embodiment of everything Glasgow resented – but also yearned towards – in her South. The protective shelter of chivalric lying, the eagerness not to face up to the truth, which seemed to her to colour all of Southern history (and literature) is summed up in the atrophied figure of Mrs Blake. 'The great blow that had wrecked her body' stands for the war that ended her old way of life, but also for the paralysis and immolation which, for Glasgow as for William Faulkner (whom she disliked) still seemed to grip the South. False romance gilding a story of violence, corruption and decline, fossilised gentility resisting shifts in class and race relations, these are what Glasgow frequently summed up by the phrase 'evasive idealism'. And Mrs Blake's disability, which both protects her and utterly isolates her from the real world, is a powerful image for a writer who suffered from severe deafness for most of her life.

Why should we care about Ellen Glasgow? Isn't she, like her Mrs Blake, a redundant figure left over from the Southern past, who might once have been a great literary beauty (a sensation with her first novel in 1897, a frequent best-seller, a Pulitzer Prize winner in 1942) but is now, irredeemably, a back number? Surely her value has been obliterated by what succeeded her in Southern writing, which she welcomed with dismay as 'literary ruffianism'[4] or 'Faulkner's school of Raw-Head-and-Bloody-Bones',[5] noting, with her own brand of genteel fastidiousness, that 'the fascination of the repulsive, so noticeable in contemporary writing, can spring only from some rotted substance within our civilisation'.[6]

Not much of her work is currently in print.[7] She features still in courses on Southern literature, where usually only the best-known of her novels (*Virginia, Barren Ground, The Sheltered Life, Vein of Iron*) are taught. But the twenty novels that made up her 'social history of

Virginia',[8] from the Civil War to the Second World War, provide an unmatchable fund of information about the customs, manners and habits of mind of her world. She is certainly an important figure in twentieth-century Southern writing. She had close connections with the intellectual movement known as the 'Southern Renaissance', and made some (rather strained) friendships with writers such as Carl Van Doren, James Branch Cabell and Allen Tate. She contributed to the Richmond magazine, the *Reviewer*, and she initiated and opened the first annual Southern Writers' Conference at Charlottesville in 1931 (where Faulkner's first and last remarks were supposed to be, 'Know where I can get a drink?').[9]

She is also, sometimes, taught and read alongside other American women writers, though she had reservations about most of them. Willa Cather's Virginian novel, *Sapphira and the Slave Girl*, was 'a bitter disappointment'; 'Even without Mrs Wharton, one Henry James is enough for any country'; 'I have the impression that [Katherine Anne Porter] will never grow larger and stronger . . . I suppose [Zora Neale Hurston's] *Mules and Men* is good Negro folklore, but what does it promise except more and more of the thing?'[10] For all her commitment to the women's suffrage cause in the 1910s and her creation of powerful, rebellious, independent heroines, Glasgow is a problematic figure for feminist studies, and the critical works which have placed her in that context[11] have to find ways of dealing with her ambivalence and defensiveness, her 'apparent conformity', her 'intellectual confusion about women's traditions', and the 'simultaneous need' (in her fictions) 'to center on heterosexual pairings and to reject them'.[12] In other words, this is a confusingly feminine feminist.

A conscientious biography by Susan Goodman, published in 1999, didn't create an Ellen Glasgow revival, but does have a painful and peculiar story to tell. Ellen Glasgow spent almost all of her seventy-two years in Richmond, Virginia (like Eudora Welty in Jackson), in the house on Main Street her father bought when she was fourteen. Her parents were of old Virginian stock, her mother from a distinguished Tidewater family, her father from Scotch Presbyterian pioneers who settled on the James River. Her father inherited the Tredegar Iron Works, run on slave labour up to the war. The marriage was a difficult one: Glasgow portrayed her mother as a woman wretchedly dedicated to service and self-sacrifice, and her father as a domineering, tyrannical

Calvinist. There were a large number of children. When Glasgow was very young her older brother died, to her mother's inconsolable sorrow; when she was ten, her mother (who had left much of Glasgow's upbringing to the black 'mammy') had a catastrophic breakdown, exacerbated, in Glasgow's version, by her father's 'sleeping with one of the colored maids' (*G*, p. 19). Glasgow came to loathe and resent her father. Like many other women writers (I describe them in 'Reading in Bed'), she defined herself through solitary rebellious reading (crucially, of Darwin) and lost her faith very young. Her sensitive brother Frank was forced into a military academy and later killed himself. Her mother died suddenly when Glasgow was twenty, a death shortly followed by the suicide of her brother-in-law, a clever young socialist lawyer who had been very influential on Glasgow's early intellectual life. His widow, her sister Cary, sank into perpetual mourning. By the time Glasgow began to write, family life seemed to her 'like living in a tomb . . . immersed in a sense of doom, of fatality'.[13]

She wrote her way out of this sense of incarceration, while living on in the family home, but her personal life was always problematic. Her incurable deafness began in her twenties and went with attacks of 'panic terror' and 'morbid sensitiveness'[14] – labelled 'neurasthenia' at the time. Though she began to make some money from her books in the 1900s, she was largely financially dependent on her wealthy engineering brother Arthur, a debt for which she doesn't seem to have been especially grateful, and which eventually 'corrupted their relationship' (*G*, p. 198). Her sexual relationships, which are portrayed in curiously shadowy and ominous tones in her autobiography, seem to have been either covert or frustrating. There was a secret passion in her twenties for a married man, the mythical-sounding 'Gerald B', which came to a climax in an ecstatic moment on the Jungfrau in the Alps in 1903, and faded out after that (she learned of his death from a newspaper). And there was a prolonged and deeply unsatisfactory engagement in her forties to a well-connected Virginian lawyer, Henry Anderson, who had a wartime affair during his work for the Red Cross in Europe with Queen Marie of Roumania – a spectacular rival whose challenge partly drove Glasgow to a suicide attempt in 1918. Their relationship trailed on for years as 'a companionate marriage which gave them no real pleasure . . . For seventeen months . . . of twenty-one years, they made one another happy' (*G*, pp. 157–8).

Her relationship with her publishers, Doubleday and Page, who found her difficult, was equally strained; her behaviour with her family, where she let her 'terrible temperament' (as she herself described it) hold sway (*G*, p. 106), was often disastrous, and ended in acrimonious fall-out over her will and her house between her siblings. Her tenderest sympathies were reserved for her dogs, and her worst girlhood quarrel with her father was over a dog he wouldn't let her keep. She was very active in the SPCA and collected hundreds of ceramic dog figurines. When her Sealyham terrier Jeremy died in 1929 she mourned him for a year and wrote: 'Nothing has mattered since – all I have wanted is to have everything over' (*G*, p. 182). The relationship that lasted longest and was most essential to her, after her sister Cary's death in 1911, was with Cary's nurse, Anne Virginia Bennett, who became Glasgow's secretary and companion, and whose long live-in intimacy with Glasgow has tended (as Patricia Matthews observes) to be consistently underestimated, challenging as it does the standard assumption that 'the marriage plot provided the only real possibility for fulfilment in Glasgow's life'.[15] Glasgow said, revealingly, of Anne Virginia, that she 'has had my interests at heart'.[16]

As that remark suggests, Glasgow's autobiography can be self-promoting and self-pitying. She praises, for instance, her mysterious allure ('Although I was not beautiful, I created the semblance of beauty for everyone who has ever loved me') and the importance of her work: 'These five novels represent, I feel, not only the best that was in me, but some of the best work that has been done in American fiction.'[17] But it is also the record of a defensive, prickly, unhappy woman, excruciatingly self-conscious about her disability, whose dedication to writing, she said herself, was made 'to compensate for the kind of life I have had' (*G*, p. 207). Appropriately, Glasgow put her own literary ambitions into the mouth of one of her unhappiest characters (in *They Stooped to Folly*, 1929), a nervy, ironical, working–class boy who has had a breakdown after the First World War, and who tells his uncomprehending, genteel Virginian father-in-law, Mr Littlepage, that he plans to write:

'Well, I shouldn't put too much faith in literature, if I were you . . . there isn't much material in Virginian history that hasn't already been exhausted.'

. . . With an air of incredible patience, the young man answered slowly, as if he were speaking to a foreigner in words of one syllable. 'But historical novels are all tosh, you know. I am interested in life, not in costume and scenery. I want to get at grips with reality.'

'Well, I shouldn't build my hopes on that kind of stuff', Mr Little-page remarked mildly but firmly; for the word 'reality' startled him . . . [18]

Mr Littlepage's anxieties are a reflection of some early local responses to Glasgow's novels, when this well-brought-up young Richmond lady began to write about degeneration and extra-marital love (*The Descendant*, 1897), scientific arguments against religion (*Phases of an Inferior Planet*, 1898), prison reform (*The Ancient Law*, 1907), and the frustrated lives of women of her own class (*The Miller of Old Church*, 1911, and *Virginia*, 1913). Though she quickly attracted big sales, some huffing and puffing went on at first about 'blunting the moral sense' and 'profanation of holy things' (*G*, p. 169). Of *Virginia*, one Southern reviewer said: 'Such books may be true to life, but we should hesitate before placing them in the hands of our trusting wives.'[19] It's hard to imagine – but it's an important part of her story – that a hundred years ago Glasgow was as shocking as Kate Chopin or Theodore Dreiser. There's a trace of this in a much later comment on her failed philosopher, John Fincastle, in *Vein of Iron* (1935): 'Nobody could earn a livelihood in America by thinking the wrong thoughts.'[20]

But there was more acclaim than criticism for a writer who had made, according to her publishers, 'realism finally cross the Potomac' (*G*, p. 168). Like other American Naturalists of the 1890s, Glasgow set herself, officially, against romance, idealisation, make-believe, the glamorisation of the old South and the nostalgic defence of lost causes. (She hated, too, being tagged as a 'local colourist' or a 'regionalist': 'I had always wished to escape from the particular into the general, from the provincial into the universal.')[21] What the South needed, she said, was 'blood and irony'.[22] When she started writing, she began 'a solitary revolt against the formal, the false, the sentimental, and the pretentious, in Southern writing'.[23] She stood for realism, truth and plain speaking: bringing the paralysed body of the South back to life. She turned her back on her mother's genteel, pious, repressed conservatism. There are a number of nice ladies in her novels happily weeping over old romances, like the Major's wife in her Civil War novel, *The Battleground* (1902), immersed in that once popular English historical novel about

Polish aristocrats, Jane Porter's *Thaddeus of Warsaw* (1803) and dismissing 'all new-fangled literature' because its heroes are 'untitled'.[24] Virginia, her epitome of stifled Southern wifehood (based on her mother) is brought up by her parents, with disastrous consequences, on 'sweet stories' (these also include *Thaddeus of Warsaw*, and her tear-stained copy of *The Heir of Redclyffe*): 'That any book which told, however mildly, the truth about life should have entered their daughter's bedroom would have seemed little short of profanation . . . the sacred shelves of that bookcase had never suffered the contaminating presence of realism.'[25]

And Glasgow does sink her teeth, not only into shocking new nineties subjects (like the persistence of savage, primitive traits in civilised peoples) derived from her reading of Darwin, Huxley and Nordau, but into very detailed, authentic, thoroughgoing accounts of corruption in Southern Reconstruction politics (*The Voice of the People*, 1900), or of the violent shifts in class structure and race relations in turn of the century Virginia (*The Deliverance*, 1904, *They Stooped to Folly*, 1929, *The Sheltered Life*, 1932), or of the effects of industrialisation on the South, most forcefully in the Depression scenes in *Vein of Iron* (1935). She can be brutal about the need for Southern gentry to regenerate themselves by marrying down (like Stella in *A Streetcar Named Desire*), or about sexual censorship, cruelty, incompatibility and predatoriness. The young wife's disgust at her elderly husband in *The Romantic Comedians* ('I didn't know how immoral marriage can be')[26] is strong, and so is teenage Jenny Blair Archbald's infantile, exploitable sexual crush on the rapacious George Birdsong in *The Sheltered Life* (1932): 'She looked up at him with her wide, shallow, devouring gaze. Beneath the stain of tears, her face was as soft as a baby's, and her small, vivid mouth was round and open and insatiable.'[27] And Glasgow, who is a funnier writer than she's given credit for, has a good knockabout time with genteel sexual hypocrisy ('He thought of his father, a Virginia gentleman . . . who had found it less embarrassing to commit adultery than to pronounce the word in the presence of a lady')[28] or intransigent piety: 'She's a good woman according to her lights, but . . . her religion has curdled.'[29]

But Glasgow's realism is a peculiar thing. Though she sets her face against 'evasive idealism', she isn't free of it. There is a great deal invested in these novels in the romance of the Southern landscape, in the heroic spirit of the old pioneers, in memory and elegy, in beauty opposed to mechanisation, and in the formative virtues of suffering and defeat. Almost all her novels are too long. Where a much greater novelist, Willa Cather, taught herself to leave things out, Ellen Glasgow liked to put everything in. So her books are lushly padded with description (some very good tobacco fields), meditations on human nature, and tremendously soppy love scenes:

'What is it?' she asked quickly, and her voice seemed part of the general radiance. 'You have been looking at the sun. It hurts my eyes.'

'No', he answered steadily, 'I was looking at you.'

She thrilled as he spoke and brought her eyes to the level of his . . . All her changeful beauty was startled into life . . . 'You know it is impossible,' he said, and kissed her.[30]

Glasgow is at her most contradictory when it comes to the two crucial ingredients in her work: race and women. There are large numbers of black characters in the novels (with far more to do and say than in Twain or Faulkner or Welty). And because she's very much influenced by Dickens, Hardy and Emily Brontë, they talk at length, in carefully presented dialect speech, which now reads condescendingly. She goes out of her way to present intimate relationships between black and white characters, to expose the sexual exploitation of black women (especially in the captain of industry who denies all responsibility for his mulatto son in *Virginia*, or in the telling figure of Memoria, George Birdsong's black mistress, in *The Sheltered Life*). And she is bitterly scathing about post-Civil-War racism in the South. But – and this makes her a difficult subject for resuscitation – she is quite unable to free herself from the white Southerner's lasting belief (which also surfaces in Flannery O'Connor and Faulkner) that the legacy of slavery – rootedness in a landscape, fidelity to a family, pastoral life – was preferable to the 'freedom' of Northern urban enslavement. Writing to Carl Van Vechten about his Harlem novel *Nigger Heaven* in 1926, she called it 'the best argument in favour of African slavery that I have ever read . . . The serene fatalism, the dignity of manner, the spiritual power, all those qualities decayed, it appeared, with the peculiar institution.'[31] And her stereotyping of 'Negro' attributes ('It is the law of African nature to expand in the sunshine')[32] undermined her political opposition to racism.

Pulling against tradition and giving in to it is the struggle at the heart of Glasgow's painful stories of women. Though these are what she's known for, she can 'do' men as well, with a vengeance: that racist, chauvinistic tobacco magnate Cyrus Treadwell in *Virginia*; the aged philosopher-General looking back over his thwarted past in *The Sheltered Life*; the self-deceiving Judge Honeywell (based unforgivingly on Henry Anderson) fooling himself into a second youth in *The Romantic Comedians*; and the anxious Mr Littlepage in *They Stooped to Folly*, fretting over the relation between changes in custom and standards of morality: 'Were there right and wrong habits of thinking? Were there right and wrong ways of behaving?'[33]

It's the women, though, who set the standards of, and are trapped by, 'right and wrong ways of behaving'. It's they who have benefited from, or been crushed by, a set of beliefs whereby the 'Southern belle' – ideally beautiful, virginal, fresh and gay, object of chivalric worship – is turned into the Southern matriarch, dedicated to a life of service and discretion. By these rules, woman's whole emotional function, according to Mrs Birdsong in *The Sheltered Life*, is this: 'A great love doesn't leave room for anything else in a woman's life. It is everything.'[34] And their purpose in life is summed up by Virginia: 'What could make her happier than the knowledge that she must surrender her will to his from the day of her wedding until the day of her death? She embraced her circumscribed lot with a passion which glorified its limitations.'[35] There are some 'types' of women in Glasgow who have fitted perfectly into this mould, and become lifelong propagandists for a system of sexual censorship and female subservience. Such is Mrs Archbald, Jenny Blair's mother, who structures 'the sheltered life' around her daughter. 'If she ever spoke the truth, it was by accident, or on one of those rare occasions when truth is more pleasant than fiction.'[36]

But alongside those bland matriarchs (usually in the same family) is a veritable army of disappointed women who have failed to conform or live up to the approved feminine model. Glasgow's novels are full of embittered old maids, spinster aunts dependent on their married relatives, locked into the memory of a single long-past romance, obsessed with their unattractiveness, or maintaining with gruesome fastidiousness antiquated standards of ladylike behaviour: 'A lady always preferred the wing of a chicken when I was young. Never the leg. It would have been indelicate to prefer the leg, even if she called it dark meat.'[37] Glasgow's wives, too, are often as bitterly redundant as their unmarried aunts and sisters: killing themselves with overwork, perpetually bullied, betrayed or ignored.

Those who resist their feminine destiny – the women artists struggling between art and passion in her earliest novels, the independent-minded girls who want freedom as well as love, the strong women who challenge the rules – frequently get collapsed back into motherhood, or are made to channel their considerable powers into keeping the home going. Glasgow's four really outstanding and impressive novels, which deserve any amount of re-reading, *Virginia*, *Barren Ground* (1925), *The Sheltered Life* and *Vein of Iron* are complex, and rigorous, in their fixing of women's lives in a place and a tradition.

The story of Virginia's utter commitment to ideals of marital subservience, resulting in her spoilt playwright husband's inevitable boredom and infidelity, her daughters' scorn and her eventual isolation and redundancy, is extremely painful to read, because it's so unrelentingly placed inside the narrow, bewildered confines of her point of view. In *Barren Ground*, Glasgow's most Hardyesque novel, Dorinda survives her girlhood betrayal by committing herself to reclaiming the 'poor land' of her family farm. But the loss of love is never appeased, and through all her long years (it's a long book) of endurance and stoicism, she drags the past with her 'like a dead fish in a net'.[38] In *Vein of Iron*, an urban survival novel, Ada Fincastle loses her young lover and re-finds him, but at the cost of 'romance'. Her long struggle to keep her family going in the Depression years is a description of a compromise – not an easy theme with which to sustain a novel – based on adaptation and realism, 'getting the better of life', 'taking the world as one found it'.[39]

But it's *The Sheltered Life* which provides the most subtle and drastic undermining of conventional ideas about women. Setting the naïve and sensation-hungry girl Jenny Blair against the wretched beauty Mrs Birdsong, who, having given all for love, is consumed with jealousy of her unfaithful husband, and surrounding them with a range of models of compromised and disappointed womanhood, works brilliantly. Best of all is Jenny Blair's inability to take Mrs Birdsong's side against her husband or to admit to her own responsibilities: it's clear that she can never break out of her 'shelter'. But would being unsheltered be better? Like the smell from the chemical factory infesting the street where the Archbalds have always lived, or the bare city blocks where the old trees have been cut down, the 'unsheltered' women Jenny Blair sees on the streets have lost all the romance that encircles poor Eva Birdsong: their eyes are 'absorbed, empty, pathetic'.[40] In the very act of denouncing 'romance' and what it does to women, the novel hankers after it and partly resists the democratisation of 'reality'.

No wonder that a peculiar sense of unreality creeps after a number of Glasgow's characters. The quality she officially celebrates in her work is 'fortitude' (it's her favourite word), and the moral of most of the novels is that the 'vein of iron' inherited from those Scotch Presbyterians is, in the end, no bad thing: it links the generations, it keeps the land going, it lasts longer than love. But though Glasgow takes every chance, for herself and for her characters, to praise fortitude and endurance, something less conclusive, more queasy and troubling, is what I finally take away from her work. It's a strange sense that there is always another potential life or self shadowing the lives her characters are forced to lead, something suppressed or half recognised, which is expressed through their stifled bodily life.

In the powerful Gothic scene in which Dorinda hears of her lover's marriage from his ghoulish old father in his rotting house, 'even her body felt numbed, as if she were asleep, and her feet, when she rose and took a step forward, seemed to be walking on nothing'.[41] The dying mother in *They Stooped to Folly*, who has always obeyed the rules, feels at last that 'she was sinking into a windy hollow of space, and that about her there was only this soundless tumult. It was as if she moved through the world and played her part in a state of suspended animation. "I am not real. I am hollow within," she repeated.'[42] That weird feeling of numbness or non-being keeps recurring, and is most drastically embodied in the half-life of the paralysed Mrs Blake in *Deliverance*.

Everyone in *The Sheltered Life* is haunted by a 'second self', a 'buried part' of their nature which has never been acted out.[43] The old General, increasingly, feels the pressure of that frustration and division: 'that hollow drumming began all over again in his ears, as if the universe buzzed with a question he could not hear clearly.'[44] What is the question that can't quite be heard? That there might be – there might have been – some other way to live?

Mr and Mrs Eliot

Here is the case for the prosecution:

T.S. Eliot, a ruthlessly ambitious young American resident in England, made a grotesque error of judgement in his first marriage to the charming, talented, vulnerable Vivienne Haigh-Wood, whose health had been fragile since childhood. Because of his own neuroses and repression, she disgusted him sexually and he was cruel to her. He manipulated her into a destructive sexual liaison with Bertrand Russell that would profit Eliot financially and socially. He used her to advance his career, in his plot to dominate literary London. She sustained him in his writing and in his breakdown. As her own mental health declined under the stress of their incompatibility, and his attentions were directed elsewhere, she became an embarrassment and a burden to him. He engineered her social ostracism, and brutally and coolly planned his abandonment of her, avoiding all contact and ensuring that he was protected by his friends and colleagues from his wife's attempts to see him. Her unswerving devotion and refusal to accept the fact of his desertion became intolerable to him, and he came increasingly to fear that she would expose his secret homosexuality, which underlay the failure of their marriage. Eventually he had her incarcerated, with the help of her brother, in a mental home. Though her behaviour was erratic, her insanity is questionable: she was starting a promising new musical career. Vivienne was left to rot in the home, while Eliot enjoyed his freedom. She died in 1947, aged fifty-eight, presumably by suicide, but in effect murdered by Eliot. He spent the rest of his life protecting his position as a famous poet and venerated publisher, by suppressing the evidence of what he had done. Since his death in 1965, his second wife Valerie Eliot has prevented all attempts at an authorised biography, and has been editing his letters with agonising slowness (she began work in 1965 and has so far produced one volume up to the year 1922). But all his available writing, particularly *The Waste Land*, the 'Sweeney' poems, *The Family Reunion* and the posthumously published obscene 'Columbo and Bolo' verses, attest to his guilt, sexual perversion, violence, repression, and obsession with wife-murder.

And this is the case for the defence:

T.S. Eliot, one of the greatest, if not *the* greatest and most influential poet and critic of the twentieth century, Nobel Prize winner and eminent publisher, was lured into a tragically unfortunate marriage, at twenty-six, to the unstable and superficial Vivien/ne Haigh-Wood (her inconsistent spelling of her name betrays her neuroses). Their incompatibility can be partly attributed to Eliot's confused sexuality (for which his domineering mother and puritan upbringing may be held responsible), which may well have involved some suppressed homosexual feeling. There are, certainly, agonised and painful expressions of misogyny and sexual anxiety in his work. Because of Vivien/ne's unstable behaviour and frequent illnesses (intensified by drug-taking), and her reckless infidelity with Bertrand Russell soon after their marriage, the relationship rapidly became intolerable to him, though Eliot tried to sustain it, asking Vivienne's advice about his work, encouraging her own writing, and sharing all their social involvements and friendships. The strain of their incompatibility, and of financial pressures, led to his breakdown in 1922, out of which came Eliot's modernist masterpiece, *The Waste Land*, in which the unhappiness and torment of his personal life is transmuted into 'something rich and strange, something universal and impersonal' ('Shakespeare and the Stoicism of Seneca', 1927).

Vivienne's state of mind became increasingly erratic and tormenting, and she alienated many of their friends. Driven to the brink by her intolerable behaviour, Eliot finally made as clean and clear-cut a break as he could, and thereafter avoided her, though racked by guilt. Vivienne, by now paranoid and uncontrolled, obsessively pursued him in public, and continued to try to force him to return to her. Eventually, her aberrant behaviour became certifiable, and her brother had her placed in a nursing home, though even then Eliot refused to sign the committal order. His guilt and suffering after her incarceration were extreme, though his religious and spiritual quest provided some consolation. Only in his last years did he find happiness with his second wife Valerie, who, in accordance with his wishes for – and right to – privacy, has not allowed any authorised biography to be written.

Which of these versions you believe depends on whose voice speaks loudest. The air around Eliot is full of voices, as a host of (mostly male) critics, editors and poets tussle over Eliot's anti–Semitism, misogyny, sexual orientation, 'impersonal' poetry and posthumous rights. There is no middle way, it seems: you must either be for him or against him. In 'Burnt Norton', 'voices' attack 'words': 'Shrieking voices/Scolding, mocking, or merely chattering/Always assail them'. 'Words' – or the true 'word' – 'Reach/Into the silence.' Eliot wrote a prayer for himself which ran, in part: 'Protect him from the Voices/Protect him from the Visions/Protect him from the tumult/Protect him in the silence.' In the tumult around Eliot, voices, words and silence are all in dispute. Voices of accusation and defence both draw what they need from Eliot's words. A conspiracy of silence is said to have grown up around the story of his first marriage. Some voices can't be heard: the complicated, scattered paper trail hasn't yielded up all its secrets yet. There are many more Eliot letters to be seen; several archives are still embargoed or under restraint (John Hayward, Emily Hale); some evidence, like Vivienne's letters to Russell, has been destroyed.

Carole Seymour-Jones's strenuous, devoted exercise in reclamation, *Painted Shadow: A Life of Vivienne Eliot*,[1] is one in a now well-established tradition of revisionary treatments of great male writers' partners or daughters, like Zelda Fitzgerald, Nora Barnacle, Lucia Joyce and Yeats's wife, George Hyde-Lees. Seymour-Jones has to make her voice very loud, or it won't be heard in the tumult. So this is a high-pitched, punitive, attack: biography as blame. It's a troubling genre, in which one life-story can only be valued at the cost of another.

The re-estimation of Vivienne which this process involves is lively, vigorous and interesting: Seymour-Jones is at her best when she is bringing her doomed heroine back to life. The young Vivienne, with her 'mock-Cockney chatter' that first amused and then irritated Eliot, her slim, stylish look, her vivid little face 'shimmering with intelligence', her flirty, quick, volatile manner, her passion and talent for dancing, is funny and alluring. In the stories and sketches she wrote for the *Criterion* (sad tales of social isolation, with a touch of Jean Rhys or Katherine Mansfield), and sometimes in the diaries and letters, you can hear a sharp witty voice, one to be reckoned with. Even at their darkest, Vivienne's writings show a grim, and startling, self-awareness. In a story of her childhood, she describes herself with 'a wild expressive look of a secret urge towards self-destruction'. As her *alter ego* 'Sibylla', she repeats in despair to herself: 'I must be independent. I must. Somehow

I must be independent.' Still, in another story, Sibylla cries out: 'But I am not an artist' (*PS*, pp. 11, 327, 425). It is no good – and Vivienne knows this herself – trying to make her out to be Eliot's literary equal, even if she was, as this book convincingly argues, his most powerful inspiration.

Her charm and talent are always, from the first, shadowed by illness. Here, the evidence can be hard to sort out. How much the childhood TB had after-effects, and how much the drugs she was given for menstrual pains and high levels of anxiety – bromide, chloral, ether, formaldehyde – contributed to her problems, seems unverifiable. Some neurotic symptoms started early – her hypersensitivity to noise, her habit of taking the sheets home from anywhere she stayed, having them washed and sending them back. The link between her depressions, anxieties and panic attacks, her physical symptoms, like colitis or neuralgia, her drug-dependency (which may have involved cocaine), and her marriage, are difficult to establish. What's not in question is that the doctors' recommendations – fasting, spinal manipulation, taking animal gland capsules, standing on her head – were no help at all. The conclusion is that 'Vivien's [Seymour-Jones's preferred spelling] predisposition to mental illness, complicated by her dependence on prescription drugs ... the bizarre experimental treatments imposed on her, and a toxic marriage which in itself produced neurotic symptoms, proved a deadly combination' (*PS*, p. 375).

Seymour-Jones doesn't believe that Vivienne was paranoid, since, after all, someone *was* out to get her. She solicits our sympathy for those terrible late scenes, after Eliot's desertion, of Vivienne wandering like a ghost at night ('I get such a horror of the streets that the streets only understand'), pretending to be someone else ('Mrs Eliot has gone away'), laying siege to him while he hid behind secretaries and in safe houses ('Tom is a great runner-away,' said his friend Mary Trevelyan), and bombarding everyone with threatening, pathetic messages: 'I take note of all things so that it will be known, in time.' But she registers the grotesqueness of such scenes, too. Vivienne once complained bitterly to a friend of Stephen Spender's, at the hairdresser's, that when she was in the street people persistently stared at her. 'My friend found this as unaccountable as Mrs Eliot did, until leaving the hairdresser's, Mrs Eliot put on her hat,' wrote Spender. 'This had stitched on it the rather garish purple and green wrapper of Eliot's play, with the letter print

MURDER IN THE CATHEDRAL very prominent around the rim' (*PS*, pp. 541, 526, 544).

One of the embarrassments for Eliot was that when Vivienne tried to ambush him in public, at theatres or in lecture halls, she would often be wearing her Blackshirt uniform. Seymour-Jones deals mildly with Vivienne's support for Mosley's Fascism, attributing it to her longing for protection and order. She even elides it with 'Eliot's right-wing beliefs' (*PS*, pp. 530, 508), as though he were to blame for her conversion. You may be sure that if *Eliot* had joined the British Union of Fascists, we would never hear the last of it.

And this biography must be judged, not only by its revaluation of Vivienne, compelling though that is, but by the case it makes against Eliot. Certainly a disturbingly vivid picture does emerge of a cold, self-interested and very peculiar man. Virginia Woolf, who with the rest of Bloomsbury gets a mostly bad press here (knee-jerk labels like 'gleeful' and 'malicious' accompany her every utterance) is, nevertheless, a compelling witness to Eliot's weirdness: 'A mouth twisted & shut; not a single line free & easy; all caught, pressed, inhibited; but a great driving power somewhere.' 'Sardonic, guarded, precise, & slightly malevolent.' 'Something hole & cornerish, biting in the back, suspicious, elaborate, uneasy, about him' (*PS*, pp. 273, 330, 386).

But since such grave charges are laid against him, the evidence needs to be looked at closely. And it must be said that there is a slapdash air to the whole book which isn't reassuring. We get great dollops of cliché: 'Under her fashionable flapper dresses beat a passionate heart'; 'He nursed a secret grief he could not share with her'; 'It was the birth of the jazz age'; 'The closet remained a prison within which his isolation grew' (*PS*, pp. 17, 79, 234, 498). It is repetitive – we hear several times, in almost identical phrasing, about Eliot's rages, or Vivienne's adoption of 'Daisy Miller' as an *alter ego*, or Eliot's belief in 'impersonal' art. There are too many quick caricatures (Pound is 'egotistical, self-obsessed and impatient', Amy Lowell is 'the wealthy and rotund lesbian') and some minor factual errors. (*Eminent Victorians* is 1918, not 1919; Mansfield's *Prelude* is 1918, not 1916.) Her paraphrase of other critics and biographers isn't always accurate. Peter Ackroyd, for example, is cited as saying in his book on Eliot that Bertrand Russell was disgusted by sex with Vivienne because she was menstruating; actually he says that 'no doubt Vivien's own physical problems had something to do with it'.[2]

Set against the passionate intensity of the biography's defence of its heroine, those are petty criticisms. But the treatment of the evidence does arouse some serious doubts. Seymour-Jones must prove at every turn that Eliot was brutal, cruel and oppressive to Vivienne. She does this partly through outraged iteration. So, Vivienne's adultery is Eliot's fault (and Bertrand Russell's, who comes out of the story as loathsome, vain and treacherous). 'Vivien's affair with Russell, rather than being . . . "a vicious sexual betrayal of Eliot", had in fact been one in which he had knowingly colluded in order to further his career, relieve himself of conjugal responsibilities, and to gain financial advantage' (*PS*, p. 365). (And also, we're told, he had homosexual feelings towards Russell.)

Eliot exploits Vivienne's intelligence ('As to Tom's mind, I am his mind') (*PS*, p. 156), when it served his purpose, for help and inspiration in writing *The Waste Land* and as a frequent contributor to the *Criterion* (the title was hers). But when she wrote a biting satire of a Bloomsbury party, in 1925 (by which time he wanted to get rid of her) under her favourite pseudonym 'Fanny Marlow' (chosen, we are told, because 'it was during her stay at Marlow that Vivienne's "fanny" was the object of Bertrand Russell's attentions') (*PS*, p. 340), he bowed to the furore it caused and agreed not to publish her any more. Why did he publish the satire, Seymour-Jones asks. 'Did he intend to sacrifice Vivien? . . . It is possible that Eliot had grown jealous of Vivien's rising success.' Two pages later, this has become: 'It is legitimate to ask whether Tom set Vivien up for her disgrace'. By the end of the paragraph this has hardened into: 'In engineering Vivien's fall Tom cleared the decks for the future' (*PS*, pp. 399, 402).

This process of cumulative reiteration happens all the time. If the word 'murder' is used often enough, T.S. Eliot becomes a murderer. *Sweeney Agonistes* is 'Eliot's own hysterical narrative, in which he explored the theme of wife murder'. Again, Eliot's 'powerful feeling that Vivien, female succuba or demon, deserved violent punishment found an outlet in *Sweeney Agonistes*' (*PS*, pp. 408, 442). In the same paragraph there's a slippage into Eliot's interest in Kyd's *The Spanish Tragedy* and in Hieronimo's quest for revenge.

'Murder, help Hieronimo', cries a woman in a 1615 woodcut advertising *The Spanish Tragedy*. 'Stop her mouth', is the stark response from the figure of Murder on the handbill, something Eliot longed to do to the wife who berated him for never speaking to her.

You have to look at this sentence for a little while before you see that Eliot is not the author of – or even the reader of – this handbill. It doesn't go without saying that *The Family Reunion* will 'seem to justify the murder of such a crazed, demonic creature' as the unbalanced wife, 'instantly recognised as the author's wife', or that Eliot enjoyed dressing as Crippen the wife-poisoner at a party 'six months after Vivien was committed' (*PS*, pp. 563, 446). Creepy, yes. Self-dramatising, yes. Scary, yes. Criminal? Pass.

The prosecution's presumption of guilt by inference is at its most inventive in Seymour-Jones's strong claims for Eliot's homosexuality. As with his anti-Semitism (which is taken for granted here and lumped together with misogyny), the argument over Eliot's sexuality is long-running. In 1952, John Peter interpreted *The Waste Land* (as does Seymour-Jones, exhaustively) as a love poem for Eliot's friend Jean Verdenal, dead in the war. Eliot threatened to sue *Essays in Criticism* (a sure sign of guilt, we learn); the edition was pulped, and the piece only reprinted in 1969. Since then the evidence for Eliot's homosexuality – his dandyish 'extérieur pimpant' (Richard Aldington's phrase), his noted use of make-up, the chilling misogyny lurking in some of his poems – has been much debated. Seymour-Jones has no doubts at all. The flat he rented from 1923 at Burleigh Mansions under the name Captain Eliot, the rumbustious 'Columbo' verses – all balls and buggery and bungholes – the male evenings *chez* John Hayward, with much scatological fun, the contact with the 'largely homosexual' circles at All Souls, the friendships with priests, and the expressions of solidarity with 'Les Boys', MacNeice, Auden, Spender and David Gascoyne, are more than enough evidence to confirm Eliot's 'membership' of 'the international fraternity of gay men in literature and arts between the wars'. Never mind that Hayward called himself 'the most un-homosexual man in England' (*PS*, pp. 566, 579). Never mind that Peter Ackroyd argues that 'it would be the tritest form of reductionism to assume that Eliot, because he could not adequately deal with female sexuality, was therefore homosexual'.[3] Never mind that Eliot married Valerie.

The problem with Seymour-Jones's approach to this subject is twofold: first, as elsewhere, there is her deployment of the evidence; and secondly there is her tone of indictment. Take the case of Eliot and Massine. Eliot's interest in the Russian Ballet and in Massine's dancing is well known. A long passage in Ronald Schuchard's *Eliot's Dark Angel* (1999), for instance, looks at Eliot's fascination with Massine's mixture of vulgar music-hall parody, ritualistic stylisation and intensity. Eliot was delighted to meet Massine in 1922 through Mary Hutchinson: 'I quite fell in love with him,' he wrote to her. ('There is no record of a further meeting,' Schuchard writes.)[4] But for Seymour-Jones the meeting illustrates the 'pull of that other twilight world'; it marked his decision to 'lay the foundations for his secret life'. Next we hear that Eliot liked Nancy Cunard, 'who prided herself on demonstrating the pleasures of heterosexual relationships to otherwise confirmed homosexuals'. Eliot, we learn, met Nancy at the Russian Ballet, because of his 'new friend' Léonide Massine. The Russian Ballet was a cult for 'men about town': these were men, comments Seymour-Jones, who went about 'under the guise of robust heterosexuality'. Eighty pages later, we hear that in 1926 Ottoline Morell thinks Eliot must be in love with somebody, and that the Russian Ballet was back in town. 'Was Eliot still in love with Massine, who was living close to Burleigh Mansions?' (No evidence is given that Eliot visited him.) Mary Hutchinson remembered often seeing Eliot at the ballet, walking in the corridors of Covent Garden. Then we get one of Vivienne's poems, about the Underworld, which we are told 'implied that in entering the gay world of Diaghilev, Eliot was entering the underworld'. The poem is quoted; it contains references to acrobats and suffocating corridors, though not to the Russian Ballet. 'Perhaps it was after Anton Dolin's acrobatic feats in *Le train bleu*, Cocteau's last ballet for Diaghilev, that Vivien ran from the "suffocating" corridor. In the final years of the Ballets Russes, the atmosphere at performances became more overtly "decadent" or homosexual' (*PS*, pp. 331–5, 415, 419–21). (No evidence is given of Eliot's seeing *Le train bleu*.) Just to clinch it, there's then a description of a 'Sailor Party' (there's no evidence that Eliot was there), organised by some well-known homosexuals,

> attended by many Bright Young Things, to celebrate the revival of *Les Matelots*, in which Massine danced the French sailor for the first time.
>
> There was certainly talk in London that Eliot enjoyed the company of sailors.

A photo of Massine is included in the illustrations, naked to the waist and looking very sexy; he is described in the caption as an 'intimate of Eliot'. These are illegitimate tactics. But, worse than that, they seem to re-criminalise homosexuality. The innuendoes about Eliot's secret vices suggest that it is as shameful to be gay as it is to be an anti-Semite or a wife-murderer.

Seymour-Jones trawls Eliot's poetry and plays relentlessly for evidence of his moral iniquity. And certainly Eliot is a very disturbing, sometimes appalling, poet. I find it hard to read the 'murderous amatory hatreds' (Christopher Ricks's phrase) of *Sweeney Agonistes* ('Any man has to, needs to, wants to/Once in a lifetime, do a girl in') as an example of 'how he managed to transmute almost maddening states of mind into a universal drama'.[5] But even when Eliot's cruel perversity scares me to death, I don't want to collapse his writing entirely into autobiography. I want to recognise the life in the work, *and* to see how it's transformed. Seymour-Jones will have none of this. Although she often tells us that Eliot wore a mask and was like an actor, she cannot see the work as performance, as the play of voices. It is all just a vehicle for shameful secrets and private feelings. Eliot's theory of the impersonal, of 'the separation of the man who suffers and the mind which creates' is, for her, a nasty and successful trick, a smokescreen, a way of 'warning off critics who were tempted to make connections between art and life' (*PS*, p. 153). In this she is at one with her heroine, one of whose desperate letters to Eliot's brother – asking for help, which as usual never came – ends: 'Goodbye Henry. And *be personal*, you must be personal, or else it is no good. Nothing's any good. Vivien.'

A Secret Self: May Sinclair

What do most of us know about May Sinclair, the English novelist who lived from 1863 to 1946? Probably that she applied the term 'stream of consciousness' to Dorothy Richardson's writing in her review of *Pilgrimage*, a term which then came to be applied, not always usefully, but frequently, to the work of Woolf or Joyce. Possibly that she was involved in the early days of the British psychoanalytical movement; that she was interested in and wrote about the Brontës; that she had an awkward friendship with the poet Charlotte Mew; and that two of her novels, *Mary Olivier: A Life* and *Life and Death of Harriett Frean*, were based on the experience of an oppressive, bourgeois Victorian childhood and treated the lives of her heroines like case studies in repression. Because reputations are so implicated in publishing history, it's those two novels, of the three that Virago reprinted in the 1980s, which are still the best known. But I would guess that, until the publication of Suzanne Raitt's biography, *May Sinclair: A Modern Victorian*, in 2000,[1] pretty much everything else about May Sinclair had sunk without trace. Her early poetry, her 'New Woman' novels of 'unpleasant' social realism and difficult issues, her wartime writings, her essays on Imagism, her book on Idealism, and her late novels of the 1920s, are not in demand. Yet this was a prolific and for a time a famous author. She wrote twenty-three novels, six collections of stories, two books on philosophy, and some sixty essays or introductions.

In part, it's a well-earned neglect. Her only previous biographer, the American critic Theophilus M. Boll (who has sunk into even deeper obscurity than his subject), in his 1973 attempt to resuscitate the reputation of Sinclair, trudged doggedly through plot summaries and appreciations of every one of her novels ('Dialogue is supreme in a variety of moods . . . Actuality trickles through the book . . . Naturalism in sex has its moments'). Suzanne Raitt, by contrast, doesn't even bother with the late novels, is guarded about the war writing and, though she makes a serious case for the early poems, what she quotes is hard going: 'Everywhere/Self-abnegation is the starting-point/For each, and union with the Highest Self/The final goal of all' (*MS*, p. 50).

Partly, Sinclair's neglect is due to her marked reclusiveness, and the fact that she outlived her own powers: from the late 1920s to her death in 1946 she sank into what Raitt terms the 'twilight years' of Parkinson's disease. But it's also to do with an established account of modernism. Women writers who fitted awkwardly or not at all into the version of high modernism dominated by the figures of Pound, Eliot, Joyce, Woolf, Stein or Lewis – because of their political concerns, interest in Victorian subject-matter, vacillations between traditional and experimental forms and literary inconsistencies – have fallen into minoritised or uncategorisable positions. Among these are Rebecca West, Charlotte Mew, Dorothy Richardson, Willa Cather and, certainly, May Sinclair. This modernist hierarchy is now being much disputed (by critics such as Lyn Pykett, Bonnie Kime Scott, Ann Ardis and Marianne de Koven), who argue that such women writers demand a reconfiguration or redefinition of what modernism can include. By positioning Sinclair as a transitional figure, a late Victorian who developed an interest in the aesthetic revolutions of younger writers, Raitt hopes to move her 'from the bottom to the centre of the page'. And certainly when the histories of modernism are rewritten, no one will be able to ignore May Sinclair again.

She partly wanted to be ignored, though, and this makes her a tricky subject for a literary biography. Raitt has tracked down (and dates to 1907 or 1908) an autobiographical sketch of 'The Miss-May-Sinclair', 'this very curious and interesting animal', which reads like a cross between Beatrix Potter and Kafka:

> It wd. seem to be fond of retirement. Its habit is to hide itself in its outer burrow, or studio, during the forenoon, when the little creature applies itself, with comic fury, to building up a heap of manuscripts wh. wd. seem to serve it for purposes of protection & indeed nutrition. (*MS*, p. 269)

Raitt begins her book by emphasising Sinclair's reclusiveness ('she spent much of her time alone'), her horror of biography as 'a dangerously invasive form', and her extreme reticence and secrecy about her private life (coexisting with her frankness in *Mary Olivier* about 'her own mental development'). Her third novel, the one which made her name, *The Divine Fire*, is concerned, 'Gissing-like', 'with the vulnerability of poverty-ridden authors, the corruption of the literary press, and the increasing commercialisation of the bookselling trade' (*MS*, p. 86). (It sets a domestic library, rare, historical and private, against a bookshop, vulgar, new and venal.) She cut bits out of her letters, left no diary, had no widower to husband her remains, resented explanations of women writers' lives in terms of a secret love interest, and 'was determined to give nothing away'. And perhaps there was not much to give away. It's hard for us now, Raitt suggests, to imagine a life led entirely without sex, intimacy, romance or domestic involvements, a life of work and private thinking. Certainly it means that the emphasis here has to be placed on Sinclair as a writer and an intellectual.

But there is a mournful childhood story to be told. May Sinclair is yet another of the women writers I've been writing about in this book who withdrew from early unhappiness into an intensive private life of reading and self-education. We see her first, in her father's library in Ilford, absorbed in Gaskell's *Life of Charlotte Brontë*, 'a book that told of lives even more restricted than her own'. Her mother, whom she would live with and look after until she was nearly forty, was 'an unimaginative and inflexible woman', a Northern Irish Protestant horrified by her daughter's developing agnosticism. Her father failed in his shipping business and died of alcoholism when Sinclair was seven. Her five older brothers, with whom as a child she competed for parental attention, all died young, one by one, of heart disease. As a young woman, Sinclair struggled, like any mid-Victorian doubter, to translate her lost religious faith into 'some kind of reconciliation between theology and philosophy', an 'agnostic ethics'. Out of this crisis of faith came the earnest Idealist poetry and the loss of two relationships, one with a theology student awaiting ordination, the other with a married professor of ecclesiastical history. Raitt makes what she can of Sinclair's 'trading sexual intimacy for intellectual independence', her probable regret at her childlessness, the possibility that she was romantically involved at the time of her mother's death, and the obsessive interest in her fiction in celibacy, sexual frustration and sublimation.

But the more visible drama is the translation, in the 1890s, after the years of poetry and philosophy, of this reclusive Victorian spinster into the author of outspoken 'modern' novels on sex, feminism and domestic tyranny. These were books – of adultery and illegitimacy and women with a past – which fell foul of the 'chaste columns' of American magazines (where Sinclair was lionised but censored) and of which one West African missionary felt bound 'to make a solemn holocaust'. Sinclair's 'issue' novels, her involvement with the suffrage movement, her dedicated interest in the lives and work of the Brontës as 'pioneers of modern femininity', brought her fame and success, but still she was more of a 'New Woman', an 1890s figure, than a modernist.

The First World War acted as a spur for Sinclair towards a new kind of writing and a new sense of self. She behaved very oddly in the war, hurling herself with excitement, even avidity, into the possibility of a life of action, but unable to cope with the realities. She went to Belgium with Hector Munro's Ambulance Corps (he was one of the directors of the Medico-Psychological Clinic), but her position was ill-defined and she seems to have been mainly in the way. There are bizarre stories of her being pushed off an ambulance full of wounded men, taken off nursing duties in Ghent for incompetence, and sent home to England. Rebecca West described Sinclair's war journal as if written by 'a little girl sitting on a tin trunk at a railway station and watching the people go by' (*MS*, p. 164). Her war novels, propagandist and anti-pacifist, mix up erotic relationships, sexual jealousy and women's desires to take part in the war.

Yet Sinclair was also coming much more in touch now with new movements in aesthetics and thought; the war years seem to have been transformative for her. She became involved with a network of (sometimes contradictory) influences which changed her as a writer, gave her a significant voice as a critic, and inspired her best work. The key ingredients in this transformation were her relationship with Charlotte Mew, her friendship with Pound and her interest in what he and his friends, H.D., Richard Aldington and Eliot were doing in poetry, and her involvement with psychoanalysis, which had begun before the war. In 1913 she became one of the founding members of the Medico-Psychological Clinic, the first British institute devoted to psychotherapy, which, from 1917 onwards, treated large numbers of shell-shocked soldiers. Sinclair (who was never analysed herself) developed 'her own idiosyncratic versions of classic Freudian and Jungian formulations like repression and sublimation' (*MS*, p. 139) – concepts which were at the heart of her novels, from *The Three Sisters* (1914) onwards. This is an intense and complex stage in Sinclair's intellectual life, and Raitt writes about the mixture of forces affecting her in the late 1910s very intelligently and illuminatingly.

Sinclair's peculiar friendship with Charlotte Mew, in which the poet seems to have been the eager pursuer and Sinclair a wary recipient of unwanted emotions, has prompted more interest than any of Sinclair's other relationships. For a full sense of Mew's strangeness, need and intensity, we have to go to Penelope Fitzgerald's brilliant and haunting short biography (1984). Raitt treads carefully through what might be sensationalised as a narrative of thwarted lesbian passion, and dismisses as malicious gossip the much-told story of Mew chasing Sinclair into her bedroom and forcing her to jump over the bed five times to escape her. What interests her most is the influence of Mew's macabre Gothic excesses and her raw dramatic performances on Sinclair's imagination. Raitt argues that Sinclair's attraction to Mew's passion and intensity is in conflict with her interest in the formal, spare, classical objectification of the Imagists. Her overlapping and conflicting cultural allegiances – to Mew, to Pound, to Eliot, to Imagism, to Vorticism, to psychoanalysis – established her 'as a mediator between the older and the younger generation' but also as a writer caught between 'Victorian emotional drama' and 'literary modernity'. Ezra Pound mockingly annotated the draft of an article she was writing on his poetry in 1922, in which she mused, with some nostalgia (as Raitt observes) on writers like Tennyson or Swinburne who had influenced her own early poetry: 'You cannot conceive him taking a great, passionate human theme & treating it greatly, passionately, tenderly'. Pound responded caustically: 'Wotcher mean by great,pash.human theem.??' (*MS*, p. 209).

In this minefield of contradictions (Jungian symbolism was a very different thing from Imagism, and the free association of Jungian psychology quite at odds with Imagism's desire for 'poetry that is hard and clear, never blurred nor indefinite'), Sinclair began to forge her own idea of literary modernism, in which 'the mind and its forms' were the key to 'the spirit of modernity'. She works this out through her pieces on Richardson, Eliot and other modern writers in the *Egoist* and the *English Review* between 1918 and 1922. Raitt writes particularly well on Sinclair's famous application of the phrase 'stream of consciousness' to *Pilgrimage*, pointing out that this was not, as so often said, necessarily derived from William James. The phrase was frequently used in the texts Sinclair was reading for her book on Idealism, in her friend Evelyn

Underhill's book on mysticism, and in many nineteenth-century writings on psychology, and it usually refers not to perception but to questions of selfhood and identity. Sinclair's interest in *Pilgrimage* is in self-knowledge and the establishment of the self 'as an autonomous subject'. Her readings in contemporary writing and in psychology all point towards her exploration of this subject in her autobiographical novels of the developing (and thwarted) self, *Mary Olivier* and *Harriett Frean*. These extraordinary novels translate traditional novelistic materials into interiorised modernist narratives, the first with the utmost inclusiveness, the second with the utmost economy. They make a savage, ironical (and, in *Harriett Frean*, undeviatingly bleak) analysis of Victorian family life, and can be set alongside *The Way of All Flesh*, or *Father and Son*, or *To the Lighthouse*, or *The Fountain Overflows*, for their subversion and rewriting of the author's childhood. It is an extremely sad fact of literary history that having discovered, after many years of writing, how to do this, Sinclair sank back into more conventional methods *en route* to the dark silence and invisibility of her late years.

Bittersweet: Rosamond Lehmann

As a teenage reader in the early 1960s I had an addiction to fated heroines driven by one all-consuming, unsatisfactory love, like *The Constant Nymph* (a favourite of Rosamond Lehmann's) or Elizabeth Bowen's dangerous innocents, Emmeline and Portia. I couldn't get enough of Lehmann's Olivia Curtis, or those scenes in *Invitation to the Waltz* and *The Weather in the Streets* where she meets the handsome Rollo Spencer, exuding upper-class confidence, first on the terrace at the ball where he rescues her from her shy awkwardness, and years later in a train's restaurant car. The moment Rollo enters, in a tweed overcoat, with a dog under his arm and a copy of *The Times*, orders sausages and scrambled eggs, and smiles across at her, you know that Olivia has met her fate. Doomed Chick Lit, this might be called, and it's a *passé* genre, alas – only Anita Brookner, who was a friend of Lehmann's, still does it. Lehmann's heroines want to please and be loved, give up their lives to one man, are exploited or betrayed, and suffer loneliness and rejection – not to mention secret abortions, social ostracism, or the loss of a child. There is no political agenda – 'I dislike feminist demonstrations,' Rollo tells Olivia, and she quickly agrees – but there is a compelling intimacy with these women's vulnerable lives.

At thirteen I read her for the emotions; twenty years later, returning to her in the Virago green-backs that re-ignited her reputation, I became aware of her brilliant social detail, sharp ironies, and vivid, naturalistic dialogue. Her life-story began to intrigue me – were these all autobiographical novels? And she featured in so many other people's stories! She was the great beauty who swept Goronwy Rees, that slippery chancer, from under Elizabeth Bowen's nose at Bowen's Court. (The greater writer eventually forgave her rival.) She was the devoted friend of Strachey and Carrington, the intimate of the strange, inscrutable Henry Yorke, the one woman friend and writer who seemed to pose no threat to Virginia Woolf. In the 1980s, I saw her once or twice, out with Carmen Callil, the friend and champion of her late years: a vast, moon-faced, grand apparition in floating colours, violet-white hair and lashings of make-up. As John Bayley once said, she loomed over you like a ship's figurehead.

Now she gets her own life-story, from another addicted childhood reader who had the advantage – and the challenge – of knowing her intimately, through family connections. Selina Hastings keeps this information back to the very end, but her close knowledge of Lehmann colours the whole picture in *Rosamond Lehmann: A Life*.[1] And a gorgeous piece of work it is, exactly right for its subject: fast-paced, vivid, bursting with characters, gossip, physical sensations and strong emotions, a book you want to gobble up like the box of chocolates which was Hastings's last present to the eighty-nine-year-old Lehmann, eagerly received. But some of these chocolates have bitter centres.

Hastings is as good as her subject at social class and English life-styles, and she gives an eloquent picture of the middle-class childhood on the banks of the Thames, the place Lehmann often returned to in her imagination, with the dilettantish, charming, sportsman father, the puritanical New England mother, and the talented, beautiful children, three of whom were made for the arts. Like their sister, Beatrix the Communist actress and John the poet and editor could take themselves very seriously in later life: as Stephen Spender (always in combat with John Lehmann) once said, the Lehmanns think they're the Brontë sisters, but in fact they're the Marx Brothers. Hastings takes quite a tough line with these glamorous egotists. She doesn't spare the quarrels between the siblings, or John's 'monstrous self-absorption', or Rosamond's snobbishness and 'tremendous ego'. But she is also profoundly sympathetic to a story often as painful as that of any of Lehmann's heroines.

Rosamond had her heart broken at Cambridge (1920s Girton is perfectly described) by her favourite type, a cool, dashing Etonian, and made a disastrous marriage, on the rebound, to Leslie Runciman, of a tough Methodist ship-owning family. 'Our sex life was a disgrace to sex,' she wrote later. As he had a neurotic horror of having children, she had a traumatic abortion. This was what she would call, snootily, her 'bleak period of exile in the detested North of England', in Liverpool and Newcastle. (It provided powerful material, 'far from gay', for her second novel, *A Note in Music*.) She escaped by writing – her first book, *Dusty Answer*, an intense, poetic story of thwarted young love, was a huge success – and through a love-affair with the alluring upper-class painter, Wogan Philipps. Yet, after a long battle for divorce, this second marriage in turn became a conflict between two self-absorbed, beautiful charmers. 'Ros and Wog' created an enchanted but short-lived idyll at their Oxfordshire house at Ipsden, surrounded by Bloomsbury friends like Siegfried Sassoon and Dadie Rylands. (Remember, Virginia Woolf told her at one particularly bucolic free-spoken Bloomsbury party in the early '30s, 'we won this for you'.) But there were tensions over her absorption in their two children, Hugo, and, especially, Sally; over Wogan's infidelities, and his escapades in Paris and the Spanish Civil War. Though Lehmann wrote her best novels during this period, and had great success (*The Weather in the Streets* was a tremendous hit, in France even more than in England and America), the marriage ended wretchedly.

The catalyst was her affair with Goronwy Rees, whose involvement with Burgess and Blunt would come back to haunt her, and who – typically – let her down badly. Some fine autobiographical stories, published in *The Gypsy's Baby*, come from this time: 'Life doesn't arrange stories with happy endings any more, see? *Never again,*' the heroine of 'A Dream of Winter' tells herself. She was right: the pattern was repeated in her forties with the next great love of her life, the poet Cecil Day-Lewis, who vacillated ineffectually and selfishly for eight years between his wife and his glamorous but impossibly demanding mistress, and then took a brutal and sudden route out of the impasse, going off with the much younger, and sexier, Jill Balcon. (Hugo, who hated Day-Lewis, had a point, when he burst out as a schoolboy: 'He only wants you for his poetry!') Rosamond's lifelong state of 'entrenched vindictiveness' towards the Day-Lewises is seen to be as grotesque as it was pitiful. (There's a frightful scene when she hits him, very hard, at a Chatto & Windus party in 1955.) But this gruesome story is quickly overtaken by the next appalling tragedy in her life, the sudden death, at twenty-four, of her daughter Sally, recently married to the poet Patrick Kavanagh.

Rosamond's devotion to Sally and the unbearable blow of her death plunged her into an intense commitment to spiritualism. She convinced herself that Sally was not dead, and that she was in contact with her. A touching late book, *The Swan in the Evening*, shows how deeply she had made herself believe that we 'go on' in the immaterial world. This is a difficult area, and Hastings treats it admirably, making us see that she *had* to 'shut down her reason' to survive, but allowing herself some dry humour (unlike Lehmann) at the information provided by 'sensitives' like Mrs Ena Twigg (Sally was being advised by St Francis how to teach the unborn birds to sing) and the psychic expert Tudor Pole, 'only a part-time visitor to Planet Earth'. Hastings is restrained, however, in comparison to Lehmann's sceptical Bloomsbury friends, like Dadie Rylands, who used to read out Rosamond's contributions to the journal of the College of Psychic Studies with screams of laughter over breakfast. The most measured and wise response came from Stevie Smith, who, reviewing *The Swan in the Evening*, wrote: 'If you believe in God you will let the dying go, glad that the pain of loss is ours, not theirs.' But Rosamond found this hard to forgive.

Hastings's tone darkens as Lehmann becomes the difficult older woman she knew, always avid for attention and admiration – the woman who wrote sadly, in her fifties, to her friend Bernard Berenson (who told her flatteringly that she had replaced Edith Wharton in his life) that she wanted 'a hand in mine, that, once taken and given, will never let mine go'. Many late affairs and friendships foundered on the rock of her 'ceaseless demands', her 'illusions and self-deceptions', her 'destructive emotional games'. So much emphasis is placed on this that I wonder if the conflicts Hastings had with her in life have skewed the portrait, in the end, too much towards the grotesque. It is probably much harder to write a *Life* of someone whose demanding, difficult, insistent physical and emotional presence looms large in the biographer's own life. Could Lehmann's courage and endurance, her commitment to public service (her international work as President of PEN, for instance), her lasting appetite for friendship, have been more emphasised? And Hastings's briskly rational approach, her clear plot summaries, don't quite catch the elusive, haunting, almost dream-like shimmering quality of those magical young woman's novels of the 1920s and '30s. But it's the mark of a fine and compelling biography that one immediately wants to sit down and have an argument with its author.

Worn Paths: Eudora Welty

Eudora Welty (1909–2001) who lived for most of her life – and set much of her work – in Jackson, Mississippi, became a Southern monument before her death. A two-volume Library of America edition of her works was published in 1998, lightly but usefully annotated by the novelist Richard Ford and the academic Michael Kreyling (who in 1991 wrote an interesting account of Welty's vital literary relationship with her agent Diarmuid Russell, the son of 'AE').[1] One volume contains her five novels. The other has the forty-one stories on which her reputation largely rests, her evocative, evasive memoir, *One Writer's Beginnings*, with its illustrations, and a selection of her essays. It misses the opportunity, though, to reprint the introduction to her book of Mississippi Depression photographs, or her telling essays on, and reviews of, Henry Green, Katherine Anne Porter, Chekhov, Willa Cather and Virginia Woolf. And, disappointingly, there's no introduction: I'd have liked to read Ford's views on Welty.

In addition to this, a respectful, affectionate, lightweight unauthorised biography by Ann Waldron was published by Doubleday, also in 1998, which justifies writing the story of Welty's life in the teeth of her lifelong resistance to a biography in these terms: 'Why, then, did I go against her wishes and produce an unauthorised biography? Because I *had* to.' (And anticipates that, whatever Welty's preference for, as she puts it herself, having 'her private life kept private', there will be many more biographies.)[2] A patchy collection of essays on Welty's late novels, co-edited by two Danish academics and introduced by Reynolds Price, shows in its bibliographies the enormous attention Welty's work receives, with books on her 'feminist intertextuality', her 'aesthetics of place', and her 'love of story-telling', tribute volumes (*Eudora Welty: A Form of Thanks*) and collections of critical essays treating Welty as traditional Southerner, or modernist, or myth-maker.[3]

In all this canonising and canonisation of Welty, what is often remarked on is her slipperiness, her ambiguity, her reluctance to be monumental. Waldron's gossipy *Life* ends, significantly, with Welty's comment on her co-editing of *The Norton Book of Friendship* in 1992: 'We should have made another book with all the things we had to leave out.' Reynolds Price, in his introduction to *The Late Novels*, draws attention to Welty's position of 'withdrawn . . . yearning'. And many of the essays in that book describe Welty as 'cagey', mysterious, artful and elusive. The best essay, by Richard Gray, called 'Needing to Talk', takes a line from *Losing Battles* (1970) as its theme: 'People don't want to be read like books'. The more they talk, the more they tell stories, and the more they are 'read', the more it seems that something 'remains uncaught'.

In *One Writer's Beginnings*, published when she was seventy-five, Welty tells an odd little story of something she saw on one of the many three-day train journeys she took in the 1930s and 1940s between Mississippi and New York. In the late '30s these long journeys became increasingly uncomfortable and unreliable, with the trains often late or breaking down.

> Once, when my train came to one of those inexplicable stops in open country, this happened: Out there was spread around us a long, high valley, a green peaceful stretch of Tennessee with distant farmhouses and, threading off toward planted fields, a little foot path. It was sunset. Presently, without a word, a soldier sitting opposite me rose and stepped off the halted train. He hadn't spoken to anybody for the whole day and now, taking nothing with him and not stopping to put on his cap, he just left us. We saw him walking right away from the track, into the green valley, making a long shadow and never looking back. The train in time proceeded, and as we left him back there in the landscape, I felt *us*, going out of sight for *him*, diminishing and soon to be forgotten.[4]

Nothing more is said about this, though it is part of a passage about the lifelong significance to her of travel. But a page or two later, she remarks: 'What discoveries I've made in the course of writing stories all begin with the particular, never the general.' That 'particular' – the sight of the soldier walking away – could easily have been the germ of a Welty story. Often, when she comments on her work, she will say that a story has grown out of a figure seen in a landscape, something glimpsed or something overheard.

Probably the best-loved of all her stories, 'A Worn Path', which enters the life of 'an old Negro woman', Phoenix Jackson, walking alone along the old Natchez Trace to get her regular supply of medicine for her grandson – a story of endurance and hope – came from the sight of a solitary old woman seen 'at middle distance, in a winter country landscape'. 'Her persisting in her landscape was the real thing,' Welty says in an essay called 'Is Phoenix Jackson's Grandson Really Dead?' The unstoppable voice of the woman who moves out of her family home in a huff, to live in the post office, was sparked off, Welty says in an interview, by the sight of 'a little post office with an ironing board in the back through the window . . . in some little hamlet in Mississippi'.[5]

The stories and novels that grow out of these 'particulars' always dramatise figures in their landscapes and invent around them, with intense, precise, deeply rooted observation, the reasons for their life. A face, a look, a scene, a conversation, an encounter, will carry with it a whole cultural history, the whole meaning of a life. So, in *Delta Wedding* (1946), the mother of the family (a sort of Virginian Mrs Ramsay) thinks: 'One moment told you the great things, one moment was enough for you to know the greatest things.'

Welty's story-teller's 'moment' has often been compared to the photographs she took in the Depression for Roosevelt's Works Progress Administration, when she travelled all over Mississippi and took pictures of poor country people, black and white, churches, state fairs, pageants, children and the old. She brings out, in her introduction to these photographs, *One Time, One Place* (1971) the imaginative connection between her photographs and her stories: 'I respond to . . . the story of her life in her face' . . . 'The thing to wait on . . . is the moment in which people reveal themselves'.[6] Waldron tells us that the first book Welty tried to sell, in 1935, 'Black Saturday', juxtaposed her photographs and her stories. No publisher would touch it.

And the fiction does have some of the qualities of the 1930s photographs, in its search for a point of entry into a hidden life, in its social realism, and in its eye for tiny details seen in passing: a needle stuck in a woman's collar which she's forgotten, 'with the thread running through the eye' ('The Key'); or, seen from a moving car at the side of the road going south from New Orleans, 'a saucepan full of cut zinnias which stood waiting on the open lid of a mailbox at the roadside, with a little note tied onto the handle' ('No Place for You, My Love'). But the truer link might be with dreams or films, rather than with photographs. She has talked in interviews about her interest in and knowledge of cinema, particularly Hitchcock. The soldier going away from the train would make a wonderful long shot. Yet no one has ever filmed Welty's novels or stories.

Her cinematic techniques are closely connected to her fascination with travel. Like Elizabeth Bowen (with whom she had a close friendship, or even, Waldron hints unprovably, a love-affair), she is obsessed with journeys. Like Virginia Woolf, one of the writers she most admired, she loves the narrative of a chance travelling encounter. Woolf's 'An Unwritten Novel', which places two women, author and subject, opposite each other in a railway carriage, and imagines the novel that might come out of this, was an inspiration to Welty. Many of her stories are set in station waiting-rooms, on trains, on boats, in cars, with travelling salesmen or hitchhikers, where people's lives cross and pass.

Welty herself was always leaving her home in Mississippi, yet always returning to the place where she was born. By analogy, she can be read as a 'universal' writer or defined by her Southernness, in comparisons with Faulkner, or Katherine Anne Porter, or Walker Percy (as several of the essays in *The Late Novels* do, with rather dull results). Certainly her novels and stories are about stasis, return and reunions, as well as journeyings. Landscapes, neighbourhoods, houses, families, stories, are embedded in memory, layered with accretions of the past. In her small towns, everyone knows everyone else's histories. Old houses stand as markers of 'the old deserted time' ('The Wanderers') that still remain in a few memories. 'Worn paths' carry the traces of all the previous journeys made along them.

Some of her narratives are historical. *Losing Battles* goes back to the Mississippi hill country of the 1930s. In the remarkable 'Natchez Trace' stories in *The Wide Net* (1943), 'A Still Moment' imagines a strange meeting between the painter and naturalist Audubon, the preacher Lorenzo Dow and the outlaw James Murrell. 'First Love' tells the story of Aaron Burr's trial from the vantage point of a deaf boot-boy, whose deafness seems to replicate our obstructed relation to the historical past.

But in all Welty's stories and novels, a Southern community's history persists through memory and story-tellers. Choric commentators recall the dramas of the past, 'like an old song they carried in their memory' ('Asphodel'), and encourage each other to perform them. In *Delta Wedding* they call it wanting 'the ghosts kept straight'. The force of memory can be oppressive. It can distort your life for ever, like the elegies for Laurel's father in *The Optimist's Daughter*, which she feels are misrepresenting him. It can trap you: you are fixed in place by what everyone knows about you in a small town like 'Morgana', Welty's invented town for *The Golden Apples* (1949): 'Then Morgana could hold them, and at last they were this and they were that' ('June Recital'). In families (her most persistent subject, she says in *One Writer's Beginnings*), memory can be a consolation or a source of strength, but also a weapon and a punishment. In the families in 'Why I Live at the P.O.', or 'Clytie', or 'Kin', no one forgets – or forgives – anything. As one old lady says in *Losing Battles*: 'Home's the most dangerous place, after all, they say.'

But she is also interested in the free, mysterious movement of individual memories. Welty gets inside the unpredictable memory of children and of the very old, with their whole lives furled inside them: Phoenix Jackson, Solomon in 'Livvie', the grandfather in 'At the Landing'. Even Uncle Felix, in 'Kin', who has had a stroke and can't remember where he is, has his life's memory stored inside him, bursting out painfully and unexpectedly. There are no writers in Welty's books, but her characters' rememberings resemble her own processes. She has often said (sounding on this subject very like Willa Cather, whose work she admires) that writing is a kind of remembering.

Landscapes, in Welty's stories and novels, seem to draw us into a deep tunnel of feeling. This writing is slow, rich and careful, and moves between tiny, exact details and something looser and more atmospheric, but never hazy. Welty has often written about her 'visual mind', about how to 'establish a chink-proof world of appearance' (especially in 'Place in Fiction'). She knows exactly what she is doing. Very precise distinctions are made between different landscapes – the strange terrain below New Orleans, the Natchez Trace, the plantation houses, the townscapes, the hill country. What we look at is completely known, often seen through the eyes of an inhabitant:

Down an arch, some old cedar lane up here, Mattie Will could look away into the big West. She could see the drift of it all, the stretched land below the little hills, and the Big Black, clear to MacLain's Courthouse, almost, the Stark place plain and the fields, and their farm, everybody's house above trees, the MacLains' – the white floating peak – and even Blackstone's granny's cabin, where there had been a murder one time.

And Morgana all in rays, like a giant sunflower in the dust of Saturday.
('Sir Rabbit')

Nothing stays still in these scenes. The river has gone away from the old
landing stages, but can still flood up – when 'boats ran over the houses'
('At the Landing'). Sudden weather alters a whole landscape in a
second. The scene is often poised at a point of change: 'It was coming
on a rain. The day had a two-way look, like a day will at change of the
year – clouds dark and the gold air still in the road, and the trees lighter
than the sky was' ('Shower of Gold').

Just as you take it in, that particular aspect is going, never to return.
It's the same with the life-stories. So the family reunion in *Losing Battles*
(like the dinner party in *To the Lighthouse*) is passing at the moment you
see it: 'and nothing at all was unmovable, or empowered to hold the
scene still fixed . . .'

In 'Place in Fiction', Welty sums up the questions fiction asks as:
'What happened? Who's here? Who's coming?'[7] These are the sorts of
questions her garrulous chorus is always asking. But they aren't always
answered. Welty's stories have been much criticised for obscurity,
especially in her early rejection slips, of which (we learn from Waldron)
there were many in the 1930s and 1940s, before the success of *Delta
Wedding* in 1946 and *The Golden Apples* in 1949. Michael Kreyling, in
Author and Agent,[8] describes her agent Diarmuid Russell repeatedly
asking her to make things clearer.

But Welty usually preferred to keep the dark places in her stories.
The secrets of human life are her subject: 'It was as if she had shown
him something secret, part of her life, but had offered no explanation'
('Death of a Travelling Salesman'). In the earlier stories, the secrecy and
terror of life often takes grotesque form: a backward girl, a deaf and
dumb boy, a freak show, two terrible old ladies, a crazy family of
malfunctioning Southerners in 'Clytie'. (However, Welty took excep-
tion, like Flannery O'Connor, to being typecast in early reviews as a
'Southern Grotesque' or 'Southern Gothic' writer – and, like Flannery
O'Connor, she loathed Carson McCullers.) Later, her use of grotes-
querie diminishes in her investigation of the unaccountable, the hidden,
in people's lives, like the wife's disappearance in 'The Wide Net', or the
unexplained hopelessness of the couple in 'No Place for You, My Love'.
In *The Golden Apples*, the secret heart of the characters' interconnected

lives – Virgie Rainey, the MacLain brothers, Cassie, Miss Eckhart – gradually unfolds; but much remains obscure, to us and to them.

Welty's characters seem to be part of something more than they know, or to be acting in ways for which they can't quite account. So her stories edge towards myth or folklore. There are quests, trials, transfigurations. She likes to touch in, but not to insist on, an archetypal element. The longing and magic of Yeats's 'The Song of Wandering Aengus' runs under *The Golden Apples*, but so do the planetary systems and the story of Perseus and Medusa. Leda and the Swan, wood-nymphs, Greek tragedy, Grimms' fairytales, jostle with old Indian stories of the Natchez Trace, and Bible stories of the Good Samaritan, Jacob and the Angel, or the Prodigal Son. Welty has been plagued by over-allegorical explicators; her allusions, at their best, are buried and implicit.

Where spells are cast and shapes shift most effectively is in the language itself. Her imagination takes possession of things and bodies by transforming them. She is addicted to verbal metamorphoses. A crookedly fastened suitcase hangs apart 'like a stupid pair of lips'. Flowerbeds in front yards are like 'bites in the grass'. An old man has a thought 'held round in his mind, like a fresh egg'. A cat jumps to the ground 'like something poured out of a bottle'. Sometimes a sight will draw out a whole string of images, like (this is catching) handkerchiefs from a conjuror's hat. So a humming-bird is 'a little emerald bobbin . . . metallic and misty together, tangible and intangible, splendid and fairy-like, the haze of his invisible wings mysterious, like the ring around the moon'. It's as if Emily Dickinson were at work in prose.

Welty's shape-shifting imagery, like Dickinson's, comes out of close watchfulness. She uses surrogate watchers, characters who enact the author's way of looking, like the narrator of 'A Memory' recalling how as a child she used to make 'small frames with my fingers, to look out at everything', or the stranger in 'The Key' who turns on all he sees the 'hurried focusing of a very tender and explicit regard'. And some looking is a form of voyeurism, staring at a neighbour's house through a telescope ('June Recital'), spying from a secret place.

That voyeuristic looking can be sinister and troubling. When Eudora Welty talked about herself and her writing, she did so with legendary modesty and gracefulness, always accentuating the elements of hopefulness in her work. And she struck everyone who met her as an enchantingly generous, humane and humorous person. This led to an overly adulatory tone of voice: 'That Eudora Welty's work is beyond the human power of praising, I don't need to say. Everyone knows it,' says William Maxwell on the cover of one of the Library of America volumes. An essay in *The Late Novels*, by Marion Montgomery, refers, with chronic respectfulness, to 'the joyful humility and piety towards existence in Welty's work'. In reaction to this sort of thing, some dry scepticism about Welty was voiced by Claudia Roth Pierpont in the *New Yorker* in 1998. Pierpont resents what she sees as Welty's over-praised provincial idealisations, her determinedly undeviating optimism, her self-created gentility and her refusal ever to have 'willingly stepped off her front porch'.[9]

Ann Waldron's biography makes us aware that Welty's own version of her life paints a mellow picture of what could be read very differently. *One Writer's Beginnings* gives only glimpses of, or keeps silent on, some of the most painful facts of her life: her (in youth) much remarked on plainness, her father's shocking early death when she was twenty-two, her mother's morbidity and guilt-inducing possessiveness, her early rage and resistance against home life and her enforced return to the South during the Depression years, her long struggles to be published, the mental illness of one of her brothers and the deaths of both, her arduous nursing of her sick mother in the 1950s and '60s, a long ambiguous relationship with a gay friend, periods of blockage in her writing, and no stories published after 1966. Waldron makes much of these ingredients, and they make a darker story than Welty has ever told about herself.

But Pierpont's harsh view that all such darkness has been kept out of the fiction in the interests of acceptance and popularity seems to me unjust. There *is* darkness – fear, terror, cruelty and violence – in Welty's fictions. They are not benign. Terrible things happen to her characters, often with a sort of cold, brutal, accidental carelessness. Rapes, murders, suicides, sudden deaths, disastrous marriages, corrosive family feuds, abandonments, humiliations, insanity, are regular occurrences. Many of these lives (white and black – though the emphasis is usually on the white families) are lived in grief, pain, loneliness and poverty. (The two 1960s stories, provoked by the racial conflicts in Mississippi into a more explicitly politicised writing than is usual for Welty, are bitter and weary in tone, and show little hope for an end to Southern bigotry and violence.)

One woman spends most of her life waiting for her husband to come back to her, another is locked into perpetual grief for her dead child, another kills herself after a lifetime of family bullying. It's a condition of life for most people to be, in old age, 'still watching and waiting for something they didn't really know about any longer, wouldn't recognise to see it coming in the road' ('The Wanderers'). There is rage and dislike, as in *The Optimist's Daughter*, for the kind of people 'who never knew the meaning of what has happened to them.' The stories are full of incidental tragedies, just paused on and then gone, like this hitchhiker's story of his mother:

> 'Long ago dead an' gone. Pa'd come home from the courthouse drunk as a wheelbarrow, and she'd just pick up an' go sit on the front step facin' the hill an' sing. Ever'thing she knowed, she'd sing. Dead an' gone, an' the house burnt down.' ('The Hitch-Hikers)

Miss Eckhart, the German piano teacher in *The Golden Apples*, a character Welty has said she strongly identifies with, lives a life of appalling isolation, frustration and estrangement, culminating in an act of crazed desperation. One of the worst moments in these stories is when Cassie, the piano pupil, witnesses Miss Eckhart, goaded by her old mother, walk across the room and hit her in the face. And then life continues.

Welty has been rightly praised for the vigour, comedy and vitality of her story-telling voices, but they are often telling grim tales, and are at their most ebullient when they have something macabre or dreadful to talk about. A lot of this good humour is barbaric. The joviality of the female relations in *Losing Battles*, who are trying to make a young girl admit she is one of the family, by forcing her on the ground, in a kind of gang rape, to swallow the juice of a melon they are grinding into her face, is astoundingly brutal. Her greatest comic turn, 'Why I Live at the P.O.', can be read as a vicious story of revenge, spite and lies. And some of the strongest feelings in Welty's stories and novels are of savage anger against the confines of the family and the community. It's one of the great energising paradoxes in her fiction that what she most celebrates is also most resisted. We enter deep into these communal lives, but we also come to understand very well the wild, savage, secret selves of people whose feelings fail 'to match the feelings of everybody else' ('June Recital'), and who need to make a life of their own – like the soldier walking out of the train and away.

A Quiet Ghost: Penelope Fitzgerald

After her death in 2000, admirers of the marvellous work of the English novelist Penelope Fitzgerald were given two consolations: a selection of stories, *The Means of Escape* (2000), and her collected non-fiction, *A House of Air* (2003).[1] Both these posthumous editions vividly call to mind her qualities, as though a quiet ghost had come in and sat down with us. She once said to me in a radio interview (in 1997)[2] that her books were so short because she didn't like to tell her readers too much: she felt it insulted them to over-explain. So there is sometimes a sense of something withheld in her novels, as in the mysterious forest encounter in *The Beginning of Spring*, or the meaning of the story of the 'blue flower', never completed, never spelt out, although Fritz the hero does tell us: 'If a story begins with finding, it must end with searching'.[3] *The Means of Escape*, a very slim volume of eight stories, appears more cryptic and sidelong even than the novels, giving us a last, rather teasing and enigmatic look.

A conundrum, something silent or unsaid, is at the heart of most of these stories. There is an alluring, intriguing contrast between the careful, rapid, subtle and precise way she establishes the settings, which are often, like her later novels, historical and foreign – nineteenth-century Tasmania or New Zealand, Brittany in the 1880s, Turkish-occupied Greece – and the mystery of what's happened and why. A runaway convict in Van Diemen's Land ambushes a rector's daughter for help. She wants to use him, as much as he does her, as a 'means of escape', but her plot, and her desires, are hijacked by the family's silent housekeeper, a ticket-of-leave woman with a terrible past, who is fanatically devoted to the daughter. 'Her motives for doing what she did . . . were never set down, and can only be guessed at.' An English artist in Brittany, one of an absurd and serious bunch of young men committed to painting from the life (loosely and affectionately translated from the Pont-Aven group of French artists that collected around Gauguin), uses a local red-headed girl as a model, but never finds out anything about 'the experiences of her heart'. 'You don't know what I want, and you don't know what I feel,' she tells him. An artistic director, an efficient managerial type, sets out to bring back a very famous, very old conductor from his deep seclusion on Iona, for a major concert. The old man meets him with tricksy, perverse, unreadable resistance, but – hearing the young woman singer the director has brought with him to the island, humming a few bars of German *lieder* – he suddenly decides to go back to the mainland, and to music. A very poor young country boy loses the medal his godmother gave him on his birthday in 1663, inscribed with the motto 'Desideratus'. After a strange quest to the big house, what he lost is returned to him: but he will never understand what he has seen.

Like this boy, and the red-headed Brittany girl, and the silent ticket-of-leave housekeeper, the stories pay attention to those who can't speak well for themselves. Fitzgerald was always drawn to what she used to call 'the exterminatees', decent or mild-mannered people not very good at being in the world, who never have the chance to tell their stories, or who get bullied or exploited by what she calls here 'the tribe of torturers'. This book is full of obscure adversity. There's a dogsbody caretaker with a dubious past whose quiet refuge is taken over by the horribly determined 'Mrs Horrabin' (this is the weakest story because more farcical than usual); there's a clerical assistant Singlebury (reminiscent of Melville's Bartleby), a creature of habit given the sack after long service by the Company's unwilling hit-man, who returns to haunt him in a ghost story of extreme, even gleeful, ghoulishness. Before he was made redundant, he used to say that the peculiar damp smell in the office was 'the smell of disappointment': the building was requisitioned in 1942 by the Admiralty and relatives would wait there for news of people missing at sea. And 'the smell of disappointment' is something you feel Fitzgerald is very quick to detect.

Singleton is a terrifyingly quiet ghost, and quietness is Fitzgerald's mode: you have to concentrate and listen hard. The old maestro on Iona once refused to conduct Mahler's Eighth Symphony. What is your objection to it? he was asked. 'It is too noisy,' he replies. But inside the quietness there are some alarming surprises and strong notes: the 'rancid' feral smell coming off the sack which the escaped convict wears over his head 'like a butchered animal'; poison running down a boy's throat while his head is forced 'back to dislocation point'; or the sound of a woman in childbirth coming from the next room of a remote New Zealand country home, many miles from Auckland, where the husband listens in agony to sounds he had never heard before, 'not in a shipwreck – and he had been in a wreck – and not in a slaughterhouse'. Meanwhile the nearest neighbour (a wonderful invention) who has come eight miles for his half-yearly visit, is sitting unmoved and unnoticing, smoking his pipe, hoping to get some dinner eventually.

Cruelty, indifference and the exercise of power are the realities. But the stories are also filled with Fitzgerald's characteristic tender, humorous apprehension of human oddness and ordinariness, and of moments of good luck which shine through in memorable images. The boy who loses his precious medal on the hill slope outside his village, in winter, goes back to look for it: 'In a little hole or depression just to the left hand of the path, something no bigger than a small puddle, but deep, and by now set thick with greenish ice as clear as glass, he saw, through the transparency of the ice, at the depth of perhaps twelve inches, the keepsake that Mrs Piercy had given him.' The man whose wife is expecting a child in the remote house on the North Island buys a pair of racing pigeons so as to send them back to the nearest town, Awanui, as messengers, when the doctor is needed. He takes them home, 'still shifting about and conferring in their wicker basket', and when the time comes for their life-or-death mission, releases them into the air. 'How to toss a pigeon he had no idea. He opened the basket, and before he could think what to do next they were out and up into the blue. He watched in terror as after reaching a certain height they began turning round in tight circles as though puzzled or lost. Then, apparently sighting something on the horizon that they knew, they set off strongly towards Awanui.' Just occasionally in Penelope Fitzgerald's luminous, dark, unflinching world, people do find their way home, or their longed-for 'Desideratus', or their means of escape.

Because of that reticence and quietness in the fiction, it's particularly intriguing to find, in her collected essays and reviews, her likes and dislikes, her preferences and opinions, quite plainly set out. In the sympathetic, curious and knowledgeable pieces on writing, art, craft, places, history and biography that make up *A House of Air*, Fitzgerald's points of view are aired on many subjects. She believed, as a novelist (as she said to me in that interview in 1997) that 'you should make it clear where you stand'. In *A House of Air* she asks: 'What is the use of an impartial novelist?' She is forthright and candid about her moral position in her novels: 'I have remained true to my deepest convictions – I mean to the courage of those who are born to be defeated, the weaknesses of the strong, and the tragedy of misunderstandings and missed opportunities which I have done my best to treat as comedy, for otherwise how can we manage to bear it?' 'Everyone has a point to which the mind reverts naturally when it is left on its own. I recalled closed situations that created their own story out of the twofold need to take refuge and to escape, and which provided their own limitations. These limitations were also mine.' Such utterances throw a very illuminating light on the novels. But they are also rather cryptic: she expects us to understand what she means by the 'point' the mind 'reverts to naturally'; she doesn't tell us what she thinks her limitations are. She has a way of saying strange, challenging, unsettling things in a matter-of-fact way, as if these were self-evident truths. Her manner is plain and mild; her prose never shows off. She is practical, vivid, clear and exact about her subject, and leads you right to the heart of the matter: the feeling of a novel, the nature of a life, the understanding of how something or someone works, the sense of a place or a time. All the same, when you get there, you may still feel – as with her novels and stories – much left unsaid or unexplained. She says here in an essay on Charlotte Mew (which preceded her moving and eloquent biography of the poet) that she is a writer who 'refuses quite to be explained'. She is amused by Byron's impatience with Coleridge's metaphysics: 'I wish he would explain his explanation.' She likes readers to have their wits about them, and she likes exercising her own, as with her pleasure in Beckett's dialogue:

> What a joy it is to laugh from time to time, [Father Ambrose] said. Is it not? I said. It is peculiar to man, he said. So I have noticed, I said . . . Animals never laugh, he said. It takes us to find that funny, I said. What? he said. It takes us to find that funny, I said loudly. He mused. Christ never laughed either, he said, as far as we know. He looked at me. Can you wonder? I said.

She comments: 'This kind of dialogue shows us what we could say if we had our wits about us, and gives us its own peculiar satisfaction.'

Beckett's hollow laughter is a surprising preference for Fitzgerald, who is not herself a player with words or a lugubrious comic. And there are some surprises in her reviews. There are pieces on writers we might have guessed she would like – Sarah Orne Jewett for her deep, quiet knowledge of a small community, its silences, pride and cruelties; John McGahern for his poetic realism, his attention to 'small acts of ceremony' and his 'magnificently courteous attention to English as it is spoken in Ireland'; William Trevor for his empathy with the innocent and the dispossessed; Olive Schreiner for her strangeness, dreaming and courage. But there are others she champions more unexpectedly: Roddy Doyle, Kazuo Ishiguro, Carol Shields, D.H. Lawrence, Joyce (especially *Finnegans Wake*). This is not a narrow, prissy or parochial critic.

At the heart of her intellectual passions is a political commitment to an English tradition of creative socialism, a vision at once utopian and practical of art as work, and of the usefulness of art to its community. Her English heroes are Blake, Ruskin, Burne-Jones, William Morris, Lutyens. She is inspired by Morris's dedication to 'the transformation of human existence throughout the whole social order'. (Though, as in *The Beginning of Spring*, she sees the comedy and pathos of Utopianism too, manifested in the early twentieth century in 'Tolstoyan settlements, garden cities and vegetarianism tea-rooms, Shelley's Spirit of Delight . . . and the new Rolls Royce'.) She deeply admires Morris's painful mixture of neurosis, work ethic, resolution and struggle for self-control. But she likes her idealists best at their most down-to-earth: Ruskin on the joy of shelling peas ('the pop which assures one of a successful start, the fresh colour and scent of the juicy row within . . .') or the cunning arrangements at Burne-Jones's studio at the Grange: 'the huge canvases could be passed in and through slits in the walls, there were hot-water pipes, and a skylight so that it could be used for painting with scaffolding'. The work of Morris that most delights her is the Kelmscott Press and his experiments with typography.

She pays great attention to serious craftsmanship, practised skills and technical mastery. (There is always a job to be done in her novels: running a bookshop or a school, keeping a barge afloat.) The best compliment she can pay to the biographies she often reviews is 'calm professionalism'. She is just as interested in non-verbal professions; there is a great deal about art in *A House of Air*. She tells us about Francis Oliphant's failed attempts at glass-painting, William de Morgan's luminous tiles, Charles Ashbee's high-minded devotion to Handicrafts (all the same, 'he was an architect whose houses stood up'), and Edward Lear's heavenly Mediterranean paintings. She has an eye for illustrations – John Minton's decorations for Elizabeth David's first cookery book, 'a kind of delicious ballet in and out of the text', or Ernest Shepard (her stepmother's father) and his feeling for line ('You can recognize it in ... a study of ... a young man cutting long grass ... The braces are only just sketched in, but you can see how they take the strain'). She loves small well-made books, like J.L. Carr's 'delightful tiny booklets', *The Little Poets* ('I only wish I had a complete set now'). One of her favourite quotations is from the socialist woodworker Romney Green, who held that 'if you left any man alone with a block of wood and a chisel, he will start rounding off the corners'.

Romney Green was a friend of the founder of the Poetry Bookshop, Harold Monro, which flourished, in its quirky, idealistic and influential way, from the 1910s to the early 1930s. This is Fitzgerald's golden age: she doesn't like 'Georgian' to be used as a term of abuse. Born in 1916, she remembered hearing Walter de la Mare reading at the Poetry Bookshop, and many of her favourite writers are connected to that period and that atmosphere: A.E. Housman, Edward Thomas, Sylvia Townsend-Warner, Stevie Smith. Again, one of the things she liked best about the Poetry Bookshop was the look of its rhyme sheets, which, 'in the spirit of William Blake', and using some of the best illustrators of the time (including John and Paul Nash, David Jones and Edward Bawden), were designed for 'the verse and the picture to make their impression together'. 'We tacked them on our walls, above our beds and our baths.'

Harold Monro was a lost cause in the end, a pathetic and gloomy alcoholic, and the Bookshop was carried on gallantly for a while, and then wound up, by his passionate Polish widow Alida. As in her novels, Fitzgerald is drawn to failures, and some of her most vivid characterisations, in life as in fiction, are of despairing figures whose struggles and defeats are at once funny and terrible. She is drawn to the sad minor characters in minor English novels. There is the poor faded shabby-genteel Mrs Morgan in Mrs Oliphant's *The Rector* ('She cannot afford to complain. Time has robbed her of the luxury of ingratitude'). There is the 'uncompromisingly plain Anne Yeo' in Ada Leverson's *Love's Shadow*, 'hideously dressed in a mackintosh and golf-cap and "well aware that there were not many people in London at three o'clock on a sunny afternoon who would care to be found dead with her"'. There is the unmarried Monica in E.M. Delafield's *Thank Heaven Fasting*, a prisoner of early twentieth-century, middle-class, English domestic servitude: 'Heavy meals come up from the basement kitchen, clothes are worn which can't be taken off without the help of a servant, fires blaze, bells are rung, hairdressers arrive by appointment – every morning and evening bring the spoils of a comfortable unearned income. It is the only home Monica has ever known, and we have to see it turn first into a refuge for the unwanted, and then into a prison.' You might not call Penelope Fitzgerald, at first glance, a feminist writer, but she is one.

So conscious of how cruel life can be to its victims, she is generally a kind reviewer. However, she should not be mistaken for a push-over, and can be lethal about poor work. One biographer, busy seeing off his predecessor as 'conventional', is dealt with thus: 'This leads you to expect a bold treatment of some debatable points, but that would be a mistake.' Another is described as writing with 'flat-footed perseverance'. She is often at her most ironical when writing about biography, a form which fascinates and exasperates her (and which, in her lives of Charlotte Mew and the Knox brothers, she made entirely her own). She always insists on the need for the fullest possible historical context, and she knows all about the problems of the genre: 'The years of success are a biographer's nightmare.' 'The "middle stretch" is hard for biographers.' 'Perhaps the worst case of all for a biographer, nothing definable happened at all.'

In any life-story, she is alert to cruelty, tyranny or unfairness, and she has no time for horrible behaviour – severely recalling Larkin, on an Arts Council Literature Panel, saying (in response to a query about the funding of 'ethnic arts centres') that 'anyone lucky enough to be allowed to settle here had a duty to forget their own culture and try to understand ours', or summing up the character Evelyn Waugh assumed for visitors and admirers as 'the tiny Master threateningly aloof in his study, emerging with the message: I am bored, you are frightened'. Like her father, Evoe Knox, as editor of *Punch*, she will always speak out against tyrants. And she has an acute feeling for – and memory of – the vulnerability of children. She responds to writers (like Walter de la Mare, or Blake, or Olive Schreiner) who enter into the child's dreams, or feelings of exile or homesickness; she is very alert to 'the bewilderment of children growing up without love'. At her memorial service, appropriately, Humperdinck's ravishing and consolatory lullaby for the two lost children, Hansel and Gretel, was sung.

Hansel and Gretel believe in angels; Penelope Fitzgerald probably did, too. She certainly believes in minor phenomena like ghosts and poltergeists, and she does a great deal of thinking about religion, as is only natural for the granddaughter of bishops and a Knox daughter – niece of a socialist priest, a notable Roman Catholic convert and translator of the Bible, and a fiercely sceptical cryptographer. Her novels argue, quietly, over belief, and the relation between the soul and the body. 'Because I don't believe in this . . . that doesn't mean it's not true,' is Frank's position in *The Beginning of Spring*. The Russian priest he is listening to says to his congregation: 'You are not only called upon to work together, but to love each other and pity each other.'[4] Fitzgerald has described herself as 'deeply pessimistic', but she seems to believe in that sort of ideal. Writing about *Middlemarch* and George Eliot's hope that 'the growing good of the world' may depend on the diffusive effect of obscure acts of courage, heroism and compassion, Fitzgerald says, not entirely confidently: 'We must believe this, if we can.' 'Pity' is one of the emotions – or qualities – she most values, especially in comedy. She has a lively interest in little-read late-Victorian theological fiction, and a sharp eye for religious patches seeping through into secular-seeming texts, like Jane Austen's Evangelicism leading Emma to weep over 'a sin of thought', or Virginia Woolf inheriting from her father 'a Victorian nonconformist conscience painfully detached from its God'.

But she is extremely reticent about her own beliefs. The people she admires are those who have a habit of 'not making too much of things'. She takes aesthetic pleasure in control and restraint: writing about Angus Wilson's homosexuality, she says, with a rare touch of primness: 'Getting rid of the restraints didn't improve him as a writer – when does it ever?' What autobiography we get from her essays comes in glimpses – she says of her father that 'everything that was of real importance to him he said as an aside'. At one point in her life she started to write a biography of her friend L.P. Hartley, but stopped when she realised that it would give pain to his surviving relative. She thinks of him as resisting investigation; one of his characters, when unconscious, is subjected to 'a complete examination' by a famous specialist, 'which in all his waking moments he had so passionately withstood'. This is a biographer who believes in privacy. One of the very few personal details she gives us in her essays – that she once had a miscarriage – is presented as an illustration of the profound reserve of Ernest Shepard, who came to see her and handed her a bunch of flowers 'without a word'. She is interested in silence: the silence that falls after a life-story like Coleridge's, the world of Jewett's stories 'where silence is understood', the reserve which kept James Barrie from telling us what Mrs Oliphant said on her deathbed. *A House of Air* ends with Virginia Woolf's description, in her last novel, *Between the Acts* (also published posthumously) of a woman writer – a comic failure, of the kind Fitzgerald enjoyed writing about, too – leaving her audience behind ('she took her voyage away from the shore') and taking away with her some mysterious unspoken words.

Heart of Stone: J.M. Coetzee

Since his hugely acclaimed novel *Disgrace* was published in 1999, the novelist J.M. Coetzee has published three books, *Youth* (2002), *The Lives of Animals* (2002) and *Elizabeth Costello* (2003), a difficult, subtle and quizzical group of early twenty-first-century works which challenge the reader to tell fact from invention and autobiography from fiction. All three books are concerned with 'embodiment', one of Coetzee's key words. How is human life to be embodied in writing?

By comparison with the acclaim for *Disgrace* and the admiring reception of *Boyhood: A Memoir – Scenes from Provincial Life*, *Youth*, the sequel to *Boyhood*, was met in the UK with some disappointed and negative reviews ('a tortuous exercise in intellectual introspection, and not much else'; 'as fiction it is so interior and cerebral, it fails to engage'; 'not wholly satisfactory as either novel or memoir').[1] Was the tide turning against Coetzee? Or was this darkly teasing little book really so much worse than its predecessors? It's not as if we expected to be charmed. The drab early 1960s London setting is just as grim as Coetzee's South Africa ever was; the cold, dysfunctional, misogynist central character, John, is as compromised and unappealing as the disgraced David Lurie. But perhaps *Youth* was being taken too seriously, and we are meant to mock this grim young man and the solemn Conradian title that portentously frames his rite of passage.

A good deal depends on whether we read *Youth* as fiction or autobiography. The book was published in the UK without a subtitle, and with a blurb that suggests it is meant to be read like Coetzee's other novels of alienated, unresolved quests: 'He begins a dark pilgrimage in which he is continually tested and continually found wanting.' So it was reviewed as a novel with powerful autobiographical ingredients. The American edition, though, is subtitled 'Scenes from Provincial Life II', a deliberate pairing with *Boyhood*. The subtitle (also used by William Cooper in the 1960s, but that's probably been forgotten) hovers between a sense of story-telling and of remembering. Certainly the facts of this life are Coetzee's. After the uneasy South African childhood we read about in *Boyhood*, he went to the University of Cape Town in the late

1950s, where he graduated in English and maths. At the start of *Youth*, we find John in 1959, living in a flat in Cape Town, aged nineteen, paying his way with a variety of small teaching and library jobs so that he can be independent of his parents, coldly undergoing a series of disappointing and pointless affairs, revolted by 'the carnage of Sharpeville', and desperate to get out of the country before he is conscripted for the Defence Force. In 1962, like this narrator, Coetzee left for London, where he was employed by IBM, and then by its British rival, 'International Computers', as one of the first wave of computer programmers, while working on an MA thesis by correspondence for the University of Cape Town, on Ford Madox Ford. The MA was awarded in 1963, but that takes us beyond the end of *Youth*. If there were to be another memoir it would cover Coetzee's move to America (a move which the anti-American narrator of *Youth* strongly resists) to study linguistics and stylistics at the University of Texas at Austin and to write a Ph.D. thesis on Beckett. In 1968, he became a Professor of Literature at the State University of Buffalo, finished his thesis and started his first book, *Dusklands*. In 1971 he returned to South Africa to teach at the University of Cape Town, and became the J.M. Coetzee we know about.

So, is *Youth* an autobiography? Although within a page the narrator pointedly mentions Rousseau, we also find on the first page that he has taken his flat 'under false pretences' and yet that this was 'not a lie, not entirely'. As the anxious, self-questioning, third-person, present-tense narrative takes hold, it is preoccupied with discovering 'the real thing' – in love, in writing, in national identity, in the self. Evidently, if this is an autobiography, it is one which is at pains to demolish the pact which autobiography is meant to establish between writer and reader, that this is 'the real thing', 'the true story'. It's an autobiography written 'under false pretences': it is never going to tell us how much is 'the truth' about the self, because it doesn't know what that is. This makes for a disconcerting, at times irritating mixture of self-importance – 'At one moment he might truly be himself, at another he might simply be making things up' – and ironic debunking. His favourite narrative, we discover at the end, is Beckett's *Watt*: 'Just the flow of a voice telling a story, a flow continually checked by doubts and scruples, its pace fitted exactly to the pace of his own mind.'

Coetzee has always been obsessed with confession and its limits. It's a theme that keeps pace with, and in part grows out of, South African history: the censorship practised by the Apartheid regime, the torture and questioning of political prisoners, the need for concealment and secrecy in so many areas of life (not least the sexual), the pressure on the writer to be politically committed, the post-Apartheid era of accountability with the Truth and Reconciliation Commission. But it's also a private obsession, and an international one: Coetzee is as much driven by his readings of Kafka and Dostoevsky as by his South Africanness. The subject recurs, from the inconsistent and neurotic first-person monologue of *In the Heart of the Country*, or the magistrate's aghast, ineffectual observation of how torture and interrogation can be resisted in *Waiting for the Barbarians*, to the desire for ultimate anonymity and inscrutability in *Life & Times of Michael K*, or Mrs Curran's abject retraction of her past in *Age of Iron*, or the haughty refusal to confess to the politically correct committee of inquiry into sexual harassment in *Disgrace*: 'What goes on in my mind is my business, not yours.'[2] Coetzee has written a good deal about confession and resistance in his literary essays: on the parallels between South African and Soviet censorship, and their effects, in *Giving Offence* (1996); on 'Confession and Double Thoughts' (first published in 1985) in *Doubling the Point* (1992). Writing there on Dostoevsky and Tolstoy's use of fictional confessions, Coetzee dwells on the 'problems regarding truthfulness' raised by, for instance, 'The Kreutzer Sonata', or the chapter 'At Tikhon's' in *The Possessed*, where confession inevitably involves mixed motives and self-mythologising. 'The self cannot tell the truth of itself to itself and come to rest without the possibility of self-deception.'[3] Whether this loop can ever be broken, and any absolution or conclusion attained, is doubtful. Coetzee's characters spend much of their time avoiding self-knowledge, playing dumb, or resisting their interpreters or interrogators. So does he. (Witness his shyness of interviewers, his refusal ever to show up at the Booker Prize, and his protest, in the person of Elizabeth Costello, against the treatment of the writer as performing animal.) He speaks about himself and his work evasively. My favourite example was his response to a five-page written question on *Foe* (1986) from the South African critic (and Sartre specialist) Philip Wood: 'I have always resisted being nudged into the role of interpreter of my own books. In this case, moreover, you do it more fluently and convincingly than I can imagine myself doing.'[4]

No surprise, then, that in *Boyhood*, Coetzee distanced himself from his childhood through the use of the third person, as in its sequel *Youth*, or that *Boyhood* was a story of the child as secret agent or changeling, an alien in his own family, school and country. At home, he resents his closeness to his mother, tyrannises over his younger brother, and thinks of his father as an unwanted intruder. He leads a double life, and keeps his aggressive behaviour in the home completely separate from his docile, abject behaviour in school. He hides away in class so that he will never be punished. He pretends to be a Roman Catholic (this is funny) because he thinks it has something to do with Rome and his hero Horatius. Part German, part English, part Afrikaner, he doesn't know what kind of South African he is: 'since not everyone who lives in South Africa is a South African, or not a proper South African'. He secretly prefers the Russians to the Americans, but keeps this dark. (This is the late 1940s.) He loathes and fears the Afrikaners and idolises the English. He passionately loves his family farm on the Karoo, but knows that – unlike the 'Coloureds' and the Afrikaners – he has no rights of ownership there: 'he will never be more than a guest, an uneasy guest'. 'His heart is old, it is dark and hard, a heart of stone.' He wants to be singular: 'I hate normal people'. He wants to be unrelated, 'to live . . . without belonging to a family'. The fascinating paradox of *Boyhood* is that this highly observant and objective narrative tells of a person who cannot see beyond his own version of things. He is 'living the only story he will admit – the story of himself'.[5]

Voluntary self-exile seems the inevitable outcome of all this. In *Youth*, John ruthlessly turns his back on his mother and family, gets out of the country whose politics, cultural standards and dominant ideology appal him, resists any kind of political involvement, treats all the women he makes love to with cruelty, contempt or resentment (presumably to be revenged on his mother's unbearable devotion, though this isn't spelt out), and makes no close friends, though he longs for friendship. He is as proud, lonely, scornful and gloomy as Lucifer. But moral judgements on this unpleasant, snobbish, self-regarding, immature misogynist seem rather beside the point. Besides, 'the story of his life that he tells himself'[6] is so full of self-loathing that he does this for us. The null extremism of the character could be read, not censoriously (as David Lurie is always being read in *Disgrace*) but as an absurd exercise in comic futility.

Youth is a story of failed aspiration. John is attracted to the idea of cutting loose and becoming an anonymous, unidentifiable wanderer, like Michael K. But John 'is too prim, too afraid of getting caught' to sign off, to fall out of the system. Though he reads avidly about explorers and longs to be an existential stranger, he is, in fact, a timidly law-abiding character. 'He has never liked people who disobey the rules.' He 'is better at tests than at real life', and relies heavily on schedules and systems, like teaching himself (unsuccessfully) to play Beethoven by practising the same piece at first very slowly and then quicker and quicker. He wants to be isolated, without ties or human concerns, but keeps being snagged back into his ordinary humanity: by the cousin who reproaches him for his callous behaviour to her girl-friend, by the young woman whose stoicism after her abortion of his child is a reproach to him, by the Indian colleague who shows him how much worse it would be to be an immigrant of colour in England in the early 1960s. (Part of the grim pleasure of *Youth* is its horribly vivid account of how drear, unfriendly, cold and dark London could seem to its incomers at that time.) He wants to be the perfect Englishman (hence his attraction to Ford Madox Ford's Tietjens as 'the quintessence of Englishness') but knows (as once at school) that he can never really fit in. The true Londoners can spot him a mile off as 'not the real thing'. He wants to be uprooted and disinherited, but realises bitterly that his gloom is inherited from his Dutch Puritan forebears. And much as he would prefer to be free of his country and all it means to him – boredom, philistinism, 'atrophy of the moral life' – he is tugged back by the memory of the farm, and the pull of the land. He wants to be apolitical, 'an onlooker', but can't avoid historical complicity: so, with suspiciously fictional irony, he is assigned to work on the data for the development of a new British bomber, and ends up installing the software for the atomic weapons research centre at Aldermaston.[7]

Above all, he aspires to be the perfect artist, the perfect stylist, a Wildean aesthete with lines like 'Happy people are not interesting.' His unpleasantness to women comes wreathed in ridiculous ideas about how they 'love artists because they burn with an inner flame', how it is 'in quest of . . . the fire of love, that women pursue artists and give themselves to them'. They are merely stages in his acquisition of the poet's requisite dark night of the soul. Joyce's *Portrait of the Artist* – as a young alien – looms over this, and Coetzee is even harsher with his younger self than Joyce is with Stephen Dedalus's high aspirations. Like many proud isolationists, he is intensely concerned with how he appears and who to model himself on. He is attracted to writers who have made themselves at home in England: Conrad, James, Pound, above all Eliot, whose protective disguise and horror of 'spilling mere emotion on to the page' he emulates. The writers he most admires are all style, no confession, like Ford or Beckett. But his own attempt at aesthetic self-construction fails miserably. He ends up 'killing time', playing chess with himself, stuck inside a Beckettian 'endgame', passive, cynical, without grace. He writes hardly any poems, except for some computer-generated verse, the most extreme possible exercise in impersonality and formalism. *Youth* is at its most artificial in the parallels it draws between the state of mind of the character and his work on computers. Like him, the Atlas ('Britain's rival to IBM') is a 'self-interrogating' machine, 'asking itself what tasks it is performing': it has 'self-consciousness of a kind'.[8]

This all seems too Coetzeean to be true. But then what is 'true'? We go round again in the loop. 'At one moment he might truly be himself, at another . . .' *Youth* is the ultimately alienated and alienating autobiography: not an inward exploration, or an ethical indictment of the author/subject, but a self-parody.

While writing *Disgrace*, and these ambiguous, quasi-fictional, third-person memoirs, *Boyhood* and *Youth*, Coetzee (even though so notoriously wary of confessions, public appearances, tribunals and interviewers) gave some talks which took the form of lectures written by a famous Australian woman writer, Elizabeth Costello. He seemed to be at once expressing his own beliefs and masking his voice inside Costello's arguments. (On the occasion I heard him, questions were not invited.) These talks were published in 2003 as a slim volume of lectures (with footnotes) called *The Lives of Animals*. In *The Lives of Animals*, Elizabeth Costello (the name contains 'Coetzee', and echoes 'Elizabeth Curren' of his novel *Age of Iron*), who is famous for her fictional version of Molly Bloom's life, *The House on Eccles Street*, is visiting her son John Bernard and his wife Norma at an American university, where she gives two lectures. The first, called 'The Philosophers and the Animals', takes Kafka's 'Report to an Academy', in which a highly educated ape tells a learned society the story of his ascent from beast to near-man, as the basis for a harrowing indictment of our treatment of animals, using the Nazi death camps as a shocking parallel. 'Let me say it openly,' says Elizabeth Costello: 'we are surrounded by an enterprise of degradation, cruelty and killing which rivals anything that the Third Reich was capable of.' The horror of the death camps was that 'the killers refused to think themselves into the place of the victims'. By analogy, we persecute animals by dint of not imagining ourselves into their lives. But 'an animal – and we are all animals – is an embodied soul'. This lecture, or lesson, is greeted in the small-town university with a mixture of scepticism, exasperation (on the part of the daughter-in-law, a philosopher of mind), cautious academic politeness, and outrage, on the part of a Jewish poet who is appalled by her analogy between murdered Jews and slaughtered cattle.

The second 'lesson', 'The Poets and the Animals', pursues the issue of animal rights through the ways in which writers have used animals, as metaphors, as tools of argument, or in attempts to 'embody' animal life in poetry, 'to return the living, electric being to language'. In the question and answer session that follows her talk, Costello is challenged (by voices standing in for many of Coetzee's readers) about the 'Western cultural arrogance' of the animal rights movement, its sentimental Utopianism, and the philosophical shortcomings in claims for equality between animal and human understanding. She answers all these points firmly, but on the drive to the airport with her son the next day, she breaks down in distress and confusion at the disparity between her outrage over 'the animal business' and other people's equanimity. She berates herself: 'Everyone else comes to terms with it, why can't you?'

The Lives of Animals, which came out just after *Disgrace* and just before *Youth*, was received with nervous respect. It was clearly linked to the scenes in the animal-welfare clinic in *Disgrace*, and the appalling things that are done to the many dogs in that novel, in which the main character discovers he is going to have to start his life again, 'with nothing', 'like a dog'. The lesson David Lurie learns passes judgement, by implication, on a society in which groups of human beings have been oppressed and treated 'like animals'. But dogs aren't just allegorical or metaphorical figures in *Disgrace*; they are realistic, 'embodied' dogs, and they are, it's clear, as important as the humans. David Lurie argues with his daughter that 'we are of a different order of creation from the animals', but she tells him that 'there is no higher life. This is the only life there is. Which we share with animals.'[9]

Coetzee then reprinted *The Lives of Animals* (without footnotes) in his novel of 2003, *Elizabeth Costello*[10] – which doesn't call itself a novel, but 'eight lessons' (with a postscript). In addition to giving the lectures from *The Lives of Animals*, Costello makes other public appearances and engages in a series of arguments about writing. At the start of the book, she has won a big American literary award, and, looked after by her son (who feels like an attendant at the shrine of the sibyl), she is being interviewed and fêted. She gives a lecture called 'What is Realism?', which again makes use of Kafka's ape. On a cruise ship, lecturing with an irritatingly exhibitionist and self-promotingly 'exotic' Nigerian writer, she talks about 'The Future of the Novel'. Visiting the sister she hasn't seen for years, who is getting an honorary degree for her work in an African mission for the terminally ill, she argues with her over the rival belief-systems of classical humanism and Catholicism. In a coda to the visit, she tells her sister a startling story of a sexual consolation she once offered to an old, dying man, pitting the story the Greek celebration of human beauty against the Gothic Christian insistence on human suffering.

At a conference in Amsterdam, speaking on 'Witness, Silence and Censorship' (the sort of topic Coetzee has spoken on himself), Costello confronts a historian who has written a vivid account of the execution of Hitler's would-be assassins, arguing that the evil of that history has been transferred to the writer and thence to the reader, and that there are some things that are better not written about. Her own secret example is a violation she suffered in her youth (another of the shockingly physical moments irrupting into this book of arguments), which is known only to 'the committee of angelic observers' that may be watching us; she herself has buried the memory silently inside her like 'an egg of stone'.

Responding to a book on the legend of Eros and Psyche, she asks, in sensual detail, whether we can imagine what it would be like to be made love to by a god. Finally, in a deliberately clichéd, Kafkaesque allegory of purgatory, a kind of 'literary theme-park', she is held at the gate by a tribunal which requires her, before she can go through to another world, to state her beliefs. To reply that as a writer it is not her profession to believe, 'just to write', will not do, nor to pretend to a belief 'that all humankind is one', nor to express her 'faith in art': 'Her books certainly evince no faith in art ... they merely spell out, as clearly as they can, how people lived in a certain time and place.' The writer's job, she has always thought, is 'believing whatever has to be believed in order to get the job done'. Now she is beginning to think that the writer must have, if not 'beliefs', then at least 'fidelities'.[11]

In this fragmentary and inconclusive book, more like a collection of propositions about belief, writing and humanity than a novel, it's clear that animal rights is not the only issue. The creature in the zoo is the novelist her, or himself, and part of the book's driving force is an impatience with the way famous writers are required to perform like rock stars, or to provide confessions or state their beliefs. Outside the writing, why should the writer's ideas be interesting? Why should fiction be 'obliged to carry a message'? Costello isn't even very good at public speaking, and keeps telling herself not to do it. There is distaste and scorn throughout, too, for interviewers, profile- and thesis-writers, goldfish 'circling the dying whale, waiting their chance to dart in and take a quick mouthful'.

But Costello's performances, however reluctant, have serious implications for the writer's role. The 'world mirror' of realism is broken, the words on the page no longer have authoritative meanings (as the Bible used to), we can no longer say with confidence who we are, but are 'just performers speaking our part', and 'the gods' seem no longer to be watching or listening. (These are all Costello's contentions.) Yet there is still some idea of 'divinity' around the figure of the writer, some idea of inspiration coming from elsewhere – why else would people cluster around to hear and see writers? The 'humanities', however secularised, still have something to do with 'a quest for salvation'. Good and evil still have some force.

But if any of these notions are to be expressed, they must somehow be 'embodied'. Costello (and presumably Coetzee) opposes 'embodiment' – fullness, the sensation of being – against mechanical, abstract, rational cogitation. If you are to imagine yourself as the other – a person imagining what it would be like to be a bat, a male writer giving voice to a woman, a human imagining intercourse with the divine – then 'embodiment', 'inwardness', is essential. The proposition that 'all humankind is one' needs to be understood not as an abstract concept but as a felt reality. Coetzee puts Costello in the almost untenable position of mounting a reasoned attack on reason. Only by finding a position beyond the rational can we find answers to questions like 'Do we really understand the universe better than animals do?', or 'Are there other modes of being besides what we call the human into which we can enter?' Every episode in the book returns to this opposition of embodiment and reason, experience and abstraction.

Some recantation appears to be going on here (recantation is one of Coetzee's themes): the arguments about the indivisibility of the soul and body are a far cry from the prissy protagonist of *Youth* wanting to study at university in a 'Department of Pure Thought'. Coetzee has always divided his fictions between eloquent, enquiring rationalists and stone-dumb characters, their souls locked in their bodies like animals, such as the girl in *Waiting for the Barbarians*, Michael K, or Friday in *Foe*. Should the novelist, too, move towards the reticence or silence of such characters? Elizabeth Costello is beginning to wonder whether 'writing what one desires . . . is in itself a good thing . . . She no longer believes that storytelling is good in itself.' The ultimate recantation would be to stop writing fiction altogether.[12]

The postscript to Elizabeth Costello is a sequel by Coetzee to Hofmannsthal's famous letter of 1902 from 'Lord Chandos' to Francis Bacon. (Characteristically austere and allusive, Coetzee points us towards the original letter without explaining it.) Hofmannsthal's imaginary seventeenth-century writer is protesting against scientific abstractions, and asking what place there is for poetry in a world of science. He argues that there is a need for a new language, closer to nature. As yet he can find no language for the revelations he gets from ordinary things and animals. This anti-Enlightenment document, a founding text for modernism, inspires Coetzee to write another invented letter, from Chandos's wife to Bacon, speaking of the extreme states of mind of those who feel themselves 'interpenetrated by fellow creatures by the thousands'. There is no language available for this kind of 'embodiment'. Perhaps the only solution, then, as Elizabeth Costello has suggested, is to stop writing fiction. Perhaps Coetzee felt, while he was writing this, that he was going to give up story-telling for ever, and write philosophical essays instead. Judging by this difficult and unforgiving book, that would be a diminishment. But he has always been impossible to predict.

Good Show:
The Life and Works of Angela Thirkell

The essence of Angela Thirkell – English lady novelist, (1890–1961) – is resistance to change. In her clearly demarcated, well-protected fictional province, there are no shocking catastrophes and no unmanageable threats. When one of her heroines, Lilian Stoner, worries that 'everyone she cared for was in danger', she adds: 'Not ferocious danger, but danger of a little pain, a little disillusionment, a little spiritual hardening' (*Before Lunch*, p. 177).[1] Despicable cosmopolitans and foreign intrusions are always rebuffed, eventually, by the solid parochial English virtues of stiff-upper-lippery, good-sportingness, dislike of fuss, sexual unadventurousness and low-key irony. In the post-1939 novels, Hitler and the German bombs and the threat of invasion are treated with the same reductive stoicism.

This made Angela Thirkell's huge body of work extremely popular in its day, and makes Thirkell still an active cult among hundreds of addicted members of the 'Thirkell Circle' and the 'Thirkell Society', whose fan clubs stretch from Wakefield, Rhode Island, to Leeds. Their newsletters fill up with guides to Thirkell's 'Barsetshire', parody letters from her characters, expressions of satisfaction from devoted Thirkellians ('I enjoy her books so much because they are like a breath of fresh air and sanity') and Thirkell quizzes: 'To whom did the following engagement rings belong?' 'What are the addresses of these cats?' 'Can you say where and by whom the following meals were eaten?'[2] To their intense delight, numerous Thirkells were reprinted in the 1990s by American publishers.

They had nearly forty titles to choose from. Once she had got going, Thirkell blithely processed her brand of English stability in novel after novel, giving her readers the security they wanted. This was guaranteed by the 'Barsetshire' setting of most of the books. Her cunning theft from Trollope of place and family names ensured that the emotions unfairly associated with that great novelist, of nostalgia and good cheer, would colour her books from the start. Her novels provided a map of

Barsetshire, complete with funny names like 'Winter Overcotes' and 'Little Misfit'. She gave affectionate, humorous descriptions of a green, idyllic, unspoilt English countryside, though she was not especially interested in nature: 'A stream bordered with kingcups made a gentle bubbling noise like sausages in a frying-pan. Nature, in fact, was at it; and when she chooses, Nature can do it' (*High Rising*, p. 216).

So much for scenery. The real interest is in what is going on inside the little Barsetshire towns – interchangeably Worsted, Nutfield, Skeynes, Harefield. The Jane Austen of the Janeites is the reassuring model here, even more than Trollope. Thirkell's material is the doings of a few country families, the interplay of the aristocrats in the big house with the village gentry, the habits of the country doctor and the vicar, the confrontations of locals and incomers, the comic idiosyncrasies of the devoted servant class. Her pleasure is in the ordinary, the everyday and the recurrent.

> 'Well, I am really going to Mrs Perry's working-party,' said Mrs Belton, 'but I had to post some letters first and somehow it is always very difficult to get along the High Street.'
>
> 'More happens in this High Street than anywhere else in the world,' said Mr Carton. (*The Headmistress*, p. 65)

The buildings in this (usually Georgian) High Street are rock solid and you can see the people going in and out and hear them talking, just like life. (Has no one ever televised Thirkell's novels? They are crying out for it.) She has a keen eye for architecture and décor, and she loves nothing so much as a rural railway station, where she demonstrates a romantic passion for humdrum detail almost amounting to genius:

> The booking-office and entrance hall still contained one of those advertisements, now much valued by connoisseurs, of a storage and removal firm whose vans had the peculiar property of exhibiting one side and one end simultaneously; the station-master had a little office chokingly heated by a stove with a red-hot iron chimney and furnished with yellowing cracking documents impaled on spikes . . . and at the end of the down platform was a tank on four legs from which local engines still obtained their water supply through a leathern hose pipe . . . The platform was sheltered by a corrugated iron roof with a wooden frill

along its front and all the paint was an uncompromising chocolate colour. (*Before Lunch*, pp. 26–7)

She knows that this kind of station is on the way out, but by concentrating so intensely on the detail of what is habitual, she holds change at bay. That sense of willed permanency also comes from the recurrence of characters. Thirkell fans are allowed pleased sighs of recognition as the eccentric Lady Emily or the endearingly vague authoress Laura Morland return in book after book. This doesn't provide the kind of melancholy poignancy which Victoria Glendinning describes in Trollope: 'In life outside books we know some friends, or enemies, intimately for a while, and then the ways part. We hear about them, with a sudden intense curiosity, or see them unexpectedly – older, and changed – years later.'[3] Thirkell's characters are more like neighbours we haven't called on for a few weeks, and when we do, we find them still wittering on about all the same things.

Her 'types' are reassuringly recognisable. There is a revolving cast of noisy young flappers who love to dance, shy young heroines *à la* Fanny Price who need bringing out, and bossy charmless practical girls with a passion for dogs or nursing. There is often a widowed heroine who has to go back and live with her parents, or is looking after children or stepchildren on her own. She is gentle and long-suffering, makes few demands, and tends to give way unless absolutely up against it, when she will show her underlying grit. Most of the married heroines are self-denying, too. Marriage is a matter of patient toleration and humouring of infantile whims:

'Catherine, I needed you, and you were not there,' said Mr Middleton pathetically.

'I was just outside the window and I heard you at once and here I am,' said Mrs Middleton. 'What is it, Jack?'

She laid her hand on her husband's shoulder and he looked up very affectionately.

'I need your advice, Catherine, as always.' (*Before Lunch*, p. 65)

Domination through dependency is usually the husband's role. Other men in the novels are used as comic fodder (ancient eccentric earls, fussy vicars, pompous butlers called Gudgeon), ironic observers (dry

fifty-ish bachelor Oxford dons with a passion for Latin verses),
dependable helpers (no-nonsense doctors, shrewd harassed publishers)
or romantic possibilities. Thirkell's lovers come in two sorts, the
fecklessly undependable with no steady job (always the heroine's first
choice) and the 'safe and comfortable' (*Wild Strawberries*, p. 178). To
ensure that the tribe will survive and that rural Tories may continue to
run the country, it is the solid, securely employable types who get
chosen as mates. Sexual desire is severely played down; the most these
heroines ever get is a manly hug or a firm kiss. Thirkell's blithe lack of
awareness of a language of sexuality is suggested by this delightful scene
in which some of her young people are enjoying a ride, at a village fête,
on a merry-go-round made of wooden animals:

> 'I knew it was you on the ostrich,' she [Lydia] said to Delia . . . 'I say,
> someone's on my cock.'
>
> 'It's only my cousin Hilary,' said Delia. 'He won't mind changing, will
> you, Hilary . . .'
>
> Mr Grant, really quite glad of an excuse to dismount, offered his cock
> to Lydia, who immediately flung a leg over it, explaining that she had
> put on a frock with pleats on purpose, as she always felt sick if she rode
> sideways . . .
>
> . . . 'I know that once Lydia is on her cock nothing will get her off. I
> came here last year . . . and she had thirteen rides.' (*The Brandons*, pp.
> 260–2)

The strongest stirrings of unexamined sexual passion are in the
relationships between mothers and sons. Mother-love is the most
intense thwarted passion in Thirkell. Affectionate, irrepressible small
boys (like Laura Morland's train-obsessed son Tony) turn into rude,
spoilt teenagers, who come home to make a mess, get their washing
done, bully, sulk and condescend. One of her favourite themes is the
humiliation of parents by their children. In *Pomfret Towers*, there is a
popular woman novelist called Hermione Rivers, a ghastly character
whom we long to see put down. But when her revolting artist son Julian
insults her, even his naïvely doting admirer Alice is outraged:

> 'And now,' said Mrs Rivers, 'I really must be going. Julian, are you
> coming with me? I've got the car.'

'Oh, my God, can't one be left alone for one moment,' said Julian to the world at large, following this appeal by a muttered remark about blasted interference.

Mrs Rivers went quite white. She walked over to the window . . . Everyone knew she was struggling not to cry.

Alice was appalled . . . What Julian had done was beyond the bounds. It was true that his mother had been very horrid to him . . . but to be as rude as that to one's mother, before strangers, was . . . the most horrible thing anyone could do. (*Pomfret Towers*, p. 247)

A wiser parent, Mrs Belton, recognises through 'some inner freemasonry of mothers' that when people boast about how close they are to their grown-up sons, 'much of this was willful self-delusion, facade . . . a gallant making the best of things' (*The Headmistress*, p. 211).

Still, not all Thirkell's women are entirely bound by domestic ties. She is certainly no feminist, but her most interesting character-types are women with a skill or a profession. The self-pitying Caroline in *O, These Men, These Men!* is at an exceptionally loose end; most Thirkell heroines are busier than this, though Caroline's predicament does show up the limited possibilities for female activity: ' "I have nothing to do," she said in half humorous self depreciation. "I can't very well do the housekeeping when it isn't my house, and I hate the poor, and I haven't any gifts. I was rather good at having a husband and a home, but I'm out of work now" ' (*O, These Men, These Men!*, p. 82).

At the opposite end of the heroine range is Miss Sparling in *The Headmistress*, handsome, efficient and immensely competent, or Anne Todd in *High Rising*, who combines being a brilliant secretary with stoically attending to her ageing mother. But for both these single women marriage is saved up as a preferable alternative, and even Thirkell's thriving women novelists see what they do as a necessary source of income in lieu of a satisfactory wage-earning husband. This is how Laura Morland introduces herself to the publisher who asks to see her first book:

'You mightn't like it,' said Laura in her deep voice. 'It's not highbrow. I've just got to work, that's all. You see my husband was nothing but an expense to me while he was alive, and naturally he is no help to me now he's dead, though, of course, less expensive, so I thought if I could write

some rather good bad books, it would help with the boys' education.'
(*High Rising*, p. 32).

Thirkell's good bad books can be as sharp and dry as Laura Morland
is there about her dead husband. But mostly they are written to feel like
affable chat. (Her manuscript books show that this came naturally to
her. Page after page is written without a blot or mark or second thought.
Her only hesitations – and these don't look like very taxing decisions –
seem to be over her titles: for *August Folly* (1935) she tried out 'Youth in
Idleness', 'Holiday Romance', 'Chorus of Youth', 'Summer Interlude',
'Idle Hill of Summer', and 'Not Too Serious'.)[4] She had a stupendous
facility for 'not too serious' talk. She is at her best when doing nicely
differentiated kinds of speech – old-style aristocratic curtness, juvenile
slang, affectations of foreignness, absent-minded natter.

> 'I know,' said Mrs Updike sympathetically. 'One always thinks of the
> thing one wants to say just when someone else is talking. I suppose it is
> because something they are saying reminds you of a thing you want to
> say, like suddenly remembering in the Litany that you can't remember
> what it was you meant to remember to remind yourself about. I've got a
> perfect thing about remembering things at the wrong moment.' (*The
> Headmistress*, p. 177)

Mrs Updike would have sympathised with Pepys, suddenly remembering his lost lobsters in the middle of saying grace. This apparently
artless rendition of inconsequentiality comes of paying keen attention to
Jane Austen's Miss Bates or Dickens's Mrs Nickleby. Under the
influence of those writers, more talk goes on than anything else in
Thirkell's novels. True to middle-class English life, there is endless
discussion of arrangements. Visits and calls are the main events. The
novel's scenarios – a fête, a school outing, a country-house weekend, a
pre-war village production of a Greek play (which reads rather as if
Between the Acts had been rewritten by P.G. Wodehouse) – are
dominated by talk, not action. The big crises – a bull getting loose and
encountering a family party in a lane, a minor car crash, a skating
accident – are never very injurious, and are dissipated at once into
gossip and comment.

But talk in Thirkell is often a screen for loneliness or grief. Though a huge amount is said, it hardly ever expresses what people are feeling. 'Again the conversation ran lightly over secret depths' (*The Brandons*, p. 188). One character is praised for seeing through a friend's 'irrelevant flow of conversation': 'Most people don't get beyond the talk. I think she was so unhappy when her husband died that she took to talking as a kind of defence' (*Before Lunch*, p. 74). These characters are skating on thick ice. The worst thing they can possibly do is to make a fuss about their emotions. Better to have a conversation about paper clips when your heart is full (*August Folly*, p. 53). The strongest relationships are those in which 'neither would trespass on the other's reserve, now or ever' (*Before Lunch*, p. 217). It is better to go in only 'ankle deep' – the title of her first novel.

Characters who go on about their feelings or, worse still, express an interest in psychoanalysis, are marked down as ridiculous or 'neurotic'. So these light, witty, easygoing books turn out to be horrifying studies in English repression. And though Thirkell ostensibly admires the stifling of emotions, there are one or two painfully revealing outbursts from women who can only express their feelings in letters, never face to face. Still more disturbingly, in her most autobiographical novel there is a sense that severe depression is struggling to find expression within the straitjacket of social confinement: 'It is my ambition to walk to the edge of the world and the end of time and fall into an absolute nothingness for ever and ever – no feelings, no dreams. But one always has to be back for tea alas! at least at this time of year' (*O, These Men, These Men!*, p. 175).

Where reserve does not figure in Thirkell is in her airing of prejudices, bigotry and class feeling. The point of reading her now in anything other than a spirit of besotted gratification is for her minute exposé of middle-class conservative attitudes in the years leading up to the Second World War. Elizabeth Bowen, herself a much more alienated, critical and disturbing analyst of this period, admired Thirkell for her accuracy, while not sharing all her views: 'If the social historian of the future does not refer to this writer's novels' (Bowen said of *Miss Bunting* in 1944) 'he will not know his business.'[5] Thirkell is aware, up to a point, of her own attitudes, and allows herself dry jokes at the expense of the snobbery of family housekeepers, or the prejudice of old families against a professional woman for not being 'exactly out of the top drawer' (*The Headmistress*, p. 53). But this doesn't inhibit her enthusiasm for her characters' swipes at foreigners or other races: 'They're all right in their place. It's here we don't want them' (*Wild Strawberries*, p. 13). 'If he had a touch of Jewish blood, it was all to the good in his business capacity' (*High Rising*, p. 62). ' "You must have had a black mammy for your fairy-godmother, David ... I don't see how else you got that nigger touch in your voice." "Drinking rum and treacle does it," said David' (*Wild Strawberries*, pp. 87–8). The same treatment is meted out to the under-educated working-classes ('Her mind, if she can be said to have had any, was running on a bottle of bright red liquid nail polish') (*Before Lunch*, p. 37), lesbians ('She thought it had perhaps something to do with drugs') (*August Folly*, p. 210), socialists ('There won't be a single gentleman left in the Cabinet in five years') (*The Headmistress*, p. 38), and the general public: ' "I often wish," said Miss Sparling, permitting herself a quite human spark of hatred, "that one could have No Sniffing carriages on the railway as well as No Smoking." "None of them can read, or want to read; and even if they can, the words convey nothing to them" ' (*The Headmistress*, p. 93).

Such human sparks of hatred increase in frequency during and after the war years. From 1939, the Thirkell novels turned into heroic but bitter comedies of England under pressure. Like Jan Struther's legendary Mrs Miniver, Thirkell is a leading proponent of the British myth of stoic domestic resilience as an answer to German aggression, as voiced by this Major's wife who goes down to her air-raid shelter with her gas mask, ear-plugs, chocolate, cards, meat tablets and knitting. 'I suppose I'm funny that way, but what I say is, Be comfortable while you can, if you see what I mean. To be uncomfortable is just playing into the Nazis' hands – they are *out* to make us uncomfortable, but I say to myself, Now, my girl, you are fighting on the home front' (*Northbridge Rectory*, p. 103).

But the war wasn't only bringing out the best in the village gentry. It was also, to Thirkell's dismay, breaking down the social structure of the country. Her wartime and post-war novels loudly and repeatedly lament the effects of 'all this mixing' (*The Headmistress*, p. 36). By the 1950s, her writing settled into a tone of what Marghanita Laski, reviewing her in 1951, called 'high class grumbling – a sense of grievance that is rapidly overwhelming her sense of fun'. It is extremely ironic to set Thirkell's increasingly defensive portrayal of a white, wealthy and well-behaved village England against the louche bravado of her son Colin

MacInnes – the Genet, or Kerouac, of 1950s West London – here celebrating 'all this mixing' in the Notting Hill landscape of *Absolute Beginners* (1959):

> Give me our London Napoli . . . with its railway scenery, and crescents that were meant to twist elegantly but now look as if they're lurching high, and huge houses too tall for their width cut up into twenty flatlets, and front facades that it never pays anyone to paint, and broken milk bottles *everywhere* scattering the cracked asphalt roads like snow, and cars parked in the streets looking as if they're stolen or abandoned, and a strange number of male urinals tucked away such as you find nowhere else in London, and red curtains, somehow, in all the windows, and diarrhoea-coloured street lighting – man, I tell you, you've only got to be there for a minute to know there's something radically *wrong*.[6]

The stand-off, literary and personal, between Angela Thirkell and her famous bohemian, bisexual son, sums up the conflict between polite middlebrow British culture and what came to subvert it in the libertarian, anti-censorship 1960s. It exposes, too, the painful personal elements in her comic novels. To read Thirkell's life-story after her novels is to see how carefully and self-protectingly she constructed her light, bright, fictional surfaces.

Thirkell belonged to a distinguished, but not an upper-class, artistic family. (Her son wrote scornfully after her death: 'A curious aspect of her portrait of the English gentry is that she was never of them, and didn't really know them.')[7] Her maternal grandfather was Edward Burne-Jones, her father was a professor of poetry at Oxford, J.W. Mackail, her godfather was J.M. Barrie and Kipling was a cousin. Pretty and precocious, Angela was married young, to a singer, James Campbell MacInnes, who turned out to be a violent drunk. They had two sons, and a daughter who died in infancy. Angela ran away from him in 1917 and they divorced when she was twenty-six, publicly and painfully. (The headlines read 'Wife's Life of Horror', etc.) She returned, like many of her heroines, to live with her parents. In 1918 she married again, a handsome Australian engineer and army officer, Captain Thirkell. They went to Australia during the 1920s, where they had a son, Lance. It's been said that Thirkell behaved obnoxiously to the 'natives', and that her husband was an unpleasant disciplinarian who beat his children. (Lance Thirkell, however, denies this.)[8] The marriage foundered, and by the end of the 1930s Thirkell was back in London with her sons. Colin, now sixteen, could not stand her, nor she him. She tried and failed to work at the BBC (always a target for her satire). In 1933, on her forty-third birthday, she published her first novel with Hamish Hamilton, and then, at the end of the year, *High Rising*, with Laura Morland as her idealised self. By her third, *Wild Strawberries* (1934) she had settled for her Barsetshire setting. By the end of the 1930s she had become a hit in America, and was publishing a novel a year, to a chorus of praise. Meanwhile MacInnes became an art student and moved into the London underworld. When he began to write in the 1950s, he made a point of dealing with everything his mother couldn't stomach: urban squalor, racial issues, bisexuality, drugs, anarchy and decadence. He found her novels 'totally revolting', a 'sterile, life-denying vision of our land'.[9] She preserved an unyielding silence about *his* work; when she died in 1961, she had him cut out of her will.

But in this Oedipal war for literary dominance, it may be that Thirkell has the last laugh. There are still plenty of readers happy to lose themselves in her world. She provides a ludicrously gratifying dose of escapist nostalgia, for a Little Old England where all Tories were decent, and no gentleman would ever be a socialist, and rural England didn't have crime, and the countryside was all green (and white), and women wore frocks, and children had nannies, and this kind of novel could go on being written for ever.

Psychic Furniture:
Ellmann's Elizabeth Bowen

Maud Ellmann's brilliant, original and obsessional book on Elizabeth Bowen[1] is dedicated to the memory of her mother, Mary Ellmann, who wrote an inspiring and underrated work of feminist literary criticism in 1968, *Thinking About Women*. Touchingly, Mary Ellmann is frequently cited in her daughter's book, speaking with the quirky perceptiveness that admirers of *Thinking About Women* will remember: on Bowen's late style being full of question marks that 'flutter (like eye-lashes?) across the text'; on *Eva Trout* (1969) as a 'linguistic folly'; or on the 'almost pathological effect' of the 'intussusception of multiple phrases and clauses' in Bowen's style. Maud Ellmann defines 'intussusception' as 'the reception of one part within another', or 'invagination'. The *OED* gives 'to take up within itself or some other part', used, also, figuratively, of 'the taking in of notions or ideas into the mind'. Maud Ellmann seems to have intussuscepted into her own body of work parts of her mother's 'notions or ideas', since her own critique of Bowen has much to do with pathological effects, incarceration, follies and introversion. And although her book is a stringently professional, unconfessional study, which hardly ever says 'I', it admits that in 'prying into Bowen's secrets, we are likely to betray our own'.

Perhaps there is a trace of self-revelation in the emphasis placed here on Bowen's mourning for her own mother, who died when she was thirteen, with whom her relationship was exceptionally intense, and who seems 'to stalk her fiction in many guises and personae'. Ellmann's psychoanalytical and deconstructive study of Bowen doesn't vulgarly reduce her to a set of symptoms or neuroses, but it is certainly 'addicted' (to use one of Ellmann's terms) to themes of mourning, bereavement, living ghosts, 'the resurgence of obliterated histories' and the shadowing of relationships by 'a third presence'. Bowen is not read here, as she has variously been, as a social realist, a Jamesian stylist, a comic satirist of manners, a historian of the Anglo-Irish, a lesbian sensibility, an anti-romantic but passionate analyst of fatal love, a civilian war correspondent, or an elegist for lost innocence. All these aspects are touched on, but Bowen is treated above all as a novelist of the unnerving, 'shaking our assumptions, undermining our defences, and penetrating deep into the haunted chambers of the mind'.

This is a dark, spooky, Poe-like version of Bowen, dominated by crypts, vampires, concealed passageways and entombments. Ellmann is well aware of the Anglo–Irish Gothic lineage, and makes good use of Lefanu and of the Protestant owners of the Big Houses as the Undead. (One of the few things on Bowen she seems not to have read is Paul Muldoon's provocative essay in *To Ireland, I*, suggesting a tincture of old Irish stories and myths in Bowen's work.) But the real interest here is in the psychoanalytical readings that can be brought to bear on such Bowenite scenarios as the return of the phantoms of the past in *The House in Paris* (1935), the addicted cherishing of the dead in *A World of Love* (1955), or the ritual burial of objects in *The Little Girls* (1964). The main psychoanalytical model provided is the theory of 'encryptment' or 'cryptonomy', and I paraphrase Ellmann's account of it as follows.

In 'Mourning and Melancholia', Freud argues that the bereaved ego initially refuses to acknowledge loss, and regresses to fantasies of cannibalism, 'incorporating' the lost object in order to deny its death or disappearance. In the normal course of mourning, the incorporated object is eventually expelled; but when mourning intensifies into melancholia, it is the object that swallows up the ego, driving it to self-destruction. This theory was used by the psychoanalytical theorists Nicolas Abram and Maria Torok as the basis of the idea of 'encryptment'. They argue that there are good and bad ways of internalising the lost object. The good way is through 'introjection', 'whereby the ego articulates its loss in language, creating a verbal substitute for the lost object'. The bad way is through 'the psychic mechanism of incorporation', which 'hollows out a "crypt" within the ego in which the lost object is buried alive'. The 'contents of the crypt' belong to the 'incorporated object', not to the self. That is, this process of encryptment doesn't work as the repression of the unconscious, but as though a 'phantom' or 'ventriloquist' has been incorporated, whereby 'the secrets of the past transport themselves into the present'. 'What haunts are the gaps left in us by the secrets of others.' Abram and Torok conclude that 'the work of mourning can begin only when the crypt is shattered and its secrets are released'. Ellmann adds to this her own term, 'incubism' (Joyce's word for the style of the Hades/cemetery episode in *Ulysses*), from which she extrapolates box in, incubate and incubus: 'the word brings together ideas of sleep, death, and sexuality'. She sees the process of 'psychic incubism or encryptment, in which the lost object is entombed alive within the ego', and the 'disentombing' of secrets, as the major activity of Bowen's novels.

Along the way, Ellmann tries on some other Freudian models. Freud's reading of the three caskets in *The Merchant of Venice* as 'the three forms taken by the mother in the course of a man's life', the third being Mother Earth, or death, is applied to the three letters which affect Leopold in *The House in Paris*. The last 'casket' is the envelope which should contain his absent mother's letter, but is empty. That third, empty envelope (from which Leopold invents the letter his mother might have written, one of the most peculiarly moving episodes in all of Bowen's fiction) is like a 'core of silence', or a 'raided tomb'. In another example, Freud's argument in *Three Essays on the Theory of Sexuality* that 'the finding of an object of desire is always a re-finding of an object previously lost' is invoked when the anguished Portia, in *The Death of the Heart* (1938), has to learn that all love is form of plagiarism. 'Experience means nothing till it repeats itself', the disabused author tells us drily, and 'to fall in love is to succumb to this compulsion to repeat'. This, Ellmann concludes, is 'the death of the heart'.

Ellmann also makes use of Freud's theories of triangular structures of desire (for instance in *Jokes and their Relation to the Unconscious*, or in his account of the Oedipal triangle) in relation to the repeatedly triangular structure of Bowen's plots. Her couples, Ellmann observes, are always haunted by a 'mysterious third person', an uninvited guest. 'It takes three to make two' – or, in Lacan's terms, which Ellmann can't resist, there's 'an intermixing of otherness' in every structure. In an early story called 'The Shadowy Third', a married couple are haunted, as in *Rebecca*, by the husband's dead first wife. In *The House in Paris*, the lovers play out their parts under the baleful eye of Madame Fisher. In *The Heat of the Day* (1949), the war – 'the incursion of history into private life', in Ellmann's phrase – is the third presence at the lovers' table. 'No,' Bowen tells us, 'there is no such thing as being alone together'.

Often there is more than one shadowy presence. Ellmann is fascinated by Bowen's 'sexual geometry', what she stylishly calls the 'hectic permutations' of her erotic plots, with four, five, even six additional figures intruding on or interfering with the 'circuit of desire'. This is a much more subtle and interesting way of dealing with the sexual ramifications and deviations in Bowen, which often involve a young girl's obsession with an older woman, than to pin them all down as lesbian triangles or rivalries, as some critics have recently tended to do. 'Outing the heroine is not the point', Ellmann says, 'for Bowen is more concerned with number than with gender'.

These Freudian deconstructions of Bowen are extremely illuminating about her obsessions, and provide a consistent and useful explanation for the Bowen plots: children traumatised by adult secrets, haunted houses, paralysed lovers, troubling irruptions of the past into the present. (I wish she had given herself more space for Bowen's stories: her methods would be interesting for stories like 'Her Table Spread', 'The Tommy Crans', 'Foothold' or 'The Disinherited'.) Her readings are, it must be said, rather repetitive ('encryptment' is explained at least four times) and run the risk of making all the novels sound the same, even though Ellmann praises, rightly, 'the infinite variety of stories that Bowen fashions out of the limited repertoire of her addictions'. At times I felt that Bowen's comedy, her stylishness, her worldliness, were being buried alive; at times I felt a little entombed myself. Ellmann's language is at its least exciting when at its most schematic: 'In Bowen's fiction, the fourth woman represents both supplement and lack: she is lacking in the sense that she withdraws from the erotic field of action, and by doing so inaugurates the chain of substitutions that ensured the circulation of desire . . .' When she is telling us about 'the displacement of intersubjective guilt . . . onto the compulsive repetition of the signifier', there is a sense of duty being done. But she doesn't always write like that. When she breaks free from abstraction and formulae, and plunges into things and places, the results are much more exciting. Take tennis balls, for example. In *The Last September* (1929), set in County Cork during the Troubles, the net around the tennis court, meant to keep the balls from going into the shrubbery, is full of holes. Ellmann comments:

> The defences of the Big House are comparably frayed. But the same net
> has malfunctioned for so long that many of the balls recovered date back

to before the Great War. Lost balls come to signify lost gumption: a ball missing since 1906 reminds a guest of his failure to emigrate to Canada.

The satirical son of the house imagines 'a small resurrection day, an intimate thing-y one, when the woods should give up their tennis balls and the bundles of hay their needles'. Bowen's own 'meticulous inventories of household objects', Ellmann notes cunningly, similarly perform 'an "intimate thing-y" resurrection in her prose'. She writes wonderfully about the psychic life of objects in Bowen, her 'mania for things'. Her 'objects have neuroses', they 'masquerade as people'. They are like body parts. Objects in Bowen can be alarmingly hallucinatory, surreal and, above all, watchful. What we look at looks back at us, often (Ellmann's joke) in anger. 'Every house has a watchful face; every car a gamut of anxieties.' In an empty bedroom of *The Last September*, 'two armchairs faced round intently into the empty grate'; when one of the occupants sits down, 'creaks ran through the wicker, discussing him'. She is very strong on Bowen's 'malignant' dark houses, full of past, like crypts, houses that can drive you mad (like the Big Houses with their isolated, fantasising owners), characters 'shaped by rooms and corridors, doors and windows, arches and columns'. She gives a lot of house-room to Bowen's ominous furniture, which has its own morality (one of her characters speaks of people 'living under the compulsion of their furniture'), haunting its owners – most insistently in *The Death of the Heart* – with reminders of the past. The loss of furniture, of things, intensely evoked by Bowen in her wartime stories and in *The Heat of the Day*, releases people into disinherited, disembodied nothingness: a state partly terrifying and partly exhilarating, described by Ellmann as 'an intoxicating day-dream of weightlessness'.

Bowen animates new technology with as much alarming energy as she does old furniture. Ellmann is gripped by her fascination with communication systems, timetables and railway stations, travel agencies, aeroplanes and all forms of transport (the faster the better), radios and gramophones and tape-recorders, switchboards, telegraphs and tele-phones. (Bowen would surely have leaped at answerphones, email and the web as fictional materials.) Fetishised telephones, 'intruding into domestic space', reached for in the night like lovers, 'a telephone which after its brief good time, had to go back on the shelf', a woman who is surprised when the telephone rings to find that she still exists – in these examples the machine becomes humanised, the humans mechanised. Bowen famously said of her characters that they were 'perpetually in transit'. Caught up in transport or communication networks, they seem to Ellmann out of control, turned into automata: 'Bowen's characters have usually gone too far to change their minds; in fact they often seem devoid of minds to change.' They don't exactly think or choose, they are spun about and driven forward by the 'fatal momentum' of their narratives. Emmeline, frantically driving in *To the North* (1932), is driven 'by the car's dizzy terror of its driver'.

Ellmann describes a modern condition of 'nervousness' in Bowen's books, in which her characters, 'enmeshed in transport networks', 'swing between the jitters and the doldrums'. The drive is always towards nothingness: silence, self-destruction, catastrophe, instability. This drastic and apocalyptic view of what are also highly stylish, controlled and socialised novels, turns Bowen firmly into a modernist. Ellmann knows that this is difficult positioning: Bowen 'wavers on the boundary between classic realism and modernist experimentation'. But she wants to place her alongside, and as the equal of, Joyce and Beckett, Eliot and Woolf. (Indeed she thinks Bowen a better novelist than Woolf.) And she also wants to point her beyond modernism, as a precursor of postmodernism, a writer moving increasingly towards disjunction and disjointedness, fissures and friction, self-reflexiveness, 'collisions between genres', and the disruption of plot and character. 'The term "dislocation" recurs like a chronic symptom throughout Bowen's work'.

All this directs us towards *Eva Trout* (1969), Bowen's last novel, seen here as the culmination of her work. Ellmann (like Andrew Bennett and Nicholas Royle in *Elizabeth Bowen and the Dissolution of the Novel* (1994), which takes Bowen much further away from the real world into dreams, trances and hauntings) thinks it is her greatest novel; and this difficult and troubling book, written in the late 1960s, does now seem to be coming into its own. The chaotic, reckless quest for home and love of the gargantuan, dangerously innocent, alien and inarticulate Eva, the weird and jumpy collection of figments who surround her, the preposterousness of the plot she inhabits, which operates without any reassuring 'voice-over' through kaleidoscopic scenes, literary pastiche and cinematic spectacle, reads to Ellmann like 'a new kind of novel for an age in which intention is irrelevant, an age in which the world can be destroyed by accident'. I continue to find *Eva Trout* an almost unbearable fiasco, and passionately to prefer the earlier novels and stories;[2] but I have learned a great deal from Maud Ellmann's championing of it. Her book makes a powerful intervention in the still-shifting reputation of this great writer, whose reception since her death thirty years ago has been going through remarkable developments, perhaps more dramatic than any other mid-twentieth-century novelist's. This book marks an important point in those developments. It is a bold, innovative, challenging study, which should be very influential.

The Man from God Knows Where:
Remembering Brian Moore

The central character of what, unexpectedly and terribly sadly, turned out to be the last novel of Brian Moore (1921–1999), was a great nineteenth-century French magician, Henri Lambert. Lambert was enlisted by the Emperor Napoleon III to use his skills in the service of the French empire. He was sent to Algeria to impress the marabouts and their Arab followers with the superior magical powers of the French, and thereby to facilitate the subjugation of the French colony. In the course of the novel, Lambert's amazing feats of conjuring are described with the apparent simplicity and self-concealing deftness for which Brian Moore's work is so much admired. As we see the magician rehearsing and rehearsing every detail of his amazing tricks, so that hard labour will produce an appearance of the utmost control and seeming ease, you might catch the sound of the novelist saying to himself, 'Lambert, c'est moi.' Certainly when Moore came across the true story – in a Flaubert letter – of the magician Houdin (from whom 'Houdini' took his name) he recognised it as one of 'his' subjects, something he knew he could do something with.

Like *Black Robe* (1983), *The Magician's Wife* (1997) involves a mutually bewildering clash of cultures and beliefs between an incoming or colonising power and a native people. Like *Black Robe* it questions the basis of any religion, when viewed by an alien eye. And, also very characteristically, *The Magician's Wife* distances us from the central, driven figure in the story and gives him to us only through the eyes of an observer. That's how we approach the charismatic people's leader in *No Other Life* (1993), Moore's Haiti novel, or the hopelessly obsessed lover in *The Temptation of Eileen Hughes* (1981), one of his finest books. Something remains inscrutable and mysterious about these distanced characters. Moore called it his 'Gatsby method'.

There was something of that quality about Brian Moore too, even though he was not a 'difficult' or a 'highbrow' novelist. (Though a passionate admirer of Joyce, he couldn't stand Henry James or Virginia

Woolf – I used to tease him about the fact that there wasn't a single book by Woolf in *either* of his houses.) He had a horror of anything that felt to him like narcissism or affectation. He was a great debunker and deflator of pretentiousness, and many of his answers in interviews are prefaced by 'I don't want this to sound pompous'. It was his great quality and strength as a writer, but also what prevented him from being as famous as he deserved, that he was always disappearing into his books, that he never wrote the same book twice, that he had a horror of repeating himself, and that he was extremely hard to pigeon-hole. In his last interview, which was with me, broadcast on Radio 3 in October 1998, he said that his ideal reader was someone who would not think, I am reading another novel by Brian Moore, but would only be gripped and absorbed by that particular story, without reference to any earlier work. He wanted to be an invisible man.

Though his own history deeply informed his work, as it must any writer's, he did not want to write autobiographical fiction. There are no temperature charts of his own emotions in his work, no self-analysis or confessions, nothing like Philip Roth's *My Life as a Man* or Edmund White's *A Boy's Own Story*. His own experiences – his Catholic Belfast childhood and schooling, his wartime witness (of the Allied beachhead at Anzio, the invasion of southern France, the Russian retreat and the trials at Auschwitz), his flight from Ireland to Canada, the upheavals in his personal life before his long second marriage to Jean Denney, his move to California, his work in Hollywood – all these things came into his work, but not as displays of personal feeling. He has never been the hero of his own tale. For example, twice in his life he narrowly escaped death. In 1953, he was swimming in a lake near Montreal when a motorboat smashed into him; he had six skull fractures and took six months to recover. He was writing his first novel, *The Lonely Passion of Judith Hearne* (1956), at the time; the accident made him aware, he once told me, that 'I did not have unlimited time to do the writing I wanted to do.' Novels followed, for the rest of his life, at an average rate of one every two years. Then, in 1976, in Dublin, he was in intensive care for three weeks after an operation, which went wrong, for a duodenal ulcer. His luck as Lazarus, risen from the dead, provides the plot of *Cold Heaven* (1983), but not in autobiographical form.

Increasingly, in 'late' Moore – from *Black Robe* onwards – he chose his subjects from his reading, from historical or news stories he came across, taken from whatever part of the world fired his imagination. (As for many Irish writers, this would often be France.) The struggle between the Catholic Church and the Communist regime in Eastern Europe in *The Colour of Blood* (1987); the prescient story of Father Aristide, Haiti's peasant boy turned populist leader and overthrown by an American-backed military junta, in *No Other Life*; the troubles in Belfast in *Lies of Silence* (1990); the Church's complicity with Nazism in occupied France in *The Statement* (1996); the colonisation of Algeria in *The Magician's Wife* – in his treatment of these events, he was always interested and moved by the plight of the ordinary people who were caught up in the historical moment and made to suffer. He was a more political novelist than has perhaps been recognised. As his subjects became more historical and weighty, his style became increasingly lean, swift and tight. After these big subjects, he could hardly – as he said ruefully – return to writing novels about marriage and adultery, certainly not about his personal life. Intriguingly, the book he was working on when he died was about the later life of Rimbaud, what happened to him after he disappeared into obscurity. (I thought at his death about something he said to me in an interview some years ago, joking furiously: 'I've a terror of dying while I'm working on something. I think – some other bastard will finish it, the way they do!')

One of his best disguises, and one of the finest things about his work, is his ventriloquising of a woman's voice. There aren't many male writers who do this comparably well – Flaubert, Chekhov, Barnes, Trevor, come to mind. From his first to his last novel, Moore had an extraordinary, uncanny ability to imagine his way into the skin and mind and emotions and sexuality of his women characters. This begins with the sad frustrations of his Belfast spinster Judith Hearne and ends with Emmeline Lambert, the magician's wife who learns to think and act for herself. And he has done this again and again: with the startling sexual intimacy and truthfulness of *The Doctor's Wife* (1976); with Marie Davenport, the woman fighting off the possibility of believing in miracles in *Cold Heaven*; with the naïve, provincial Irish shopgirl, in London for the first time, who has aroused, quite unwittingly, a hopeless and absolute passion quite incongruous to its object, in *The Temptation of Eileen Hughes*, and with Mary Dunne, the beautiful three-times married Canadian woman, falling to bits on one day in New York as her past floods back at her and she battles with suicidal depression – what she calls 'the dooms':

> I hate being a woman, I hate this sickening female role playing. I mean the silly degradation of playing pander and whore in the presentation of my face and figure in a man's world. I sweat with shame when I think of the uncounted hours of poking about in dress shops, the Narcissus hours in front of mirrors, the bovine hours under hair driers and for what? So that men will say in the street, 'I want to fuck you, baby,' so that men will marry me and *keep* me and let's not go into that if I don't want the dooms in spades. (*I Am Mary Dunne*, 1968)

A male writer disguised as a woman, an Irishman become a Canadian, an agnostic from a Catholic family, a Canadian living in California, a stylist of magicianly skills who wants to be invisible: this is a writer extremely hard to categorise. When the BBC titled a 'Bookmark' profile of him, 'The Man from God Knows Where', he was much amused. I notice that the emphasis in the tributes to him after he died was on his Irishness; no doubt in the Canadian obituaries, which I didn't see, he was being claimed for Canada. Predictable 'hooks' have been found for him. (This always irritated him, like the frequent references to his work as 'cinematic', linked to his brief stint as a Hollywood screenwriter, working with Hitchcock on *Torn Curtain*. As he pointed out, narratives told inside a character's mind, as in most of his books, are extremely hard to translate to the screen – as the 2004 film of *The Statement* shows.)

And if he wasn't cinematic, he was 'Greeneian'. Since he was praised by Graham Greene, and since he wrote about Catholics who lose their faith (most brilliantly in *Catholics* (1972) and *Black Robe*), this tag seems to fit. But the comparison, though flattering, came to bore him, and doesn't really get us far. Moore is not writing about guilt and remorse in the shadowy hinterland of lost virtue, but much more about sudden crises of choice and responsibility, moments when the main character, in the thick of events, suddenly has to reconsider the whole shape and meaning of their life, but without much time for Greeneian introspection. I think of Greene as much the more recognisable, self-echoing writer, compared with the breathtaking prestidigitation and unpredictability of this novelist, who could write a painfully burdened, thickly emotional narrative such as *An Answer from Limbo* (1962), *and* conjure up the strange and brilliant surreal phantasmagoria of *The Great Victorian Collection* (1975), *and* plunge us into the fast, terrifying, gripping pace of *The Colour of Blood*.

It is too easy, too, to pin him down as a writer of lost faith. One obituarist (*Daily Telegraph*, 12 January 1999) said that 'his whole career as a writer had been moulded by an unsuccessful flight from religion'. This seems to me misleading (and suggests that everything he did was somehow a failure). Moore used religious faith in his work, which he lost at an early age, not as a personal dilemma, but as a powerful metaphor. The characters who are his heroes are those who accept that there is 'no other life'.

Moore's Irishness is a complex matter, too. Though he never gets away from Irish subjects and themes, either directly or indirectly, Irishness lay under layers of world-travelled, secular, international interests. 'In most of my books', he said, 'Ireland is part of the actual or remembered landscape'. But he was never a local writer in the manner of John McGahern, or the early Edna O'Brien. Seamus Heaney wrote of this eloquently in his poem for Brian Moore, 'Remembering Malibu', which hangs framed in the corridor of Moore's Malibu house. Heaney's poem compares the 'abstract sands' and 'early Mondrian' of the Pacific coast's dune-scape to the stormy Atlantic Irish shore, and asks what it would mean to 'rear and kick and cast that shoe' and make your life's choices 'beside that other western sea', 'far, far' from home. Moore agreed with Heaney that there was a conflict in his work between the 'sacro-world' of Catholic Northern Ireland and the weightless, profane spaces of the secular modern world.

I will always remember Brian with Jean, his inseparable companion, in that Malibu house, all stone and wood and great windows and the sound of the sea, looking down from the stone terrace of tropical plants over the breakers and whales and surfers of the Pacific, walking along the shore of the ocean. The house they had built in Nova Scotia, more recently, faced the Atlantic, and seemed to echo the Malibu house, though it was plainer. It was as though they had decided to go together as far to the edges of the continent as they could get. Certainly this was not a reclusive writer. Brian Moore was a very convivial man who travelled widely, knew a remarkable range of people, gossiped wickedly, and was full of stories and knowledge, curiosity and silly jokes. He was generously affectionate, keenly interested and interesting, very funny, and also – as the evenings went on – ruthless, scathing and outrageous. He loved good talk, argument, company and worldly pleasures. All the same, I think of him most going away to his study – looking out, in both houses, over the ocean – to do his work. In that last interview with me, just after his seventy-seventh birthday, he said that he had never been certain of why he was here, of the meaning of his life, and that writing was a necessary obsession to him because only there could he continue to ask – not answer – these questions. Only in his study, working quietly, with the novel 'going along', could he forget himself and everyone he knew and become 'invisible'; and that, he said, was joy.

How to End It All

Most (though not all) biographies are about the dead. Most biographers, therefore, have to decide how to deal with the death of their subject. But why 'deal with'? Doesn't biography just state the facts? No, because there is a great deal invested, always, in the death of the subject, in terms of how the death relates to the life, how the subject behaves at their death, and how, if at all, the death can be interpreted. There are also tricky questions for the biographer about tone of voice at the moment of the subject's death. If you are coming to the end of a life you've spent a lot of time with, you will tend to be moved – if only by relief. Do you let these emotions flood the page, hoping they will flood the reader too? Do you restrain your emotions and give the death clinically? If you are writing the life of a writer, do you allow yourself to describe their death as they might have done it, in their fictions or poetry? Do you, in the tone you choose, and also in matters of structure and interpretation, try to give the death meaning and derive from it some sense of a resolution of the life?

The answers to these questions will depend very much on when, and in what cultural context, the *Life* is being written. One model for changing attitudes to death, suggestive and influential, if not entirely convincing, was provided by the French social historian Philippe Ariès's books *Western Attitudes towards Death* (1976) and *The Hour of Our Death* (1981), with sources drawn mainly from French Catholic culture. Ariès famously proposed four broad historical phases of attitudes towards death.

In the first, in the early medieval period – his evidence comes from French Romances of the tenth, eleventh and twelfth centuries – there was what he calls 'tame or tamed death'. 'Death was a ritual organised by the dying person himself.' It was witnessed by family, friends and neighbours, and was dealt with as a communal ceremony expressing 'resignation to the collective destiny of the species'. In the second, in the later medieval period, the dying person is still presiding over the event, but the rise of individualism undermines the calm acceptance of death.

Ariès calls this 'the death of the self' ('la mort de soi'), in which there is an increasingly close relationship between 'death and the biography of each individual life'. This way of thinking about death, Ariès argues, dominated until the eighteenth century, when a third phase takes over, characterised by an idea of 'la mort de toi', the death of the other, or 'the beautiful death'. A romantic, emotional, even erotic, rhetoric of loss and bereavement makes itself felt on tombstones and in epitaphs. More crying and fainting went on at deathbeds, and 'the cult of memory' developed.[1] In the fourth phase, which Ariès identifies as post-industrial and contemporaneous, death is made 'invisible', taboo, hushed up, 'unnameable', hidden away in hospitals. The dying are no longer told that they are dying, and so cannot prepare their farewells. 'She didn't even say goodbye to us,' Ariès quotes a son saying at the bedside of his mother. Excessive mourning is felt to be morbid, children are protected from deathbed scenes, and it becomes indecent to let someone die in public.[2]

Many historians of social rituals of death have quarrelled with Ariès's broad-brush historical divisions.[3] Pat Jalland notes that the Evangelical model of the 'good death' is more apt for Protestant nineteenth-century England than Ariès's 'beautiful death', and was in any case in decline by the end of the century. John Wolffe argues that there was, in fact, 'no normative or ideal model' for deathbed behaviour in Britain in the nineteenth century. Douglas Davies, in *Death, Ritual and Belief*, is suspicious of Ariès's sweeping generalisation. But he does agree that the idea of how much 'control' we can have over our own deathbeds has always been a crucial part of social and cultural attitudes to dying.[4]

We would now want to add a contemporaneous phase to Ariès's periods of death, a phase in which the deaths of ordinary people are made public. This phase or moment has been made all too memorable for us by the events of 11 September 2001, since we have all shared the last words, most often words of love, which the victims of the attack spoke on their phones from the twin towers and from the hijacked planes. And we have become 'used', if used is the word to use, to hearing the last words of pilots in air crashes relayed from black box readings; we all remember reading the letter left for his loved one by a young Russian seaman perishing in the Kursk submarine. British readers in the 1990s shared the banal, everyday 'dying' experiences of journalists such as Ruth Picardie or John Diamond, whose publicly recorded stages of dying from cancer may have provided consolation to others in similar situations.

The search for exemplary deaths has a very long history. Now we find it in ordinary people's lives, not in saints' or great men's lives. But our continuing interest in exemplary deaths, 'good deaths', goes back to medieval stories of 'holy living and holy dying', and to the handbooks for exemplary deaths, the *ars moriendi* of the fifteenth century. The *Arte and Crafte to Know Well to Dye* of 1490 included instruction such as: 'To die well is to die gladly'. The exemplary death of a great man continues to impress, even when the death is not 'holy'. In the eighteenth century, both Boswell and the economist Adam Smith gave accounts of the death of the philosopher David Hume. The firm-minded Hume, renowned for his atheism, refused all false consolation on his deathbed in 1776 ('Your hopes are groundless,' he said to Adam Smith). Questioned anxiously by Boswell about immortality at their last meeting, Hume good-humouredly maintained his sceptical position: 'I asked him if the thought of Annihilation never gave him any uneasiness. He said not the least; no more than the thought that he had not been, as Lucretius observes.' Hume's death as a sceptic is rendered, both by Smith and Boswell, as a heroic, even saintly death. (Boswell and Johnson argued over it: Johnson's opinion was that Hume was lying if he said he didn't fear death.)[5]

In nineteenth-century Evangelical England, the secular *Lives* of great men – statesmen, leaders, educationalists, politicians – were often coloured by features inherited from saints' lives or classical models. In such narratives death must be heroic, must provide a lesson; a 'good death' is of the utmost importance, and 'last words' needed to be witnessed and reported. John Wolffe, in his book on the subject, *Great Deaths*, describes the widespread interest in the last moments of royalty and public figures. Disraeli's death in 1881 was a focus of 'sustained public interest': people wanted to know if it was 'a close worthy of the wonderful life'. Gladstone's death in 1898, a slow and horribly painful death from cancer of the mouth, was sanitised in public accounts to show 'how a Christian should die'. John Morley wrote an idealised deathbed scene in his *Life* of Gladstone of 1904, responding to Gladstone's daughter's plea that his suffering should not be publicly aired.[6] And there are many more examples of saintly nineteenth-century deaths. One is in Dean Stanley's 1844 *Life* of his legendary teacher Thomas Arnold, headmaster of Rugby. The book ends with a tremendously pious and prolonged deathbed scene, in which Dr Arnold, dying of a heart attack at the age of forty-seven with his family around him, thanks God for giving him this pain which is so good for him. Another is in Robert Southey's *Life of Nelson* (1832), a book which was intended as 'a manual for the young sailor, which he may carry about with him, till he has treasured up the example in his memory and his heart'. (It was published in a handy pocket-size edition for that purpose – no doubt to be whipped out on board ship in the middle of a battle or a thunderstorm to see what Nelson would have done in such circumstances.) Nelson's death in battle is a saint's death which gives the conclusive meaning to his life. His dying words on deck, barely discernible to the listeners, were, not 'Kiss me Hardy', but, 'Thank God I have done my duty ... God and my country.' Nelson, the author concludes, provides 'a name and an example, which are at this hour inspiring thousands of the youth of England, a name which is our pride, and an example which will continue to be our sword and shield'.[7]

Out of that tradition of exemplary deaths comes the curious vogue for anthologies of death, which persisted into the twentieth century. Victorian Evangelical tracts published consoling last words, some more elevated than others; Pat Jalland quotes *Clear Shining Light*, an 1880s memoir of the Evangelical Caroline Leakey, whose last words were: 'Farewell, dear drawing-room, you have long been devoted to God.'[8] Anthologies of the literature of death, like *The Art of Dying* (1930), or D.J. Enright's *Oxford Book of Death* (1983)[9] include, or are made up of, selections of famous last words. D.J. Enright is particularly keen on the 'last words' which sum up a person's work or seem to 'predicate a continuity of occupation between this life and the next', like Gainsborough's 'We are all going to heaven, and Van Dyck is of the company' (1788), Beethoven's 'I shall hear in Heaven' (1827), Adam Smith's 'I believe we must adjourn this meeting to some other place' (1790), or Turner's 'The Sun is God' (1851). Enright observes that we have become more cynical about legendary, over-apposite last words, which may well have been invented or embellished by a ghost-writer, though, as he says, it is still nice to think that Andrew Bradford, an eighteenth-century Philadelphian newspaper publisher, did cry on his deathbed, 'Oh Lord, forgive the errata!' And, echoing Ariès, he notes that the hospitalisation and, very often, the sedation of the dying have led to the 'dying out' of Last Words as an institution.[10]

Janet Malcolm, much of whose work attacks biographical inventions and intrusions, gives a sardonic warning in *Reading Chekhov* (2003) of how our fascination with last words can lead to myth-making and inaccuracy. Chekhov's death, she writes, 'is one of the great set pieces of literary history'. It is recorded in an account written by his wife, Olga Knipper, four years after the death, which took place on 21 July 1904. The Chekhovs were in a German hotel. The dying Chekhov woke up in the night and asked for a doctor. Olga asked a Russian student, Rabeneck, who was in the hotel, to go for the doctor. The doctor came, and cradled Chekhov in his arms. Chekhov said 'Ich sterbe' ('I am dying'). The doctor gave him an injection of camphor, and ordered champagne. Olga writes:

> Anton took a full glass, examined it, smiled at me, and said: 'It's a long time since I drank champagne.' He drained it, lay quietly on his left side, and I just had time to run to him and lean across the bed, and call to him, but he had stopped breathing and was sleeping peacefully as a child.

Later, in 1922, Olga embellished the account, adding a moth flying into the room after the death, the cork bursting out of the champagne bottle, an expression of serenity on the dead man's face, and the waking song of the birds. The student Rabeneck also wrote an account, fifty-four years after the death, which adds more details: the doctor sending him for oxygen, a 'strange sound coming from Chekhov's throat', and the doctor asking Rabeneck to tell Olga that Chekhov is dead. The doctor also left a (second-hand) report, which had Chekhov saying 'Soon, doctor, I am going to die', and his reaction to the doctor saying he will send for oxygen: 'Before they brought the oxygen, I would be dead.' Another second-hand account, from a Russian journalist called Iollos, who interviewed Olga on the day of Chekhov's death, added still more details. Chekhov was raving, saying something about a sailor, something about the Japanese. Then, Olga was putting an ice-pack on Chekhov's chest, and he said with a sad smile: 'You don't put ice on an empty heart.' Iollos says that Chekhov's last words were 'Ich sterbe': nothing about the champagne.

Malcolm goes on to look at how biographers of Chekhov have treated their sources, and finds all kinds of inventions and elaborations, for instance in David Magarshack's *Anton Chekhov: A Life* (1952):

> Chekhov said with a smile, 'It's a long time since I drank champagne.' He had a few sips and fell back on the pillow. Soon he began to ramble. 'Has the sailor gone? Which sailor?' He was apparently thinking of the Russo-Japanese war . . . This went on for several minutes. His last words were 'I'm dying'; then in a very low voice to the doctor in German: 'Ich sterbe' . . . Suddenly, without uttering a sound, he fell sideways. He was dead. His face looked very young . . .

Other examples, listed by Malcolm – from lives of Chekhov by Princess Toumanova (1937), Daniel Gilles (1967), Henri Troyat (1984), Irene Nemirovsky (1950), V.S. Pritchett (1988), Donald Rayfield (1997) and Philip Callow (1998) – add all kinds of extras. 'Don't put ice on an empty heart' gets turned into 'Don't put ice on an empty stomach'. Chekhov's eyes glitter, the moth flies round the room while he is dying, the sailor becomes his nephew, or a character in the story 'Ward 6'. Philip Callow, in particular, splashes on the details, for instance about the champagne:

> The doctor . . . went to the telephone in the alcove and ordered a bottle of the hotel's best champagne. He was asked how many glasses. 'Three,' he shouted, 'and hurry, d'you hear?'

And the champagne arrives with cut-crystal glasses carried by 'a sleepy young porter'. Reading this, Malcolm suddenly remembered a story she had read by Raymond Carver, called 'Errand', in the 1989 collection *Where I'm Calling From*, which makes up the details of Chekhov's death, just as Philip Callow gives them. She is bewildered – and offended – by all these fictionalisations. But what her fascinating comparative account makes clear is that all biographers want to make as much as possible of the ending of the life. It matters to us, as Chekhov's readers, whether his last words really were (as we would like them to be), 'It's a long time since I drank champagne.'[11]

We still have a great preoccupation with endings, and when I read

European or Anglo-American biographies, of the past and of the present, it seems to me that, for all Ariès's neat division into four 'phases' of thinking about death, there is, particularly in post-nineteenth-century biography, a confused and complicated mixture of ideas about how dying relates to a life-story. But why should the manner of the death and the explanations for the death of the subject still matter so much? Why should there still be so much pressure on the biographer to read the whole life of the subject in terms of the death (especially if that death is a suicide)? The Christian tradition, which has had a profound bearing on the history of Western biography, and which explains our lasting curiosity about 'last words', still makes us want the death to complete the meaning of the life. The desire reflects, in Frank Kermode's phrase in *The Sense of an Ending*, 'our deep need for intelligible Ends'.[12] We prefer not to read the subject's death, as perhaps it should be read, as without content, merely contingent, just the next fact in a series of facts: to 'de-dramatise it', as Edmund White quotes Genet as saying.[13] We feel we must stage it and interpret it, or over-interpret it. In Julian Barnes's novel *Flaubert's Parrot*, an obscure critic called Edmund Ledoux is mocked for devising an influential legend that Flaubert committed suicide, thereby ignoring the literary evidence 'of a man whose stoicism runs as deep as his pessimism':

> Ledoux's account of the suicide goes like this: Flaubert *hanged himself in his bath*. I suppose it's more plausible than saying that he electrocuted himself with sleeping pills; but really . . . What happened was this. Flaubert got up, took a hot bath, had an apoplectic fit, and stumbled to a sofa in his study; there he was found expiring by the doctor who later issued the death certificate. That's what happened. End of story. Flaubert's earliest biographer talked to the doctor concerned and that's that. Ledoux's version requires the following chain of events: Flaubert got into his hot bath, hanged himself in some as yet unexplained fashion, then climbed out, hid the rope, staggered to his study, collapsed on the sofa and, when the doctor arrived, managed to die while feigning the symptoms of an apoplectic fit. Really, it's too ridiculous.[14]

'That's what happened'; 'End of story'; 'that's that' – death as just a fact – is wittily set against the 'ridiculous' over-interpretation of M. Ledoux. But we have still not reached a point, in the writing and reading of life-stories, where 'end of story' is a neutral or simple moment. There are conflicting ways of thinking about death, mixed together in biographers' choices about how to end it all.

In Lytton Strachey's early twentieth-century biographical writing, which set out to debunk the kind of exemplary hagiography that we find in Stanley's *Life of Arnold* (Strachey's own sketch of Arnold in *Eminent Victorians* (1918) marks the difference), things are not as clear-cut, when it comes to dying, as Strachey might have wanted them to be. Here is his 1921 account of the death of Queen Victoria:

> She herself, as she lay blind and silent, seemed to those who watched her to be divested of all thinking – to have glided already, unawares, into oblivion. Yet, perhaps, in the secret chambers of consciousness, she had her thoughts, too. Perhaps her fading mind called up once more the shadows of the past to float before it, and retraced, for the last time, the vanished visions of that long history – passing back and back, through the cloud of years to older and ever older memories – to the spring woods at Osborne, so full of primroses for Lord Beaconsfield – to Lord Palmerston's queer clothes and high demeanour, and Albert's face under the green lamp, and Albert's first stag at Balmoral, and Albert in his blue and silver uniform . . . and Lord M dreaming at Windsor with the rooks cawing in the elm-trees . . . and her mother's features sweeping down towards her, and a great old repeater-watch of her father's in its tortoise-shell case, and a yellow rug, and some friendly flounces of sprigged muslin, and the trees and the grass at Kensington.[15]

And that's how his book ends. Strachey is trying out a new psychoanalytical model on the venerable Queen of England which must, at the time (only twenty years after her death) have been rather startling. She becomes just another human being, as her whole life flashes before her eyes, and her involuntary memories rush her back to the primal scene of childhood. But if this is a debunking mechanism, it is also a surprisingly sentimental piece of writing, allowing in, at the very last, the Victorian elegiac pathos Strachey has been so keen to satirise in his treatment of the age. Bruce Redford, writing on Boswell's *Life* of Johnson and on the fictive methods of biography, in *Designing the Life of Johnson* (2002), calls this 'a vivid montage', an invitation 'to relive his biography at top speed'. But, he says, 'the flashback sacrifices history to poetry ... [and] distances us by making the versatile biographer the true protagonist of his tale'. It 'sacrifices credibility to pyrotechnic display'.[16]

In contemporary biographies, especially of literary figures, you may still find that attempt to stage the whole meaning of the life and the life's work at the deathbed, sometimes with unfortunate effects, as in the ending of John Halperin's 1984 life of Jane Austen:

> From 7.p.m. on 17 July until she died the next morning at 4.30 a.m. in the arms of her sister, Jane Austen, after praying for death, lay apparently insensible. What thoughts, if any, may have raced through the fading light of her mind we of course shall never know. Did she, perhaps, dream of Chawton, its paths and gardens, and wonder how her mother might greet the news of her death? Did she recall that wonderful moonlit walk she took from Alton to Chawton the previous autumn, when, for the last time, she seemed to possess all her strength? Did her thoughts stray back to that tumultuous trip to London in the autumn of 1815 ... ? Did she remember the arrival of her 'favourite child' *Pride and Prejudice* from London in 1813, or the excitement of holding her very first publication in her hands in 1811, or the years of 'exile' in Southampton and Bath which preceded that first success? ... Did she recall the awful night at Manydown when she changed her mind about marriage ... ? Did she dream of that vibrant autumn of 1800, when she danced her feet off at the Basingstoke ball ... ? Did her thoughts wander back to Steventon, its shrubbery and its country walks ... bittersweet memories of a boy named Tom who had first touched her heart? ... How would her brothers and their children respond to the news of her death; how would her sister take it? Surely some portion of her last earthly thoughts must have been of Cassandra, with whom she had always shared everything; Cassandra, who seemed always to be there, as she was now; Cassandra, in whose arms she lay cradled; Cassandra; Cassandra.[17]

Like Strachey, Halperin runs backwards through the life as it flashes past, but it reads as a clumsy, laboriously rhetorical device for reminding his readers of the main events, and an intolerably sentimental fictionalising of his heroine. D.J. Taylor does the same thing, rather oddly, at the end of his otherwise matter-of-fact life of George Orwell

(2003). The italicised passage here seems to add nothing more to our sense of Orwell's life than a redundant, if stylish, tribute to Strachey:[18]

> Orwell's dream
>
> *And perhaps at the very end his mind moved back, back through the cloud of the years, to older and even older memories: to the rain falling over the grey sea off Jura; to the thump of the bombs going off in the streets beyond Piccadilly; and the lofted torches in the great square at Barcelona; and the electric shock of the bullet slamming home; and Eileen's face under the Church gate; and Eileen at the supper table in Hampstead ... and his mother's shadow falling across the garden; and the sound of the nightjars on summer evenings in the lanes; and the woods and the streams of Oxfordshire.*

All these biographers are using the same strategy to make the moment of their subject's death sum up and conclude the whole story of their life. Where biography leans towards fiction, this is a favoured tactic. The novelist Peter Ackroyd, in his life of Dickens (1990), brings in all the characters of Dickens's imagination to witness his death, and uses a similar device of accumulative rhetorical questions to make the fantasy work. In Ackroyd's theatrical staging, Dickens is, at his death, at the centre of the world he himself has created. Ackroyd makes much of the last words.

> 'On the ground'. His last words. And is it possible that he had in some bewildered way echoed the words of Louisa Gradgrind to her errant father in *Hard Times*, 'I shall die if you hold me! Let me fall upon the ground!'? And were his other characters around him as he lay unconscious through his last night? ... And can we see them now, the ghosts of Dickens's imagination, hovering around him as he approaches his own death? Oliver Twist, Ebenezer Scrooge, Paul Dombey, Little Nell, Little Dorrit, The Artful Dodger, Bob Sawyer, Sam Weller, Mr Pickwick [thirty-two more names of Dickens's characters listed] ... all of them now hovering around their creator as his life on earth came to an end.[19]

As well as giving to the death the conclusive meaning of the life's work, Ackroyd is also trying to emulate and even parody his subject's literary strategies and his language. (That overlap of tone between biographer and subject is often noticeable in nineteenth-century life-writing, less so, usually, in later biography.)[20] And he is also bringing his biography full circle, since he began his book with the writer on his deathbed, having his death mask taken, so as to establish the myth of a Dickens who always connected death and infancy and who feared more than anything the return of the dead.[21] Both Halperin and Ackroyd fictionalise their deathbed scenes, in attempts to be 'true', not to the realities of death, but to the spirit of the writer's life. The opposite of this is the biography that tries to unpick false or legendary associations of the life with the work or the myths which have accumulated around the writer's death, like Richard Holmes's account of the death of Shelley (with which I began this book), or Claire Tomalin's revisionary account of Dickens's death in *The Invisible Woman*, or Juliet Barker's realistic, demystifying account of Emily Brontë's death in *The Brontës* (1994). This is a dry, exact, scrupulously evidence-based account, which still can't quite resist invoking the spirit of Emily Brontë's own work. It is worth quoting at length, since it works through the slow, dogged accumulation of detail:[22]

Emily was now in the final stages of consumption, though neither she nor her family apparently suspected how close she was to death. Though the pain in her side and chest had improved, her cough, shortness of breath and extreme emaciation had not; to add to her troubles, she began to suffer from diarrhoea, though she remained adamant that 'no poisoning doctor' should come near her. 'Never in all her life had she lingered over any task that lay before her, and she did not linger now,' Charlotte later wrote of her sister . . . The evening before her death, she insisted on feeding the dogs, Keeper and Flossy, as she had always done. As she stepped from the warmth of the kitchen into the cold air of the damp, stone-flagged passage, she staggered and almost fell against the wall. Charlotte and Anne, rushing to help her, were brushed aside and, recovering herself, she went on to give the dogs their dinner. Mrs Gaskell reported how Charlotte shivered recalling the pang she had felt when, having searched over the bleak December moors for a single sprig of heather to take in to Emily, she realised that her sister had not even recognised her favourite flower. On the morning of Tuesday, 19 December 1848, she insisted on rising at seven as was her habit. Combing her hair before the fire, the comb slipped from her fingers and fell into the hearth; she was too weak to pick it up, and before Martha Brown arrived and retrieved it for her, a large part of it had been burnt away by the flames. Neither Martha nor Charlotte dared to offer assistance as Emily slowly dressed herself and made her way downstairs. Still struggling to keep up an appearance of normality, she even attempted to pick up her sewing . . .

By midday, Emily was worse. Her unbending spirit finally broken, she whispered between gasps for breath, 'If you will send for a doctor, I will see him now.' Dr Wheelhouse was summoned immediately but, of course, it was too late: there was nothing he could do. Tradition has it that Emily refused to the last to retire to bed, dying, as unconventionally as she had lived, on the sofa in the parsonage dining-room. This seems unlikely, as there is no contemporary source for the story and Charlotte later movingly described how Emily's dog Keeper 'lay at the side of her dying-bed'. In all probability, therefore, Emily was carried upstairs to her own little room over the hall, which had once been the 'children's study' . . . She fought death to the end. And it was a bitter end. There was no time for consolatory words or acceptance of the inevitable. After 'a hard, short conflict', Emily was torn from the world, 'turning her dying eyes reluctantly from the pleasant sun'. At two o'clock in the afternoon, aged thirty, she died: the relentless conflict between strangely strong spirit and fragile frame was over.

Note 'This seems unlikely'. Barker (whose vast book on the Brontë sisters sets out to correct all previous versions of their lives, especially idealised accounts of Charlotte) will not be moved by the popular myth. She is like Janet Malcolm, refusing to accept unquestioningly the legendary story about Chekhov and the champagne. Barker takes care to provide her source materials – all the more poignant because so scrupulously placed, as with Gaskell's reminiscence of Charlotte's evidence about Emily not recognising her favourite flower. Yet Barker is not entirely clinical, after all, in her retelling of this agonising story. There's a definite symbolic touching up of that comb, 'burnt away by the flames'. And she allows echoes from Emily's own poetry to infiltrate, at the last, this apparently clinical narrative. The struggle in Brontë's poem 'The Philosopher' between the 'quenchless will' and the 'little frame', and the dauntlessness of 'no coward soul is mine', are deliberately echoed.

A desire to echo the subject's tone, in a spirit of tenderness and sympathy, is often heard in the closing pages of *Lives* of nineteenth-century writers. Victoria Glendinning's *Life* of Trollope (1992) ends like a Victorian novel, telling us what happens to all the characters, and concluding with the modest, affecting and affectionate last words of Trollope's *Autobiography*: 'Now I stretch out my hand, and from the further shore I bid adieu to all who have cared to read any among the many words that I have written.'[23] Jenny Uglow's biography of Elizabeth Gaskell (1993) ends with a mention of one of the minor characters who appeared at her funeral at Knutsford: 'And of all people, among the mourners was one of her protégés, Hamilton Aidé, who had walked across from Tatton. He was the man who wrote so badly but sang so beautifully, to Elizabeth's huge amusement. She would have liked that.'[24] Her ending maintains to its very last word this biography's loving attention to detail, its tone of sympathy, attention and humour – qualities which mirror Elizabeth Gaskell's own characteristics.

Such attempts, however scrupulous or persuasive, to make the moment of death somehow match up to, fulfil, or re-enact the *imaginative* life of the writer-subject can lead biographers of writers into difficulties. Proust is a particularly interesting case here, since so much of his writing is *about* death and our attitudes to it. Accounts of Proust's long-drawn-out and heroic death (on 18 November 1922, from pneumonia, septicaemia, and damage to the lungs from asthma) by André Maurois (1950) and George Painter (1965) turn Proust into the writer as saint, meeting his end with 'stoic disregard', 'indescribable dignity' and 'heroic courage'.[25] Maurois cannot resist citing Proust's fictional account of the death of the writer Bergotte, in which the immortality of the artist is movingly suggested by the continuing existence of his books. Painter, whose whole thesis of the life of Proust is based on Proust's guilty love-hate relation with his mother, and on Proust's idea of 'two paths' or 'two ways', the natural self and the acquired self, interprets the death according to his thesis. Proust, he says, is supposed to have said 'Mother' at the end. Painter comments: 'Now only the young mother, restored from before the beginning of Time Lost, before she had ever seemed to withhold her love, remained. At half-past five, calm and motionless, his eyes still wide open, Proust died.' Painter concludes: 'As he predicted, the Two Ways had met . . . the self we are born with and the self which we acquire, always join at last . . .'[26]

A dry warning note is sounded against that heroic, meaningful, anticipated and resolved account of a writer's death, in which the life and the death are validated in terms of the work, in Beckett's 1965 essay on Proust, which he prefaces: 'There is no allusion in this book to the legendary life and death of Marcel Proust', and in which he says this about death: 'Whatever opinion we may be pleased to hold on the subject of death, we may be sure that it is meaningless and valueless. Death has not required us to keep a day free.'[27] Jean-Yves Tadié's 1996 biography of Proust seems to take warning from Beckett in its attempt very scrupulously and carefully to sort out the death from the writing. It doesn't give 'Mother' as a last word, and it doesn't try to fit Proust's account of the death of Bergotte into his own death.[28] Tadié is much more concerned with the story of the writing life. He does note that Proust is writing sentences to do with the death of Bergotte on his own deathbed. This includes a passage on the 'frivolity of the dying', where Bergotte, at his last gasp, is allowed to ask for all the food and drink which had previously been forbidden to him as a dead man. 'I couldn't have some champagne?' he asks. Perhaps he had been reading about Chekhov.

Proust was violently opposed to biography, as many novelists are, because it is a rival to their own art-form. These versions of Proust's death suggest, indeed, that it is almost impossible for biographers not to try to be like novelists, not to make the death of a writer simply a fact, devoid of conclusive meanings or of relation to the writer. Even when a modern, secular biographer is trying to be completely clinical about their subject's death, to describe it just in all its contingency and physical awfulness, it may still be hard to resist colouring the moment of death with the subject's own attitude to death. The poet and biographer Andrew Motion, in *Philip Larkin* (1993), replaces sentiment with a mercilessly detailed account of every physical indignity of the death, but is still writing – as is perhaps inevitable – in the shadow of the writer's own voice and feelings:

> [In 1985] when Larkin should have been travelling to and from Buckingham Palace (to collect the Companion of Honour), he was at home, dazzled by fear and pain. The prospect of death, acknowledged

but unnamed, raged out at him, concentrating the terrors he had kept before him all his life . . . In his fifties, the dread of oblivion darkened everything. Death, he said, 'remains a sort of Bluebeard's Chamber in the mind, something one is *always* afraid of'. As he entered his sixties his fear grew rapidly. Reviewing D.J. Enright's *Oxford Book of Death* in 1983 he said, 'Man's most remarkable talent is for ignoring death. For once the certainty of permanent extinction is realised, only a more immediate calamity can dislodge it from the mind' . . . Now he told Monica he was 'spiralling down towards extinction' . . . As Friday [28 November 1985] wore on Larkin grew steadily weaker. In the evening, trying to get into his chair in the sitting-room, he fell to the ground and picked himself up with difficulty . . . Later Larkin collapsed again in the downstairs lavatory, jamming the door shut with his feet. Monica was unable to force the door open. She couldn't even make him hear her – he had left his hearing-aid behind – but she could hear him. 'Hot! Hot!' he was whispering pitifully. He had fallen with his face pressed to one of the central heating pipes that ran round the lavatory wall. The next door neighbour was called again, the door was opened, and Larkin was carried into the kitchen. He asked for some Complan . . . When the ambulance arrived he looked up at [Monica] wildly, begging her to destroy his diaries. [He is taken to hospital where he is heavily sedated.] . . . Larkin had died at 1.24 a.m., turning to the nurse who was with him, squeezing her hand, and saying faintly, 'I am going to the inevitable.'[29]

Perhaps I should have called this essay 'From Champagne to Complan'. Yet even here, with all the clinical detail and the physical humiliation – a far cry from Arnold's or Nelson's heroic deaths, or Chekhov's romanticised last moments – there is still a belief in the significance and value of the last words, and an irresistible echo of the work of the poet himself, in the phrases: 'dread of oblivion darkened everything', 'dazzled by fear and pain', 'raged out at him'. Larkin's biographer is thinking of 'Aubade': 'The dread/Of dying, and being dead/Flashes afresh to hold and horrify./Most things may never happen; this one will/ And realisation of it rages out/ In furnace fear when we are caught without/ People or drink.' And other lines from Larkin haunt this death scene: 'Why aren't they screaming?' ('The Old Fools'); 'Beneath it all, desire of oblivion runs' ('Wants').

It is still unusual for contemporary biographers to accede to Beckett's idea of the meaninglessness and contingency of the death. Some twentieth-century biographies of the most problematic figures of that century, such as Stalin and Freud, still insist on the death as the moment when the myth is fixed, or perpetuated – as though returning to Ariès's earliest 'phase' in which the dying man controls the event. Alan Bullock, in *Hitler and Stalin*, describes Stalin making a terrifying deathbed gesture, as though 'bringing down a curse' and thereby preserving 'his image of himself intact to the end'. Peter Gay, in *Freud: A Life for Our Time*, describes Freud's dying gesture of 'greetings, farewell, resignation', whereby 'the old stoic kept control of his life to the end'.[30]

There is an interesting commentary on this dying gesture by Adam Phillips in 'The Death of Freud', collected in *Darwin's Worms* (1999). Phillips argues that Freud was preoccupied, bizarrely, with controlling his own version of his life – bizarrely, since his life's work was to ask 'how do people become who they are' and 'what constitutes evidence for this'. Yet he himself was anxious to 'keep control of the stories' that people would tell about him. He destroyed his papers, and (like Proust) he was extremely hostile to the idea of any biography. Biography, with its attempt to tell the conclusive truth about a life – particularly the life of an artist – seemed to Freud like a travesty or parody of psychoanalysis. Biography maintains, unlike psychoanalysis, that the meaning of a life can be finalised. Biography diminishes or travesties the human project, which is 'to die in our own way'. Freud wanted his death 'to *belong* to him', not to his biographers. What, then, asks Phillips, do Freud's biographers, Ernest Jones and Peter Gay, do with the death of Freud, a slow, torturing, lingering process of death from cancer which ended when he asked his doctor to kill him? Jones (very like some of the other biographers I've been considering) writes an 'exemplary and heroic' death scene, 'a triumph of Freud's belief in the reality principle', a picture of 'a man facing his fate without wish or illusion'. Jones compares Freud's final gesture to Hamlet: 'It said as plainly as possible, "The rest is silence."' (So the biographer is Horatio). Gay makes no reference to Hamlet, but still places the emphasis on Freud's keeping control of his life, dying in his own fashion. Phillips comments: 'For both Jones and Gay, the death, Freud's death, must say something about the life; must prove that the life was discernibly of a piece and that the death, therefore, was of a piece with the life . . .

Freud had unified himself.' But the whole basis of Freudian analysis,
and part of Freud's dislike of biography, was precisely that a life does
not lend itself in this way to 'straightforward intelligibility'. Thus the
biographers, while making Freud the hero of the deathbed, are also
betraying Freud's own desire for self-fashioning. 'Freud's heroic image
of self-definition, of self-fashioning, is the notion that we want to die in
our own way. The subject of a biography' (Phillips concludes, appearing
to concur with Freud at last) 'always dies in the biographer's own
way.'[31]

In conclusion: biographical readings of their subject's end in which a
gesture, a last word or a final act are given value and significance, or in
which the subject's work is invoked at the moment of death, sustain the
old tradition of the deathbed scene that concludes the meaning of the
life; but this may be quite incongruous for our post-Freudian, post-
Beckettian, times. Yet it is still very unusual for death in biography to
occur as random, disorderly, without meaning, without relation to the
life lived, and without conclusiveness. How to 'treat' the death seemed
to me one of the most difficult challenges in writing a biography of
Virginia Woolf, whose death invites interpretation and mythologising.
In her life, she was shadowed by death from childhood onwards. She
persistently found ways of turning her grief for her lost dead, and her
preoccupation with death, into fiction. But if the novel as 'elegy' was
one of her main inventions, she also wanted to sabotage the traditional
presentation of deaths in fiction. This is how she kills off Mrs Ramsay,
in brackets, in *To the Lighthouse:*

> [Mr Ramsay stumbling along a passage stretched his arms out one dark
> morning, but, Mrs Ramsay having died rather suddenly the night before,
> he stretched his arms out. They remained empty.][32]

After the strong emotions which have gathered around Mrs Ramsay in
the first part of the book, the abrupt parenthesis is shocking. Nothing
could be further from the prayers and weeping and solemn family
gatherings of the traditional Victorian deathbed. Virginia Woolf goes
out of her way in her fictions to avoid the melodramatic, necrophiliac
lamentations which filled the darkened rooms of Hyde Park Gate after
her mother's death. Though almost all her novels are dominated by a

death, in almost all the death is not written in. Rachel, the young heroine of *The Voyage Out*, whose mother died when she was eleven, can barely say what she feels ('I am lonely,' she began. 'I want –').[33] She misremembers and can hardly mention her mother, who exists in the book as a gap or a silence. When Virginia Woolf does return to the death of the Victorian mother, in *The Years*, where at the start of the novel the Pargiter children are wearily waiting for it to happen, she writes a brilliantly alienated and unfeeling deathbed scene, which makes a cruel satire on the Victorian genre. These fictional death scenes parallel her desire for biographies not to be like respectful obituaries or monuments.

So, faced with her death, which itself refused ceremony, attendance or observation, the biographer encounters an acute problem of treatment. The causes of her death seem apparent. She had a history of suicidal breakdowns. War was placing her under great stress, with her houses in London bombed, air raids overhead and the imminent expectation of invasion. She and Leonard knew they were on Hitler's blacklist, and, like many of their friends, had made suicide plans. She felt extremely isolated living in the country. She was depressed on finishing her novel, *Between the Acts*, and convinced that it was worthless. She was making a distressing return to her childhood in her autobiography. She was, as at earlier moments of danger, finding it almost impossible to eat or sleep. She was obsessed by her own thoughts, her inner voices. All these are well-known factors. None of them, though, can ultimately explain the horrible and obscure moment of her suicide in the River Ouse on 28 March 1941, over sixty years ago.

But explanation is exactly what is wanted for such a death, and the explanations and making of myths began the moment the death was known. An accidental feature, the coroner's misreading of the suicide note at the inquest, contributed to the myth-making. What Virginia Woolf had said in one of her notes to Leonard was: 'I feel certain that I am going mad again: I feel we cant go through another of those terrible times.' What was read out in court, and reported in the papers, was: 'I feel I am going mad. I cannot go through these terrible times.' Whereupon the wife of the Bishop of Lincoln wrote an outraged letter to the *Sunday Times*, commenting on the coroner's remark that Mrs Woolf must have felt 'the general beastliness of things more than most people'. This, said the Bishop's wife, 'belittles those who are carrying on unselfishly for the sake of others'. And Leonard Woolf had to write letters to the papers explaining that this was not what Virginia had said.[34]

So the story of the feeble authoress giving up on the war effort began to be built into the posthumous myths of Virginia Woolf. That image of a nervous aesthetic creature, too fragile for her own good, was also being processed in the weeks after her death, by the (mostly male) writers who were paying their tributes to her, culminating in the special issue of *Horizon* in May 1941. When *Between the Acts* was published in July, the respectful reviews which greeted it persisted with the image of a thin-blooded, exquisitely imaginative writer, described by one reviewer as 'a war casualty'.[35] Since then, debate has continued over the death: on how much Leonard Woolf can be held responsible;[36] on how far back into childhood the causes of her death can be traced, and on whether her suicide was an act of insanity, or (as I read it) a rational act of courage. And now the death has been simplified, or Ophelia-ised, by the film of *The Hours*,[37] as the romantic immersion of a beautiful young woman with a very long nose, in beautiful still waters, with music playing.

My view, when I wrote my biography, was that Virginia Woolf's suicide should not be made to fit a theory; and that all the information and all the interpretations should be written, or rewritten, as accurately as possible. But what I didn't want to do, or didn't feel I could do, was to write an account of her death which gave the impression that there was nothing mysterious and nothing obscure about that act. I could describe, as far as I knew it, how she ended it all, but I couldn't entirely – and nor can anyone – say why.

Notes

Introduction: Writing about Lives

1 Carlyle, review of Croker's edition of Boswell's *Life of Samuel Johnson*, in *Fraser's Magazine*, April 1832, pp. 253–9, reprinted in James L. Clifford, ed., *Biography as an Art*, Oxford University Press, 1962, pp. 82–3.

2 Quotation from the *Quarterly Review*, 1856, copied by Gaskell into her manuscript of *The Life of Charlotte Brontë* (1857), quoted in Jenny Uglow, *Elizabeth Gaskell: A Habit of Stories*, Faber, 1993, p. 406.

3 Richard Holmes, *Footsteps: Adventures of a Romantic Biographer*, Flamingo, 1995, p. 27.

4 Henry James, 'James Russell Lowell', *Atlantic Monthly*, February 1892; quoted in Leon Edel, *The Life of Henry James*, Vol. II, pp. 28–9, and in David Ellis, *Literary Lives*, Edinburgh University Press, 2000, p. 124.

5 Samuel Johnson, *The Rambler*, 60 (13 October 1750), reprinted in Clifford, ed. *Biography as an Art*, p. 42.

6 Virginia Woolf, 'The Art of Biography' (1939), in *The Crowded Dance of Modern Life*, Penguin, 1993, p. 149.

7 John Dryden, 'The Life of Plutarch', prefixed to *Plutarch's Lives, Translated from the Greek by Several Hands* (1683), in John Dryden, *Of Dramatic Poesy and Other Critical Essays*, Everyman, Vol. II, 1962, p. 9.

Shelley's Heart and Pepys's Lobsters

1 Ian Donaldson, 'Biographical Uncertainty', *Dictionary of National Biography* Seminar, Oxford, January 2003.

2 Julian Barnes, *Flaubert's Parrot*, Cape, 1984, p. 38.

3 Hermione Lee, *Willa Cather: A Life Saved Up*, Virago, 1989; 1997, p. 330.

4 Charlotte Yonge, 'Sir Thomas More's Daughter', in *A Book of Golden Deeds*, 1864; Partridge, 1932, p. 176.

5 See, for variant versions, F.B. Pinion, *Thomas Hardy: His Life and Friends*, Macmillan, 1992, and Molly LeFebure, *Thomas Hardy's World*, Carlton, 1997.

6 Michael Paterniti, *Driving Mr Albert: A Trip across America with Einstein's Brain*, Little, Brown, 2000.

7 Joseph Hone, *W.B. Yeats, 1865–1939*, Macmillan, 1942, pp. 477–9; R.F. Foster, *W.B. Yeats: A Life*, Vol. II, *The Arch-Poet*, Oxford University Press, 2003, pp. 728–9.

8 Richard Holmes, 'Introduction', *Shelley: The Pursuit*, Weidenfeld & Nicolson, 1974; *Footsteps: Adventures of a Romantic Biographer*, Hodder & Stoughton, 1985, pp. 152–3. 'Death and Destiny', on Shelley's afterlives, was first published in the *Guardian*, 24 January 2004, pp. 4–6, and delivered as a lecture at the National Portrait Gallery in the series 'Interrupted Lives', on 29 January 2004. Holmes chaired an early version of my talk on 'Shelley's Heart' at a conference

on 'Biographical Knowledge', University of Cambridge, Centre for Research in the Arts, Social Sciences and Humanities, 31 March 2003.

9 Holmes, *Shelley*, pp. x–xi.

10 Ibid., p. 732; Ian Hamilton, *Keepers of the Flame*, Hutchinson, 1992, p. 131, Timothy Webb, *Shelley: A Voice not Understood*, Manchester University Press, 1977, pp. 14–15.

11 Roger Smith et al., *The Shelley Legend*, Scribner's, 1945, p. 305.

12 Holmes, *Shelley*, p. 353; William St Clair, 'The Biographer as Archaeologist', in *Mapping Lives: The Uses of Biography*, ed. Peter France and William St Clair, Oxford University Press, 2002, p. 232.

13 Andrew Bennett, 'Shelley's Ghosts', in *Romantic Poets and the Culture of Posterity*, Cambridge University Press, 1999, p. 171.

14 Holmes, *Shelley*, p. 730; William St Clair, *Trelawny: The Incurable Romancer*, John Murray, 1977, p. 217, David Crane, *Lord Byron's Jackal: A Life of Edward John Trelawny*, HarperCollins 1998, p. 48.

15 Edward Trelawny, *Recollections of the Last Days of Shelley & Byron*, Edward Moxon, 1858, Ch. 12; 1858 version also in T.J. Hogg, *The Life of Shelley*, Vol. II, Dent, 1933.

16 Crane, *Lord Byron's Jackal*, p. 50.

17 See Webb, *Shelley*, p. 13; William St Clair and Leslie A. Marchand, 'Trelawny on the Death of Shelley', *Keats–Shelley Memorial Bulletin*, 4 (1952), pp. 9–34; Richard Holmes, 'Death and Destiny', *Guardian*, 24 January 2004, p. 4.

18 *The Letters of Edward James Trelawny*, ed. H. Buxton Forman, Oxford University Press, 1910, p. 12; Marchand, 'Trelawny on the Death of Shelley', p. 21; Trelawny, *Records of Shelley, Byron and the Author*, Basil Montagu Pickering, 1878, 'Appendix', Vol. II, p. 241.

19 Leigh Hunt, *Autobiography*, 1850; ed. J.E. Morpurgo, Cresset Press, 1948, pp. 326–7, 331.

20 H. Buxton Forman, quoted by H.J. Massingham in *The Friend of Shelley: A Memoir of Edward James Trelawny*, Cobden-Sanderson, 1936, p. 174.

21 Edward Dowden, *The Life of Percy Bysshe Shelley*, 2 vols, Kegan Paul, Trench & Co., 1886, pp. 576–9.

22 John Gisborne, 'Shelley's Heart: A Memorandum by John Gisborne', in *Shelley and Mary*, 1882, Vol. III, pp. 867–8, and quoted in *Maria Gisborne and Edward Williams: Shelley's Friends, Their Journals and Letters*, ed. Frederick L. Jones, University of Oklahoma Press, 1951, p. 88.

23 'The Real Truth about Shelley's Heart', *My Magazine*, 29, 285 (November 1933), pp. 939–43. F.L. Jones, ed., *The Letters of Mary Shelley*, University of Oklahoma Press, 1944, p. 187.

24 Miranda Seymour, *Mary Shelley*, John Murray, 2000, p. 306.

25 Holmes, 'Death and Destiny', p. 4.

26 Mary Shelley to Maria Gisborne, 15 August, c. 27 August 1822, *The Letters of Mary Shelley*, ed. Betty T. Bennett, Johns Hopkins University Press, 1980, pp. 253, 254.

27 *The Journals of Mary Shelley*, ed. Paula Feldman and Diana Scott-Kilvert, Clarendon Press, 1987, p. 444: 11 November 1822.

28 Crane, *Lord Byron's Jackal*, p. 57.

29 Holmes, *Shelley*, pp. 658, 730.

30 Holmes, 'Death and Destiny', p. 4.

31 Marcel Schwob, 'Introduction' to *Vies imaginaires*; transl. Ian White, *The King in the Golden Mask and Other Writings*, Carcanet, 1982, p. 115. I am grateful to Ann Jefferson for telling me about Schwob.

32 Claire Tomalin, *Samuel Pepys: The Unequalled Self*, Viking, 2002, pp. 62, 83.

33 Ibid., p. 74.

34 Ibid., p. 306.

35 Ibid., p. 158; *The Diary of Samuel Pepys*, ed. R. Latham and W. Matthews, Viking, 1970–83, Vol. IV, p. 306: 13 September 1663.

36 Tomalin, *Samuel Pepys*, p. 164; Pepys, *Diary*, Vol. VIII, p. 303: 29 June 1667.

37 Tomalin, *Samuel Pepys*, pp. 261, 186; Pepys, *Diary*, Vol. VII, p. 164: 13 June 1666.

Virginia Woolf's Nose

1 Conference on 'Writing the Lives of Writers', Senate House, London, Centre for English Studies, London, 1–3 June 1995; proceedings published as *Writing the Lives of Writers*, ed. Warwick Gould and Thomas F. Staley, Macmillan, 1998.

2 Ted Hughes, in the *Independent*, 20 April 1989, quoted by Jacqueline Rose in *The Haunting of Sylvia Plath*, Virago, p. 67.

3 See, for a drily ironic version of such battles, Ian Hamilton, *Keepers of the Flame*, Hutchinson, 1992.

4 Holograph, Department of Manuscripts, British Library, reproduced in Hermione Lee, *Virginia Woolf*, Chatto & Windus, 1996, pp. 756, 759–60. The other note to Leonard Woolf is reprinted in *The Letters of Virginia Woolf*, ed. Nigel Nicolson and Joanne Trautmann, The Hogarth Press, 1980, Vol. VI, Appendix A, opposite p. 489.

5 Elaine Showalter, 'Introduction', *Mrs Dalloway*, 1925; Penguin, 1992, p. xxi.

6 'The Cinema', in *The Crowded Dance of Modern Life*, Penguin, 1993, p. 56.

7 *Mrs Dalloway*, p. 23.

8 *The Diary of Virginia Woolf*, ed. Anne Olivier Bell and Andrew McNeillie, The Hogarth Press, 1977–84, Vol. II, p. 263: 30 August 1923.

9 *Diary*, Vol. II, p. 207: 14 October 1922.

10 *Mrs Dalloway*, p. 10.

11 Elaine Showalter, 'Introduction', *Mrs Dalloway*, p. xxxvi, citing Woolf's Introduction to the Modern Library edition of 1928.

12 Some argue that it's set on 13 June 1923, some on 20 June; David Bradshaw, in his notes to the Oxford World's Classics *Mrs Dalloway* (2000), pp. 182–3, argues for an 'imaginary' Wednesday in June.

13 *Diary*, Vol II, p. 283: 9 January 1924.

14 Michael Wood, review of *The Hours*, in *New York Times Book Review*, 22 November 1998, p. 6.

15 Michael Cunningham, *The Hours*, 1998; Fourth Estate, 1999, p. 211.

16 Ibid., pp. 117, 33, 114, 153.

17 Ibid., p. 83.

18 Ibid., p. 8.

19 *Mrs Dalloway*, p. 10; Cunningham, *The Hours*, p. 8.

20 Michael Wood review, op. cit.; Seymour Chatman, '*The Hours* as Second-

Degree Narrative', forthcoming in *A Companion to Narrative Theory*, ed. James Phelan and Peter J. Rabinowitz, Blackwell's, 2005. Quoted by permission of the author.

21 This point was made by Mary Desjardins in a panel discussion of *The Hours* at the Virginia Woolf Conference, Smith College, 6 June 2003.

22 Sean O'Connell, Review of *The Hours*, *Filmcritic.com*, 2003.

23 Aidan Elliot, 'Our Finest Hour', *Oxford Student*, 6 February 2003, report on Hermione Lee's interview with Stephen Daldry at the Phoenix Cinema, Oxford, *www.oxfordstudent.com/2003–0206/culture/1*.

24 Cunningham, *The Hours*, p. 151.

25 Mark Doty, *London Review of Books*, 14 November 2002, p. 8. Quoted with permission of the author.

26 Philip Hensher, *Daily Telegraph*, 24 January 2003.

27 Ed Gonzalez, *Slant Magazine*, 2003; Hermione Lee, interview with Daldry, op. cit.

28 Angela Wintle, 'Decrying Woolf', *The Times*, 29 January 2003, T2, p. 7; Virginia Nicholson, letter to Hermione Lee, 11 February 2003, quoted by permission of the author.

29 Roberta Rubenstein, 'Outlook', *Washington Post*, 26 January 2003, B, p. 3.

30 Maria Alvarez, 'Woolf at Our Door', *www.theage.com.au/articles/2003/01/29/1043804404038.html*.

31 Woolf's nose has been a bone of contention since well before *The Hours*. Brenda Silver, in *Virginia Woolf Icon*, an account of all the images, representations and versions of Virginia Woolf, writes on how the long, aristocratic Stephen nose encouraged those critics who wanted to attack her as an upper-class snob. *VW Icon*, Chicago, 1999, pp. 139, 141.

32 Patricia Cohen, 'The Nose Was the Final Straw', *New York Times*, 15 February 2003, A, 19–21; Michael Cunningham, email to Hermione Lee, 19 February 2003, quoted by permission of the author.

33 David Hare, 'Introduction', *The Hours*, Miramax Books, 2002; Daniel Mendelsohn, 'Not Afraid of Virginia Woolf', *New York Review of Books*, 13 March 2003; Panel discussion on *The Hours*, with Brenda Silver (Chair), Michèle Barrett, Daniel Mendelsohn, Leslie Hankins, Mary Desjardins, Virginia Woolf Conference, Smith College, 6 June 2003. Quoted by permission of the participants, and with thanks to Brenda Silver, Daniel Mendelsohn and Michèle Barrett.

34 *Orlando*, 1928; Penguin, 1993, p. 213; *To the Lighthouse*, 1927; Penguin, 1992, p. 202.

Reading in Bed

1 Richard Ellmann, *Literary Biography*, Clarendon Press, 1971.

2 Robert Darnton, 'What is the History of Books?', in Cathy Davidson, ed., *Reading in America*, Johns Hopkins University Press, 1989, p. 45.

3 *The Diary of Virginia Woolf*, ed. Anne Olivier Bell and Andrew McNeillie, The Hogarth Press, 1977–84, Vol. IV, p. 173: 24 August 1933.

4 Letter to Ethel Smyth, 29 July 1934, in *The Letters of Virginia Woolf*, ed. Nigel Nicolson and Joanne Trautmann, The Hogarth Press, 1975–80, Vol. V, p. 319.

5 Letter to Vita Sackville-West, 29 December 1928, *Letters*, Vol. III, p. 570.

6 Virginia Woolf, 'Hours in a Library' (1916) in *The Essays of Virginia Woolf*, ed. Andrew McNeillie, Vol. II, The Hogarth Press, 1986.

7 Kate Flint, *The Woman Reader*, Oxford University Press, 1993. See also *The Practice and Representation of Reading in England*, ed. Helen Small, James Raven and Naomi Tadmor, Cambridge University Press, 1996.

8 Richard de Bury, *The Philobiblion*, 1344; trans. E.C. Thomas, City of Birmingham School of Printing, 1946.

9 Jean-Baptiste de la Salle, *The Rules of Christian Decorum and Civility*, trans. R. Arnandez, 1703; Lasallian Publications, 1990, p. 43. Cited in Alberto Manguel, *A History of Reading*, Flamingo, 1997, p. 159.

10 Armando Petrucci, 'Reading to Read', in *A History of Reading in the West*, ed. Guglielmo Cavallo and Roger Chartier, trans. Lydia Cochrane, Polity Press, 1999, pp. 362–4.

11 Judith Fetterley, 'Reading about Reading', in *Gender and Reading*, ed. E. Flynn and P. Schweickart, Johns Hopkins University Press, 1986, p. 151.

12 Dora Thornton, *The Scholar and his Study*, Yale University Press, 1996, pp. 90, 92.

13 Anne (or Mary) Cary, *The Lady Falkland: Her Life*, ed. Barry Weller and Margaret W. Ferguson, University of California Press, 1994; Barbara Kiefer Lewalski, *Writing Women in Jacobean England*, Harvard University Press, 1993, p. 184.

14 Jacqueline Pearson, *Women's Reading in Britain, 1740–1835*, Cambridge University Press, 1999, pp. 219, 42, 155, 158.

15 Flint, *The Woman Reader*, pp. 101–2; Martyn Lyons, 'New Readers in the Nineteenth Century', in *A History of Reading in the West*, pp. 318–24.

16 Stendhal, *The Red and the Black*, 1830; ed. Ann Jefferson, trans. Scott Moncrieff, Everyman, 1997, Book 2, Ch. 13.

17 Antonia Fraser, ed., *The Pleasure of Reading*, Bloomsbury, 1992, pp. 43, 127, 183, 143, 159.

18 Elizabeth Bowen, 'Out of a Book' (1946), in *The Mulberry Tree: Writings of Elizabeth Bowen*, ed. Hermione Lee, Virago, 1986; Vintage, 1999, p. 52.

19 Elizabeth Bowen, 'Coming to London' (1956), ibid., p. 86.

20 Elizabeth Bowen, 'Rider Haggard: *She*' (1947), ibid., p. 249.

21 Ibid.

22 Bowen, 'Out of a Book', ibid., p. 50.

23 Ibid., p. 53.

24 Hermione Lee, *Willa Cather: A Life Saved Up*, Virago, 1989; 1997, p. 37.

25 Ellen Glasgow, *The Woman Within*, 1954; University of Virginia Press, 1994, p. 90.

26 Eudora Welty, *One Writer's Beginnings* (1984), in *Eudora Welty: Stories, Essays, & Memoir*, The Library of America, 1998, pp. 842, 862.

27 Eudora Welty, *The Optimist's Daughter* (1972), in *Eudora Welty: Complete Novels*, Library of America, 1998, pp. 54–5.

28 Mary Gordon, in *A Passion for Books*, ed. Dale Salwak, Macmillan, 1999, p. 124.

29 Holbrook Jackson, *The Anatomy of Bibliomania*, Faber, 1950, pp. 261–4.

30 Manguel, *A History of Reading*, pp. 153, 160.

31 Cynthia Ozick, *Art and Ardor*, New York, 1983, quoted in Manguel, p. 160.

32 Edith Wharton, 'The Great Miss Netherby', unpublished TS, Beinecke Rare

Book and Manuscript Library, Yale University Library, reprinted by permission
of the Estate of Edith Wharton and the Watkins/Loomis Agency.

33 Edith Wharton, 'Literature', TS, Beinecke Library, Yale.

34 Edith Wharton, *A Backward Glance*, Scribner's, 1934; Century, 1987, p. 69.

35 Edith Wharton, 'Life and I' (n.d.), in *Novellas and Other Writings*, ed. Cynthia
Griffin Wolff, Library of America, 1990, cited in Candace Waid, *Edith
Wharton's Letters from the Underworld: Fictions of Women and Writing*, University
of North Carolina Press, Chapel Hill, 1991, p. 11.

36 Wharton, *A Backward Glance*, p. 66.

37 Edith Wharton, *Hudson River Bracketed*, 1929; Virago, 1986, pp. 59, 65, 318,
322.

38 See Hermione Lee, *Virginia Woolf*, Chatto & Windus, 1996, p. 43.

39 Ibid., p. 142.

40 Leslie Stephen, 'The Study of English Literature' (1887), in *Men, Books and
Mountains*, ed. S.O.A. Ullmann, The Hogarth Press, 1956.

Jane Austen Faints

1 *Persuasion*, Chs 17, 21.

2 'caustic': Margaret Kirkham, *Jane Austen, Feminism and Fiction*, The Athlone
Press, 1983, p. 59; 'touched up': B.C. Southam, ed., *Jane Austen: The Critical
Heritage*, Routledge & Kegan Paul, Vol. II, p. 4; Marilyn Butler, 'Simplicity',
London Review of Books, 5 March 1998, p. 3.

3 See Bruce Stovel, 'Further Reading', in *The Cambridge Companion to Jane
Austen*, ed. Edward Copeland and Juliet McMaster, Cambridge University
Press, 1997, pp. 227–43, and Deirdre Le Faye, *Jane Austen: A Family Record*,
British Library, 1989; 2nd edn, Cambridge University Press, 2004. Kathryn
Sutherland, 'Introduction', James Edward Austen-Knight, *A Memoir of Jane
Austen, and Other Family Recollections*, Oxford University Press, 2002, p. xxv.

4 Claire Tomalin, *Jane Austen: A Life*, Viking, 1997, p. 122; Deirdre Le Faye,
Jane Austen's Letters, Oxford University Press, 1995, pp. xiv–xviii; Carol
Houlihan Flynn, 'The Letters', in *The Cambridge Companion to Jane Austen*, pp.
100–14; Sutherland, 2002, p. xxx.

5 Le Faye, *Jane Austen: A Family Record*, 2004, pp. 143–4.

6 Constance Pilgrim, *Dear Jane: A Biographical Study*, Pentland Press, 1971,
described by John Wiltshire, in *Recreating Jane Austen*, Cambridge University
Press, 2001, p. 13, as 'a wonderful, ridiculous book'; Joan Rees, *Jane Austen:
Woman and Writer*, Robert Hale, 1976, p. 88; John Halperin, *The Life of Jane
Austen*, Johns Hopkins University Press and Harvester, 1984, p. 133. On
'pathological' readings, Claudia L. Johnson, *Jane Austen: Women, Politics and the
Novel*, University of Chicago Press, 1988, p. 120. On Cassandra's invention,
David Nokes, *Jane Austen: A Life*, Fourth Estate, 1997, p. 243; 'mistily
romantic': Tomalin, *Jane Austen: A Life*, p. 179.

7 'A very domestic woman': Marilyn Butler, 'Simplicity', p. 3; 'veneration': Carol
Shields, *Jane Austen*, Weidenfeld & Nicolson, 2001, p. 146; Henry Austen,
'Biographical Notice', 1818, reprinted in the Penguin edition of *Northanger
Abbey*, 1972, p. 31; 'ladylike image': Jan Fergus, 'The Professional Woman
Writer', in *The Cambridge Companion to Jane Austen*, p. 12.

8 James Austen-Leigh, *A Memoir of Jane Austen*, 1870, reprinted in the Penguin

edition of *Persuasion*, 1994, pp. 331, 387, 389. On its characteristics and reception, Kirkham, *Jane Austen: Feminism and Fiction*, pp. 58–9; 'a comfortable, approachable figure': Southam, ed., *Jane Austen: The Critical Heritage*, Vol. II, pp. 2–5. 'We might and we did': Clara Tuite, *Romantic Austen: Sexual Politics and the Literary Canon*, Cambridge University Press, 2002, p. 25.

9 Deirdre Lynch, *Janeites: Austen's Disciples and Devotees*, Princeton University Press, 2000, p. 7.

10 Butler, 'Simplicity', p. 3.

11 'Regulated Hatred: An Aspect of the Work of Jane Austen', *Scrutiny*, 8 (1940), pp. 346–62, in Ian Watt, ed., *Jane Austen: A Collection of Critical Essays*, Prentice-Hall, 1963, p. 169; Marvin Mudrick, *Jane Austen: Irony as Defence and Discovery*, Princeton University Press, 1952.

12 Marilyn Butler, *Jane Austen and the War of Ideas*, Clarendon Press, 1975; against her view, Alistair Duckworth, *The Improvement of the Estate: A Study of Jane Austen's Novels*, Johns Hopkins University Press, 1971; 1994, p. xxv, and Jon Mee, 'Jane Austen's Treacherous Ivory', in *The Post-Colonial Jane Austen*, ed. You-Me Park and Rajeswari Sunderrajan, Routledge, 2000, p. 76.

13 Nigel Nicolson, *The World of Jane Austen*, Weidenfeld & Nicolson, 1991, cited in Wiltshire, *Recreating Jane Austen*, p. 37. Susan Watkins, *Jane Austen in Style*, Thames & Hudson, 1996, p. 7, first published 1990 as *Jane Austen's Town and Country Style*. 'Golden age': Mary Evans, *Jane Austen and the State*, Tavistock Publications, 1987, p. x; 'harmonious refuge': Deirdre Lynch, 'At Home with Jane Austen', in *Cultural Institutions of the Novel*, ed. Deirdre Lynch and William B. Warner, Duke University Press, 1996, p. 172; 'angelic dismay': Ivor Morris, *Jane Austen and the Interplay of Character*, Athlone Press, 1987, p. 163.

14 For good summaries of the different critical positions on Austen, see Rajeswari Sunderrajan ('gendered public–private ascription'), 'Austen in the World: Postcolonial Mappings', in *The Post-Colonial Jane Austen*, pp. 3–25; Deirdre Lynch on the Austen industry in 'At Home with Jane Austen', pp. 159–92, Clara Tuite on the 'canonical constructions' of Austen in *Romantic Austen*, Lynch, *Janeites*, and Claudia L. Johnson, 'Austen Cults and Cultures', in *The Cambridge Companion to Jane Austen*, pp. 211–26. For Austen as 'deeply involved', see Duckworth, *The Improvement of the Estate*, p. xxv.

15 On Chapman's editions, see Johnson, 'Austen Cults and Cultures', pp. 217–19, and Southam, ed., *Jane Austen: The Critical Heritage*, Vol. II, pp. 99–100. 'fleas': Roger Sales, *Jane Austen and Representations of Regency England*, Routledge 1994, p. 10. Critical of capitalism: Evans, *Jane Austen and the State*, p. 1. Jane and Cassandra: Terry Castle, 'Sister-Sister' [headlined by the *LRB* editor, 'Was Jane Austen Gay?'], *London Review of Books*, 3 August 1995, reprinted in *Boss Ladies, Watch Out!*, Routledge, 2002. Edward Said, 'Jane Austen and Empire' (1989), in *Culture and Imperialism*, Vintage, 1994. 'Green core' in Clara Tuite, 'Domestic Retrenchment and Imperial Expansion: The Property Plots of *Mansfield Park*', in *The Post-Colonial Jane Austen*, p. 112.

16 Carolyn Heilbrun, *Writing a Woman's Life*, 1988; Ballantine Books, 1989, pp. 30–1.

17 Jane Austen to Cassandra Austen, Sat. 27–Sun. 28 October 1798, *Jane Austen's Letters: New Edition*, ed. Deirdre Le Faye, Oxford University Press, 1995, p. 17.

18 Le Faye, *Jane Austen: A Family Record*, 2004, p. 128.

19 Sutherland, 2002, p. xl. Wiltshire, *Recreating Jane Austen*, 2001, p. 17.

20 On the Leavisite construction of 'Augustan Austen', Johnsonian and satirical, writing a comedy of civilised life, see Tuite, *Romantic Austen*, pp. 2–5.

21 John Mullan, *Sentiment and Sensibility: The Language of Feeling in the Eighteenth Century*, Clarendon Press, 1988, p. 217. Emma Austen-Leigh, *Jane Austen and Bath*, 1939; republished with intro. by David Gilson, Routledge, 1995, p. 13; A.C. Bradley, 'Jane Austen' (1911), in *A Miscellany*, Macmillan, 1929, p. 71.

22 John Wiltshire, *Jane Austen and the Body*, Cambridge University Press, 1992, pp. 8, 12, 140.

23 'Timid': Jon Mee, in *The Post-Colonial Jane Austen*, p. 87. 'Green nook': Lynch, 'At Home with Jane Austen', p. 89. 'Bath': Tuite, *Romantic Austen*, p. 163. 'Enjoying herself': Margaret Kirkham, *Jane Austen, Feminism and Fiction*, 1983; revised edn, Athlone Press, 1997, pp. 61–3.

24 Bruce Stovel, 'Further Reading', in *The Cambridge Companion to Jane Austen*, p. 229. Halperin, *Life of Jane Austen*, pp. 123–4, 132. Park Honan, *Jane Austen: Her Life*, Weidenfeld & Nicolson, 1987, pp. 155–6.

25 Tomalin, *Jane Austen: A Life*, pp. 75, 261, 142, 205, 170–5.

26 Shields, *Jane Austen*, pp. 150–1, 73–83.

27 Nokes, *Jane Austen: A Life*, pp. 220–2, 254, 350–1, 410, 491.

28 Wiltshire, *Recreating Jane Austen*, p. 35.

29 *Mansfield Park*, Ch. 22.

On Being Ill

1 See Hermione Lee, *Virginia Woolf*, Chatto & Windus, 1996, Ch. 10; Thomas Caramagno, *The Flight of the Mind: Virginia Woolf's Art and Manic-Depressive Illness*, University of California Press, 1992.

2 *The Diary of Virginia Woolf*, ed. Anne Olivier Bell and Andrew McNeillie, The Hogarth Press, 1977–84, [*Diary*], Vol. III, p. 287, 16 February 1930.

3 *Diary*, 5 September 1925, III, p. 38.

4 Ibid. Letter to Vita Sackville-West [VSW], 7 September 1925, in *The Letters of Virginia Woolf*, ed. Nigel Nicolson and Joanne Trautmann, The Hogarth Press, 1975–80 [*Letters*], III, p. 204; *Diary*, 14 September 1925, III, p. 40; Letter to Roger Fry, 16 September 1925, *Letters*, III, p. 208; Letter to VSW, 13 October 1925, *Letters*, III, p. 217; Letter to VSW, 26? October 1925, *Letters*, III, p. 218; Letter to VSW, 16 November 1925, *Letters*, III, p. 221; *Diary*, 27 November 1925, III, p. 46.

5 *Diary*, 27 November 1925, III, p. 47.

6 *Diary*, 14 September 1925, III, p. 41.

7 Letter to T.S. Eliot, 3 [should be 8] September 1925, *Letters*, III, p. 203.

8 Letter to T.S. Eliot, 13 November 1925, *Letters*, III, p. 220.

9 *Diary*, 7 December 1925, III, p. 49.

10 *Diary*, 2 September 1930, III, p. 315.

11 Virginia Woolf [VW] to 'Anon', 10 December 1930, *Letters*, IV, p. 260.

12 In *The Moment and Other Essays* (1947) and in *Collected Essays*, ed. Leonard Woolf, Chatto & Windus, 1967, Vol. IV. The *Forum* edition of 'On Being Ill' is in *The Essays of Virginia Woolf*, ed. Andrew McNeillie, Vol. IV The Hogarth Press, 1994, IV, pp. 581–9. The 1930 version is reprinted as a separate volume by the Paris Press, 2002.

13 VW to Edward Sackville West, 6 February 1926, *Letters*, III, p. 239.

14 *On Being Ill*, Paris Press, 2002, p. 14.

15 *The Tempest*, IV, i, line 155.

16 *Antony and Cleopatra*, IV, xiv, line 10.

17 VW to VSW, 23 September 1925, *Letters*, III, p. 214.

18 Here she improves on her source, which has a 'window blind' rather than a plush curtain: 'This blind told me of her intense suffering, for there was the clutch of her fingers, as they wrinkled the surface in her anguish. There was writing in the folds caused by her squeeze that told more than words could of the heart's despair.' Augustus Hare, *The Story of Two Noble Lives. Being Memorials of Charlotte, Countess Canning, and Louisa, Marchioness of Waterford*, London, George Allen, 1893, Vol. III, pp. 23–4.

19 For other accounts of VW and Romanticism, see Hermione Lee, 'A Burning Glass', in Eric Warner, ed., *Virginia Woolf: A Centenary Perspective*, Macmillan, 1983; Ellen Tremper, *Who Lived at Alfoxden?: Virginia Woolf and English Romanticism*, Bucknell, 1998.

20 'Impassioned Prose', in *The Essays of Virginia Woolf*, Vol. IV, 1994, p. 366.

21 Thomas De Quincey, 'Suspiria de Profundis', Blackwood's *Edinburgh Magazine*, 57 (1845), pp. 742–3; in *Confessions of an English Opium-Eater and Other Writings*, Oxford University Press, 1996.

22 De Quincey, *Confessions of an English Opium-Eater*, pp. 112, 71.

23 *William Wordsworth: The Poems*, ed. John O. Hayden, Penguin, 1977, Vol. I, p. 581.

24 'Impassioned Prose', p. 366.

25 'De Quincey Dines', in De Quincey, *Literary Reminiscences*, ed. E. Blunden, 1821–2, p. 101.

26 Charles Lamb, Letter to Bernard Barton, 25 July 1829, in *Charles Lamb & Elia*, ed. J.E. Morpurgo, Carcanet, 1993, p. 75.

27 'The Decay of Essay Writing' (1905), in *The Essays of Virginia Woolf*, Vol. I, 1986, p. 25.

28 Charles Lamb, 'The Convalescent', in *Last Essays of Elia*, ed. G.E. Hollingsworth, London, 1932, pp. 42–6; 'Popular Fallacies: That We Should Rise With the Lark' (1826), in Morpurgo, ed., *Charles Lamb & Elia*, p. 71.

29 Virginia Woolf, *The Waves*, Penguin, 1964, p. 119.

30 *On Being Ill*, p. 19.

Father and Son: Philip and Edmund Gosse

1 Virginia Woolf, 'Sketch of the Past', in *Moments of Being*, ed. J. Schulkind and H. Lee, Pimlico, 2003, p. 92. Peter Abbs's introduction to the Penguin edition of *Father and Son*, 1983, argues that it should be defined as autobiography.

2 Henry James to Edmund Gosse, 10 November 1907, in *Henry James: A Life in Letters*, ed. Philip Horne, Allen Lane, 1999, p. 453.

3 Evan Charteris, *The Life and Letters of Sir Edmund Gosse*, Heinemann, 1931, pp. 309–11; Adrian Frazier, *George Moore, 1852–1933*, Yale University Press, 2000, p. 559, note 249.

4 George Moore to Edmund Gosse, 15 November 1907, in Frazier, *George Moore*, p. 371.

5 In Charteris, *Life and Letters*, p. 305.
6 Ann Thwaite, *Edmund Gosse: A Literary Landscape 1849–1928*, Secker & Warburg, 1984, p. 437. Hereafter *EG* in the text.
7 Edmund Gosse, *Father and Son: A Study of Two Temperaments*, Heinemann, 1907, Preface. Hereafter *FS* in the text.
8 Ann Thwaite, *Glimpses of the Wonderful: The Life of Philip Henry Gosse*, Faber, 2002, pp. 2, 113, 235. Hereafter *PG* in the text.
9 Anna Shipton, *Tell Jesus: Recollections of Emily Gosse*, Morgan & Chase, 1864, p. 22. Parts of P.H. Gosse's 'Memorial of the Last Days on Earth of Emily Gosse' are reprinted in *Areté*, ed. Craig Raine, 7 (2001), pp. 69–88.
10 Edmund Gosse, *The Life of Philip Henry Gosse, FRS*, Kegan Paul, 1890, p. 279.
11 Ibid., p. viii, Charteris, *Life and Letters*, p. 222.
12 Edmund Gosse, 'Biography' (1902), *DNB*, 1911.
13 Edmund Gosse, *Tallemant des Réaux, or the Art of Miniature Biography*, Clarendon Press, 1925, pp. 9, 23.
14 Charteris, *Life and Letters*, pp. 269, 305.
15 Ibid., p. 411.
16 See David Amigoni, *Victorian Biography: Intellectuals and the Ordering of Discourse*, Harvester Wheatsheaf, 1993; Joseph Bristow, *Effeminate England*, Oxford University Press, 1995; Trev Lynn Broughton, *Men of Letters, Writing Lives*, Routledge, 1999; Michael Roper and John Tosh, *Manful Assertions: Masculinities in Britain since 1800*, Routledge, 1991.
17 Virginia Woolf, 'The New Biography' (1930), in *Collected Essays*, Vol. IV, p. 234, ed. Leonard Woolf, Chatto & Windus, 1967.
18 Edmund Gosse, *Tallemant des Réaux*, p. 21.
19 Edmund Gosse, *The Life of Philip Henry Gosse, FRS*, p. 350.

An Appetite for Writing: Thurman's Colette

1 Judith Thurman, *Secrets of the Flesh: A Life of Colette*, Knopf, 1999, pp. 28, 149, 208, 346. Hereafter *C* in the text.
2 Judith Thurman, interview with Jean Strouse, *New York Times Review of Books*, 9 November 1999.

The Sheltered Life: Ellen Glasgow

1 *The Deliverance*, Doubleday, 1904, p. 50.
2 Ibid., p. 74.
3 Ibid., pp. 485–6.
4 *A Certain Measure*, Harcourt, Brace & Co., 1938, p. 15
5 Letter to Irita Van Doren, 8 September 1933, *Letters of Ellen Glasgow*, ed. Blair Rouse, Harcourt, Brace & Co., 1958, p. 143.
6 *The Woman Within: An Autobiography*, posthumously published in 1954; University Press of Virginia, 1994, pp. 268–9.
7 The University of Virginia keep in print *Virginia* (1913), *Barren Ground* (1925), *The Romantic Comedians* (1926), *The Sheltered Life* (1932) and *Vein of Iron* (1935).
8 *A Certain Measure*, p. 3.
9 Susan Goodman, *Ellen Glasgow: A Biography*, Johns Hopkins University Press, 1998, p. 186. Hereafter *G* in the text.

10 Letter to Hudson Strode, 22 May 1941; to Van Wyck Brooks, 4 October 1939; to Harry Scherman, 14 January 1937, *Letters*, pp. 285, 257, 216–17.

11 Linda Wagner, *Ellen Glasgow: Beyond Convention*, University of Texas Press, 1982; Elizabeth Meyer, *The Social Situation of Women in the Novels of Ellen Glasgow*, Exposition Press, 1978; Pamela Matthews, *Ellen Glasgow and a Woman's Traditions*, University Press of Virginia, 1994.

12 Matthews, *Ellen Glasgow*, pp. 14, 19, 24.

13 *The Woman Within*, p. 101.

14 Ibid., p. 152, quoted Goodman, *Ellen Glasgow: A Biography*, p. 52.

15 Matthews, *Ellen Glasgow*, p. 72.

16 *The Woman Within*, p. 216.

17 Ibid., pp. 158, 270.

18 *They Stooped to Folly*, The Literary Guild, 1929, p. 76.

19 *A Certain Measure*, p. 94.

20 *Vein of Iron*, 1935; University Press of Virginia, 1995, p. 38.

21 *The Woman Within*, p. 128.

22 *Ellen Glasgow's Reasonable Doubts*, ed. Julius Rowan Raper, Louisiana State University Press, 1988, p. 72.

23 *A Certain Measure*, p. 8.

24 *The Battleground*, Doubleday, Page & Co., 1902, p. 199.

25 *Virginia*, Doubleday, Page & Co., 1913, p. 53.

26 *The Romantic Comedians*, 1926; University Press of Virginia, 1995, p. 198.

27 *The Sheltered Life*, 1932; University Press of Virginia, 1994, p. 245.

28 *They Stooped to Folly*, p. 30.

29 *Vein of Iron*, p. 76.

30 *The Voice of the People*, Doubleday, Page, & Co. 1900, pp. 230–1.

31 Letter to Carl Van Vechten, 28 July 1926, *Letters*, pp. 80–1.

32 *Barren Ground*, 1933; Harcourt Brace, 1985, p. 420.

33 *They Stooped to Folly*, p. 136.

34 *The Sheltered Life*, p. 55.

35 *Virginia*, p. 203.

36 *The Sheltered Life*, p. 173.

37 *They Stooped to Folly*, p. 161.

38 *Barren Ground*, p. 369.

39 *Vein of Iron*, p. 326.

40 *The Sheltered Life*, p. 232.

41 *Barren Ground*, p. 150.

42 *They Stooped to Folly*, p. 260.

43 *The Sheltered Life*, p. 105.

44 Ibid., p. 180.

Mr and Mrs Eliot

1 Carole Seymour-Jones, *Painted Shadow: A Life of Vivienne Eliot*, Constable, 2001. Hereafter *PS* in the text.

2 Peter Ackroyd, *T.S. Eliot*, Hamish Hamilton, 1984; Abacus, 1985, p. 84.

3 Ibid., pp. 309–10.

4 Ronald Schuchard, *Eliot's Dark Angel*, Oxford University Press, 1999, pp. 110–15.

5 Lyndall Gordon, *Eliot's New Life*, Oxford University Press, 1988; 1989, p. 62.

A Secret Self: May Sinclair

1 Suzanne Raitt, *May Sinclair: A Modern Victorian*, Oxford University Press, 2000. Hereafter *MS* in the text.

Bittersweet: Rosamond Lehmann

1 Selina Hastings, *Rosamond Lehmann: A Life*, Chatto & Windus, 2002.

Worn Paths: Eudora Welty

1 Eudora Welty, *Complete Novels* and *Stories, Essays and Memoir*, Library of America, selected and annotated by Richard Ford and Michael Kreyling, 1998. All quotations from the novels and stories are from this edition.
2 Ann Waldron, *Eudora: A Writer's Life*, Doubleday, 1998, p. 3.
3 Jan Nordby Gretlund and Karl-Heinz Westarp, eds, *The Late Novels of Eudora Welty*, University of South Carolina Press, 1998.
4 Eudora Welty, *One Writer's Beginnings*, Harvard University Press, 1984, p. 96.
5 See *Conversations with Eudora Welty*, ed. P.W. Prenshaw, Washington Square Press, 1985, p. 285.
6 Eudora Welty, *One Time, One Place*, Random House, 1971, p. 7.
7 Eudora Welty, 'Place in Fiction', in *The Eye of the Story: Selected Essays and Reviews*, Random House, 1978, pp. 116–33.
8 Michael Kreyling, *Author and Agent*, Farrar, Straus & Giroux, 1991.
9 Claudia Roth Pierpont, 'The Myth of Eudora Welty', *New Yorker*, 5 October 1998.

A Quiet Ghost: Penelope Fitzgerald

1 Penelope Fitzgerald, *The Means of Escape*, Flamingo, 2000; *A House of Air* (with an introduction by Hermione Lee), Flamingo, 2003.
2 'The View from Here', Penelope Fitzgerald interviewed by Hermione Lee, producer Erin Riley, BBC4, 1997.
3 Penelope Fitzgerald, *The Blue Flower*, Flamingo, 1995, p. 112.
4 Penelope Fitzgerald, *The Beginning of Spring*, Flamingo, 1988, p. 121.

Heart of Stone: J.M. Coetzee

1 J.M. Coetzee, *Youth*, Secker & Warburg, 2002, reviewed by Jason Crowley, Rosemary Goring and Geoff Dyer.
2 *Disgrace*, Secker & Warburg, 1999, p. 51.
3 *Doubling the Point*, Secker & Warburg, 1992, p. 282.
4 *The Writings of J.M. Coetzee*, ed. M.V. Moses, Duke University Press, 1995, p. 194.
5 *Boyhood*, Secker & Warburg, 1997; Vintage, 1998, pp. 18, 79, 123, 78, 91, 161.
6 *Youth*, p. 130.
7 Ibid., pp. 141, 97, 52, 102, 104, 83.
8 Ibid., pp. 14, 30, 66, 61, 143.
9 *Disgrace*, p. 74.

10 *Elizabeth Costello*, Secker & Warburg, 2003.
11 Ibid., pp. 193–225.
12 Ibid., pp. 156–82.

Good Show: The Life and Works of Angela Thirkell

1 All quotations from Thirkell's novels are given in the text. Editions referred to are published by Moyer Bell: *The Headmistress* (1995), *Growing Up* (1995), *O, These Men, These Men!* (1995), *Miss Bunting* (1995), *The Demon in the House* (1996), *Ankle Deep* (1996), or by Carroll & Graf: *Northbridge Rectory* (1991), *Before Lunch* (1988), *Pomfret Towers* (1986), *High Rising* (1994), *Wild Strawberries* (1989), *The Brandons* (1987), *August Folly* (1995).
2 Issues of the *Angela Thirkell Society Journal*, 1981—, Brotherton Library Special Collection, University of Leeds. I am grateful to Chris Sheppard for access and help.
3 Victoria Glendinning, *Trollope*, Hutchinson, 1992, p. 215.
4 Thirkell Papers, Brotherton Library Special Collection, University of Leeds.
5 Elizabeth Bowen, quoted in Margot Strickland, *Angela Thirkell: Portrait of a Lady Novelist*, Duckworth, 1977, p. 138.
6 Colin MacInnes, *Absolute Beginners*, Allison & Busby, 1959; 1980, p. 47.
7 Colin MacInnes, 'Mum's the Word', *New Statesman*, 1963, in *Absolute MacInnes*, ed. Tony Gould, Allison & Busby, 1985, p. 146.
8 Strickland, *Angela Thirkell*, p. 59; Lance Thirkell, talk given to 'The Sixty-Three Club', 11 December 1983, Thirkell Papers, University of Leeds.
9 MacInnes, 'Mum's the Word', in *Absolute MacInnes*, p. 146.

Psychic Furniture: Ellmann's Elizabeth Bowen

1 Maud Ellmann, *Elizabeth Bowen: The Shadow across the Page*, Edinburgh University Press, 2003. All quotations in the text are from Ellmann.
2 For my version of Bowen, see Hermione Lee, *Elizabeth Bowen*, Vintage, 1999.

How to End It All

1 Philippe Ariès, *Western Attitudes to Death*, Marion Boyars, 1976, pp. 11, 55, 37, 68.
2 Ariès, *The Hour of Our Death*, trans. Helen Weaver, Allen Lane, 1981, p. 569.
3 See Douglas Davies, *Death, Ritual and Belief*, Cassell, 1997; Claire Gittings, *Death, Burial and the Individual in Early Modern England*, 1984; Peter Jupp and Claire Gittings, eds, *Death in England*, Manchester, 1999; Pat Jalland, *Death in the Victorian Family*, Oxford University Press, 1996; R. Houlbrooke, ed., *Death, Ritual and Bereavement*, Routledge 1989; John Wolffe, *Great Deaths*, Oxford University Press, 2000.
4 Jalland, *Death in the Victorian Family*, p. 8; Wolffe, *Great Deaths*, p. 61; Davies, *Death, Ritual and Belief*, p. 7.
5 David Hume, *Dialogues concerning Natural Religion*, ed. Norman Kemp Smith, Nelson, 1981, pp. 243–8; James Boswell, 'An Account of My Last Interview with David Hume, Esq.', from *The Private Papers of James Boswell*, ed. G. Scott and F. Pottle, Vol. XII (1931), pp. 227–32; Bruce Redford, *Designing the Life of*

Johnson, Oxford University Press, 2002, pp. 143–4. I am grateful to Tony Nuttall for alerting me to Hume's deathbed words.

6 Wolffe, *Great Deaths*, pp. 158, 178.

7 Robert Southey, *Life of Nelson*, 2 vols, John Murray, 1813; vol. 1 1832, pp. 290, 296.

8 Jalland, *Death in the Victorian Family*, p. 33; see pp. 33–7 on nineteenth-century last words.

9 *The Art of Dying*, ed. Francis Birrell and F.L. Lucas, The Hogarth Press, 1930; *The Oxford Book of Death*, ed. D.J. Enright, 1983, 1987.

10 Enright, *Oxford Book of Death*, 1987, p. 314.

11 Janet Malcolm, *Reading Chekhov*, Granta, 2003, pp. 63–73.

12 Frank Kermode, *The Sense of an Ending*, Oxford University Press, 1966; 1968, p. 8.

13 Edmund White, *Genet*, Chatto & Windus, 1993, p. 729.

14 Julian Barnes, *Flaubert's Parrot*, Cape, 1984, p. 181.

15 Lytton Strachey, *Queen Victoria*, 1921; Penguin, 1971, p. 246.

16 Redford, *Designing the Life of Johnson*, pp. 9–10.

17 John Halperin, *The Life of Jane Austen*, Harvester, 1984, p. 352.

18 D.J. Taylor, *Orwell: The Life*, Chatto & Windus, 2003, p. 424.

19 Peter Ackroyd, *Dickens*, Sinclair-Stevenson, 1990, Ch. 21.

20 See David Amigoni, *Victorian Biography: Intellectuals and the Ordering of Discourse*, Harvester, 1993.

21 Ackroyd, *Dickens*, pp. xi–xii.

22 Juliet Barker, *The Brontës*, Weidenfeld & Nicolson, 1994, p. 576.

23 Victoria Glendinning, *Trollope*, Hutchinson, 1992.

24 Jenny Uglow, *Elizabeth Gaskell: A Habit of Stories*, Faber, 1993, p. 616.

25 André Maurois, *The Quest for Proust*, Cape, 1950, p. 332.

26 George Painter, *Marcel Proust*, Chatto & Windus, 1965, pp. 363, 364.

27 Samuel Beckett, *Proust*, John Calder, 1965, p. 17.

28 Jean-Yves Tadié, *Marcel Proust*, 1996; Viking, trans. Euan Cameron, 2000.

29 Andrew Motion, *Philip Larkin*, Faber, 1993, p. 521.

30 Alan Bullock, *Hitler and Stalin: Parallel Lives*, HarperCollins, 1991, p. 1067; Peter Gay, *Freud: A Life for Our Time*, Dent, 1988, p. 651.

31 Adam Phillips, 'The Death of Freud', in *Darwin's Worms*, Faber, 1999, pp. 67–111.

32 Virginia Woolf, *To the Lighthouse*, 1927; Penguin, 1992, p. 140.

33 Virginia Woolf, *The Voyage Out*, 1915; Oxford University Press, 2001, p. 62.

34 Hermione Lee, *Virginia Woolf*, Chatto & Windus, 1996, Ch. 40.

35 Malcolm Cowley, *New Republic*, 6 October 1941, in *Virginia Woolf: The Critical Heritage*, ed. Robin Majumdar and Allen McClaurin, Routledge, 1975, p. 449.

36 See Phyllis Grosskurth, *Times Literary Supplement*, 31 October 1980, pp. 1225–6, reviewing the last volume of Virginia Woolf's letters, and suggesting foul play ('In the official search, how thoroughly was the river dragged? . . . How could her body have been wedged in some underwater debris? It would surely have required some very heavy rocks to have held it down, until it was found three weeks later, floating like a decomposed Ophelia') and Nigel Nicolson's response to these suggestions as 'absurd' (*TLS*, 23 January 1981).

37 See my earlier chapter on 'Virginia Woolf's Nose'.

Index